CASES IN
AGRIBUSINESS
MANAGEMENT
SECOND EDITION

Edited by

George J. Seperich
Arizona State University

Michael J. Woolverton
The American Graduate School
of International Management

James G. Beierlein
The Pennsylvania State University

David E. Hahn
The Ohio State University

Gorsuch Scarisbrick, Publishers
Scottsdale, Arizona

Damage: extensive highlighting + some underlining
Date: 2/15 BZ

President: John W. Gorsuch
Publisher: Gay L. Pauley
Editor: Diana Clark Lubick
Developmental Editor: Katie E. Bradford
Production Editor: Carma Paden
Marketing Manager: Renee W. Rosen
Sales Manager: Shari Jo Hehr
Cover Design: John Wincek, Aerocraft Charter Art Services
Typesetting: Andrea Reider

Gorsuch Scarisbrick, Publishers
8233 Via Paseo del Norte, Suite F-400
Scottsdale, AZ 85258

10 9 8 7 6 5 4 3 2

ISBN 0-89787-133-2

Printed in the United States of America.

Contents

Preface

Case studies have a long history as effective teaching tools at the most respected business schools. Teachers of agribusiness have increasingly turned to the case-study method as a way to increase teaching effectiveness. Students tend to like cases because they serve as an interesting way to learn how to apply analytical tools in true-to-life agribusiness settings.

At the urging of our colleagues around the country, we have assembled a new edition of *Cases in Agribusiness Management*. The first edition has been used at all levels of higher education at many schools by agribusiness teachers. Some cases in the first edition have become classics, rated as "must use" in some agribusiness classes.

The agribusiness environment has changed. It is time for new cases that reflect changes in industry structure, technology, global competition, and cost/profit relationships. The case studies in this edition have been carefully selected to expose students to the new realities of agribusiness. We have kept a few cases from the first edition, those that our colleagues and students have told us we must keep. Each new case was written by a professional agribusiness teacher, recognized as a master classroom teacher. Every case has been proven in the classroom.

The cases are arranged according to subject area—such as marketing, finance, management, and so on—so that teachers can easily locate the cases needed to complement classroom instruction. Nothing increases the credibility of a teacher more than for students to see how classroom material can be used directly in an agribusiness firm to solve problems. Better yet, students can see how they can be successful in agribusiness careers by gaining confidence in the knowledge and skills learned in the classroom. By preparing solutions to these cases, students will learn about a variety of agribusinesses, managerial styles, and decision-making situations.

These cases vary in complexity and are designed to meet the needs of a range of students, from those taking their first course in agribusiness to those studying at the graduate level. In some functional areas, a teacher can utilize several cases by beginning with a less sophisticated case and progressing to more difficult cases. This casebook has been designed to be used with a number of textbooks by presenting a variety of agribusiness situations.

We hope this casebook represents a continuing effort to support agribusiness teaching. We encourage agribusiness teachers to develop their own cases so that the best ones can be included in the next edition. We hope you will find this book a useful addition to your instructional materials and valuable in educating your students in agribusiness management topics.

George J. Seperich
Michael W. Woolverton
James G. Beierlein
David E. Hahn

Introduction to the Case-Study Method

The case-study method may be new to you. Experience has shown that case studies bring interesting, real-world situations into the classroom study of agribusiness marketing, finance, and management. The case studies in this book have been carefully selected to provide you with opportunities to apply the analytical tools you have studied and in the process learn about decision making. You will learn how business is conducted in many agribusiness industries and how to make decisions in a variety of complex, changing agribusiness environments.

As you discuss these cases with your fellow students, you will learn that decision making is often a confrontational activity involving people with different points of view. Most important, you will learn how to work toward consensus while tolerating legitimate differences of opinion.

Decision making is what managers do. The decisions of managers directly influence revenues, costs, and profits of an agribusiness firm. If you are to be successful in an agribusiness career, you must learn to be a good decision maker. You must develop the ability to apply classroom training in business and economics to agribusiness problem solving so that you can learn how to (1) make decision making easier, (2) improve the analytical quality of decisions, (3) reduce the time required to make decisions, and (4) increase the frequency of correct decisions.

After completing a few case studies, you should find them an interesting and rewarding way to learn. You will soon discover, however, that case studies require an approach that is different from normal homework assignments. Each case can have more than one right answer depending on how the problem is defined and which assumptions are made. Students commonly spend several hours preparing the solution for a case assigned for classroom discussion. The time you spend working on case studies will be well spent because it will prepare you to confidently take on a position in agribusiness in which decision-making challenges face you each day.

Success in your career will be the real reward for the work you do in preparing solutions to the case studies in this book.

■ ATTACKING THE CASE

Your first reaction upon reading a case will probably be to feel overwhelmed by all the information. Upon closer reading, you may feel that the case is missing some information that is vital to your decision. Don't despair. Case writers do this on purpose to make the cases represent as closely as possible the typical situations faced by agribusiness managers. In this age of computers, managers often have to sift through an excessive amount of information to glean the facts needed to make a decision. In other situations, there is too little information and too little time or money to collect all the information desired. One definition of management is "the art of using scanty information to make terribly important, semi-permanent decisions under time pressure." One reason for using the case-study method is for you to learn how to function effectively in that type of decision-making environment.

When assigned a case that does not contain all the information you need, you can do two things: First, seek additional information. Library research or a few telephone calls may provide the necessary facts. Second, you can make assumptions when key facts or data are not available. Your assumptions should be reasonable and consistent with the situation because the "correctness" of your solution may depend upon the assumptions you make. This is one reason that a case can have more than one right solution. In fact, your teacher may be more interested in the analysis and process you used to arrive at the decision than in its absolute correctness.

In some cases, the case writer(s) have provided questions to guide your analysis; in other cases it is up to you, the case analyst, to decide which questions are relevant in defining the problem. This too is by design. In an actual agribusiness situation you will have to decide which questions to ask, and certainly no one will give you a list of multiple-choice answers. This is why it is suggested that you not limit your analysis to the questions at the end of a case.

The Seven Steps of Problem Analysis

Using an organized seven-stem approach in analyzing a case will make the entire process easier and can increase your learning benefits.

1. *Read the case thoroughly.* To understand fully what is happening in a case, it is necessary to read the case carefully and thoroughly. You may want to read the case rather quickly the first time to get an overview of the industry, the company, the people, and the situation. Read the case again more slowly, making notes as you go.

2. *Define the central issue.* Many cases will involve several issues or problems. Identify the most important problems and separate them from the more trivial issues. After identifying what appears to be a major underlying issue, examine related problems in the functional areas (for example, marketing, finance, personnel, and so on). Functional area problems may help you identify deep-rooted problems that are the responsibility of top management.

3. *Define the firm's goals.* Inconsistencies between a firm's goals and its performance may further highlight the problems discovered in step 2. At the very least, identifying the firm's goals will provide a guide for the remaining analysis.

4. *Identify the constraints to the problem.* The constraints may limit the solutions available to the firm. Typical constraints include limited finances, lack of additional production capacity, personnel limitations, strong competitors, relationships with suppliers and customers, and so on. Constraints have to be considered when suggesting a solution.

5. *Identify all the relevant alternatives.* The list should include all the relevant alternatives that could solve the problem(s) that were identified in step 2. Use your creativity in coming up with alternative solutions. Even when solutions are suggested in the case, you may be able to suggest better solutions.

6. *Select the best alternative.* Evaluate each alternative in light of the available information. If you have carefully taken the preceding five steps, a good solution to the case should be apparent. Resist the temptation to jump to this step early in the case analysis. You will probably miss important facts, misunderstand the problem, or skip what may be the best alternative solution. You will also need to explain the logic you used to choose one alternative and reject the others.

7. *Develop an implementation plan.* The final step in the analysis is to develop a plan for effective implementation of your decision. Lack of an implementation plan even for a very good decision can lead to disaster for a firm and for you. Don't overlook this step. Your teacher will surely ask you or someone in the class to explain how to implement the decision.

The Report

The course instructor may require a written or an oral report describing your solution to the case. The high quality of your analysis or the brilliance of your insights will do you little good if your solution is not expressed clearly. The teacher is more likely to accept your solution, even if he or she does not agree with it, if you are able to identify the issues, explain the analysis and logic that led you to choose a particular alternative, and lay out a good plan for implementing the decision.

Written Reports

You probably will be asked to write reports for at least some cases. The following guidelines will help you write an effective case analysis. First, in business communications a short report is usually considered better than a long report. This does not mean that in your report you can skip key points, but rather that you state relevant points clearly and concisely. Do not include trivial matters.

Second, the report should be well written. It should be typed and not contain spelling or grammatical errors. The report you hand in for class should be equivalent in quality to a report you would write for your boss, a senior manager of an agribusiness company. In the early years of your career, particularly in a large firm, you are likely to become known for the quality of your written reports.

A well-written report would contain the following elements:

1. *Executive summary.* This is a concisely written statement, less than one page, placed at the front of the report. It briefly summarizes the major points of the case and your solution. It should describe the major issue, the proposed solution, and the logic supporting the solution.
2. *Problem statement.* Present the central issue(s) or major problem(s) in the case here. Do not rehash the facts of the case; assume that anyone reading the report is familiar with the case.
3. *Alternatives.* Discuss all relevant alternatives. Briefly present the major arguments for and against each alternative. Be sure to state your assumptions and the impact of constraints on each alternative.
4. *Conclusion.* Present the analysis and logic that led you to select a particular solution. Also discuss the reasons you rejected the other alternatives.
5. *Implementation.* Outline a plan of action that will lead to effective implementation of the decision so that the reader can see not only why you chose a particular alternative but how it will work.

Oral Reports

In some instances the instructor may specifically require an oral report on a case. One student or a team of students will be assigned an oral report in advance. In many classroom situations, each student must be prepared to discuss any aspect of a case if called upon or to comment on ideas presented by other students. It is not uncommon for a large portion of the course grade to be based on the frequency and quality of a student's oral participation in classroom discussions. Preparation of an oral case report should include the following:

1. *Description of the case situation.* Present a brief overview of the situation in the case. Sometimes a teacher will ask a student to start off the classroom discussion with this overview.

2. *Problem statement.* Describe the major issue(s) or problem(s) in the case.

3. *Analysis of the key alternatives.* Present the results of your analysis of relevant alternatives in a concise manner. Depending on the type of analysis, this is sometimes called "running the numbers."

4. *Conclusion.* Briefly describe the logic that led you to choose the alternative. Summarize why the other alternatives were not chosen.

5. *Implementation.* Present your implementation plan.

Sometimes the teacher will assign a full-case presentation. In that situation you go through the presentation point by point. In a class discussion setting, however, even though you must be prepared, you will almost never make a full-case presentation. You will be asked to present pieces of your presentation. For example, you may be called upon or volunteer to present your conclusion. You are likely to be interrupted, and count on being asked to defend your statements.

■■■ CONCLUSIONS

The analysis of case studies may be among the most challenging assignments given to a student. Cases are not just "busy work" given to fill up a student's time. Approached properly, case analysis can be extremely beneficial in preparing you for a career in agribusiness management by giving you a chance to develop decision-making skills in the classroom so that you will be better prepared to meet the challenges of your after-graduation job.

By preparing solutions to the cases studies in this book, you will be exposed to a variety of agribusinesses, management roles, and business situations. Your decision-making skills will be enhanced as you sift through large volumes of information to identify problems, determine corporate goals, define relevant alternatives, and develop plans to implement decisions. You will hone your ability to apply analytical tools in true-to-life agribusiness situations. By preparing reports, you will learn how to express yourself succinctly, both orally and in writing. You will also develop the ability to defend the logic of your analysis and conclusions. These are all valuable skills for a future agribusiness manager and will help you go a long way in a rewarding career.

MARKETING

CASES

Sabina Farmers Exchange

It was January 1988, and Ed Kuehn, owner–manager of Sabina Farmers Exchange, had just purchased the lumberyard adjacent to his feed and farm supply business in Sabina, Ohio. Ed's parents had originally purchased the company in 1955, and Ed had become president and majority stockholder in 1972. By late 1987, Ed had built his business to a gross sales level of $30 million and employed 52 people. He manufactured his own line of livestock feed and marketed more than 7,000 tons annually under the Premier name. Ed's firm also had the largest grain elevator in the area, with 3.5 million bushels of grain storage capacity.

Although enjoying tremendous success, Sabina Farmers Exchange had always marketed products using traditional methods and through traditional channels—Ed had five salesmen on the road making farm calls and sales. His firm also utilized a small retail showroom where he inventoried animal health products and miscellaneous farm supplies.

Ed was considering how to make the best use of the lumberyard. For some time he had been mulling over the idea of opening a drive-through farm supply operation. This facility would have roll-type garage doors on either end and a lane through the middle so that customers could drive through and shop without leaving their cars. Merchandise would be displayed and inventoried on either side of the middle lane. Ed believed that speed and convenient service would be well received by customers in his trade area. The lumberyard property housed a 9,600-square-foot building that Ed felt could easily be remodeled to accommodate this type of business.

Ed had purchased the property for $120,000 and was willing to invest an additional $30,000 in remodeling it. In addition, he felt that it would need to be stocked with approximately $45,000 of inventory. These anticipated

This case was prepared by John C. Foltz, Assistant Professor of Agribusiness Management, Department of Agricultural Economics and Rural Sociology, University of Idaho; and Jay T. Akridge, Associate Director, Center for Agricultural Business and Associate Professor, Department of Agricultural Economics, Purdue University, as a basis for classroom discussion rather than to illustrate either effective or ineffective handling of a business situation.

expenditures made him think about the sales goals and margins he should consider for this addition to his business.

Exhibit 1 shows U.S. Department of Agriculture statistics for livestock and crop acreages in the surrounding counties. Sabina is located midway between Washington Court House and Wilmington, the county seats of Fayette and Clinton counties—about 10 miles from each. In 1988, Sabina's population was about 2,800, Wilmington was home to roughly 10,500 people, and approximately 12,800 residents lived in Washington Court House. Ed was aware of a number of residents who lived in one town and worked in the other. Generally, their commute took them through Sabina.

Sabina Farmers Exchange had enjoyed a solid, profitable business. In 1988, the customer base was roughly 75 percent rural and farm customers and 25 percent in-town or "backyard farm" customers. The firm's sales by department for the previous year were: grain-handling income (storage, drying, and marketing income), 53 percent; feed, 25 percent; agronomy department (fertilizer, seed, and chemicals), 18 percent; animal health, 0.5 percent; and farm supplies, 2.5 percent.

Retail farm supply competition in the area was strong, provided in part by the statewide co-op, Countrymark, which had stores in both Wilmington and Washington Court House. In fact, Countrymark's branch in Washington Court House had a drive-through as part of its operation. From a feed and farm input standpoint, additional competition came from two private firms: Buckley Brothers in Wilmington, and Master Feed Mill with branches in Wilmington and Hillsboro. On the farm chemical side of the business, competitors included Mid-Ohio Chemical, with six outlets in the four-county area, and Terra International, located in Melvin and Sabina.

Ed had done a little research and had accumulated some additional information. One source was a map of the four-county area that Sabina Farmers Exchange considered its market (Exhibit 2). Ed also had a floor plan of the building (Exhibit 3) in which he was considering opening his drive-through operation. He had recently read an article in *Feed and Grain Times* (Attachment A) that described some changes occurring in production agriculture and discussed what these changes could mean for farm suppliers. Finally, an article from *Agri Marketing* (Attachment B) describing the growth of the sundowner market had caught his attention, and he felt it might be of use.

Armed with this background information and his "feel" for the market, Ed had some ideas he wanted to try. One option was to use this new property as warehouse space. Sabina Farmers Exchange, however, had been innovative before, and he thought the drive-through concept might be worth trying.

EXHIBIT 1   Market area: Numbers of livestock and crop acreages.

COUNTY	CATTLE AND CALVES	MILK COWS	HOGS	CHICKENS (3 mos. +)
Clinton	15,000	1,500	93,000	3,654
Fayette	12,000	*	58,000	2,140
Greene	19,000	*	75,000	1,652
Highland	25,000	2,800	43,000	2,251

COUNTY	HENS, PULLETS (LAYING AGE)	BROILERS, TURKEYS	HARVESTED ACREAGE Corn	HARVESTED ACREAGE Soybeans
Clinton	*	239	73,200	73,200
Fayette	2,021	*	71,800	98,300
Greene	1,487	296	66,200	54,200
Highland	2,046	532	63,200	61,200

Source: Ohio Agricultural Statistics, 1987.
*Government does not release data that may reveal the status of individual operations.

EXHIBIT 2   Southwestern Ohio market area.

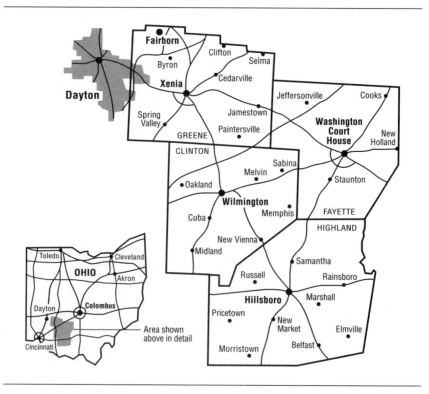

EXHIBIT 3   Floor plan for proposed drive-through operation.

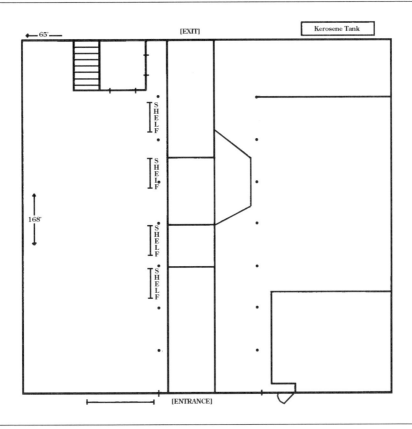

▬▬▬ QUESTIONS

1. What target market should Ed try to appeal to with this drive-through approach?
2. Given your brief market research (based on the exhibits), was this a growing target market? What are the long-term prospects for this market?
3. Would full-time farmers benefit from this type of merchandising/marketing?
4. What should be the characteristics of potential products in the drive-through? (Address issues such as ease of handling and ability of customer to choose among products.) Give two examples of specific products you would recommend to be carried in the drive-through, and explain why you would recommend them.

5. What type of pricing strategy might be appropriate for Ed's drive-through? Are there any economies of scale/efficiency concerns that would help this type of approach, or would this convenience add to the cost of marketing the products? (Essentially, look at the costs and benefits of the proposed drive-through.)

6. How should Ed convey information to customers at the drive-through? Think through some options both for promoting products and for communicating with customers.

7. What other adjustments might be necessary in Sabina Farmers Exchange operations to support this strategy? (Hint: Think of changes in personnel, appearance of store, traffic flow, and so on.)

8. Based on what you know about the case, how many employees would be needed for this operation?

9. Using the floor plan of the proposed drive-through, determine how you would arrange products for optimum space use, convenience, and accessibility.

Attachment A

The Emerging New Agriculture: Implications for Feed and Grain Dealers

It is absolutely clear that dramatic change is sweeping across agriculture, leaving a totally new environment in its wake. Feed and grain dealers are faced with unprecedented challenges that can mean new opportunities for growth and profit—if they understand what is going on and are able to take advantage of the situation.

Many people believe that the worst is over—that we have turned the corner. It's true that much of agriculture has experienced substantial improvements in the past two years—thanks to some government programs and the exceptionally strong livestock and poultry sectors.

But these improvements follow many painful changes. We have downsized American agriculture dramatically in recent years. Not only are there fewer farms, there are far fewer dealers, both on the supply and marketing side. We have restructured much of agriculture into a far more efficient machine.

But the adjustments are not yet complete, and probably will never be! In fact, change seems to be occurring at an even faster rate. By stepping back and looking at these changes, managers can gain a far better understanding of the emerging new agriculture and, more importantly, develop appropriate strategies for dealing with this exciting, but challenging, new world. That's what management is all about.

The changing structure of agriculture

Many of the changes we are experiencing are major structural changes that are reshaping agriculture, creating a totally different market environment for the feed and grain industry. Let's examine some of those structural changes.

Concentration of production. There is a clear and dramatic trend toward concentrating production decisions into the hands of fewer and fewer producers. Experts predict that by the year 2000, less than 50,000 farms will produce 75 percent of all farm products. The poultry industry has already moved far in this direction and livestock is shifting dramatically. Even grain production is becoming far more concentrated.

This means there is a great concentration of power into the hands of

W. David Downey. (June/July 1988). The emerging new agriculture: implications for feed and grain dealers. *Feed and Grain Times,* pp. 22–23.

fewer and fewer large farmers whose purchasing and marketing decisions are of great importance to the feed and grain industry at every level. Learning to be more responsive to their needs without giving in to unrealistic demands will be a major factor in a dealer's success. The fact is that large progressive farmers have very different needs and must be serviced very differently than smaller traditional farmers. This difference will be a key to success for many firms.

Aggressively pursuing the large farmer market means developing creative new business strategies. Professionally run businesses must be staffed by highly competent professionals who can respond immediately to the needs of customers. Understanding how to deal with a complex farm business management and ownership structure can be critical to marketing success. Compounding the problem is the fact that personnel are sometimes intimidated by the size and sophistication of large operators.

Growing part-time farmer market. Ironically, the number of smaller farmers who depend on non-farm jobs for a major portion of their income is rapidly growing. Part-time farmers frequently have substantial acreage and offer significant business opportunity. Many are yesterday's "average" farmers who are struggling for survival by turning to off-farm jobs. Coupled with the growing number of hobby farmers, this "sundowner" market offers substantial new opportunities for dealers who understand their different needs.

But this market requires a very different approach. Off-farm obligations create the need for different hours and types of service. Learning to cope with the demands of smaller customers, and making money doing it, is a new experience for many dealers.

New marketing and merchandising techniques are necessary. Sometimes, just convincing personnel who have spent a lifetime working with "real farmers" to have the patience to work with part-timers is a challenge. And, of course, a fundamental question must be answered: Should I try to serve both the commercial and part-time markets?

Industrialization of farm production. Farming has truly become an industrialized process—and it becomes more so each day. Technology has allowed us to separate land ownership, labor and management. Today, purchase decisions in larger operations are often made by specialists hundreds of miles from the farm operation. A purchasing agent mentality, where bids are requested for written specifications and methods of purchase, are increasingly common. The ability to "talk commodity markets" intelligently becomes as important, or more important, than personal relationships. All of this smacks of a truly industrialized business.

It is not enough to simply handle grain or sell feed. Increasingly, dealers must be concerned with meeting the business needs of the customers—selling the products the way the customer wants to buy and providing related grain marketing services. This means understanding the business needs of larger operations and being creative in how you do business.

Technicalities of agriculture. Technology is a close companion of industrialization. The necessity for efficiency and productivity in farming has made information a critical farm supply itself—for large and small farmers alike. Computer technology has made information flow an intricate part of farming. Access to market information and what it means has itself become a major industry. Dealers who are ill equipped to communicate at this level will have a tough time dealing with progressive customers who demand to do business with "people who know."

Many people feel we are on the verge of major breakthroughs in biotechnology. Genetic engineering promises exciting new production methods that may revolutionize agriculture—possibly creating totally new crops and markets. While we are still on the threshold of major breakthroughs, dealers must be poised and ready to capitalize on opportunities that arise. Already breakthroughs in feed additives and genetic engineering are threatening to have a major impact on the dairy industry. Because of our ability to bring new ideas into the market very quickly today, new technologies will likely make sweeping changes almost overnight—offering great opportunities for firms that are ready.

Globalization. Everywhere we look we see evidence that we have become a global marketplace. Probably no ag industry has been more affected than the grain industry. The U.S. marketplace has become a "supplier of last resort" for many of our traditional customers. Economic policies for developing countries and other major exporters seem to have more effect on the fortunes of feed and grain dealers than domestic conditions. Even a weaker dollar has not been able to restore the United States to its former dominant position in the world marketplace. The bottom line is that we are intricately and permanently interconnected to every other major grain producer in the world.

Our once predictable world has been replaced by sudden shifts in direction caused by complex world events, confusing new distribution systems and intense new competition with different values. Feed and grain dealers must face the inevitable—an intensely competitive, rapidly changing environment where alliances with suppliers, timely access to markets and the flexibility to adjust to rapidly changing conditions are crucial. Monitoring changing circumstances and maintaining the ability to respond quickly will be an essential key to dealer success.

Keys to dealer success

While no one can predict the future with certainty, the trends that have been described here have a high probability of continuing. The resulting environment poses challenges for dealers that will prove highly profitable for some and disastrous for others. Here are some important keys for taking advantage of the emerging new agriculture.

Marketing the feed and grain business. Never has marketing been as important as it is in the emerging new agriculture. The wide difference in customers from large progressive high-tech operations to small part-time farmers brings this issue clearly into focus. Dealers must become much better at defining who they want to target in the market and designing specific marketing plans to reach these target segments profitably.

Marketing encompasses a wide range of activities—far more than just selling. It includes the choice of products and services offered, quality of personnel, pricing policies, promotional activities, competitive reaction, etc. But most importantly, it requires intentional and regular analysis of potential customers and their needs.

Professional personnel. "People are our most valuable asset." This common adage has much truth, but the demands placed on personnel in the emerging new agriculture is far greater than ever before. The process begins with hiring people who have the ability to perform up to the level of customer expectation. But it must continue with frequent development programs. Feed and grain dealers who hope to be competitive must recognize the importance of and invest in staff who can do the job.

Efficiency. In the highly competitive world we have described, there is little room for inefficiency. Often success or failure is determined by tenths of percentage points. Most of the inefficient operators have already been forced out of business. Those who remain today have already squeezed most of the excess out of their business. Still, a significant competitive edge can be gained by having a cost advantage over a competitor.

This underscores the importance of maintaining close control over operating costs and managing margins and cash flow carefully. There is no longer room for sloppy management.

Flexibility. There is every reason to believe that the markets ahead will continue to change rapidly, and some-times unpredictably. Dealers must position themselves to respond quickly. Long-term capital expenditures that commit a firm to a single direction should be made very cautiously, because the cost of error is tremendously high. Alternative "what if" scenarios should be considered to determine if the firm could withstand the "worst case" situation. Computerized spread sheets may be a dealer's best friend in looking to the future.

This restructuring process has already taken its toll. There are far fewer feed and grain dealers in the market today than a few short years ago. Further reductions in acreage and grain to be handled will add still further pressures. But many dealers who have made important adjustments are well positioned to take advantage of opportunities in the emerging new agriculture. Those who understand what is going on, and are willing to make tough decisions, will likely find the next decade an exciting and profitable time.

Attachment B

The Unknown Farmer: In Pursuit of the Elusive but Lucrative "Sundowner" Market

Sometimes they're called sundowners, sometimes gentlemen farmers, sometimes part-timers. They're the little guys—small-acreage farmers who often have a full-time off-farm job. They may not be Class 1A farmers, but numerically they represent the only group of farm operators that is steadily growing. And, collectively, they have significant purchasing power.

While some marketers have carved out a niche by selling to the part-time farmer, there seems to be great confusion as to just what the part-time farmer is.

The U.S. Census Bureau says part-time farmers work off the farm 50% or more of the time. For Doane Marketing Research Inc., St. Louis, the "sundowner" has a full-time job and farms with profit in mind. The National Farm & Power Equipment Dealers Association, St. Louis, makes a further distinction: Part-time farmers derive 20% to 79% of their income from farming; "hobby farmers" derive up to 19% of their income from farming.

"I wish we had better data on this market," says Pat Carroll, advertising and public relations manager for Kubota Tractor Corp., Compton, Calif., one of the companies that has done well targeting this group of consumers. "We know they are out there and getting bigger all the time."

Defining the market

The hardest part in targeting the part-time farmer is coming up with a solid demographic picture of the market, especially as the line between the full-time and part-time farm operator blurs. In the past 12 years, for example, the number of farm operators who work off the farm has doubled to 88%.

"It's a good market and it's growing," says Don Van Hook, advertising manager for Deere & Co., Moline, Ill. "But it's a broad market that runs the gamut from the guy farming small acreage who thinks of himself as a full-time farmer and works off-farm to support the farm, to 'gentlemen farmers' who like to play farmer on the weekend."

Just what, then, is the definition of the part-time, or sundown, farmer? If the market is defined as operators with yearly gross income from farming of $40,000 or less, these operators

Kelly O'Brien and Stephanie Johnston. (November & December 1987). The unknown farmer: In pursuit of the elusive but lucrative "sundowner" market. *Agri Marketing,* pp. 30–33.

are a fairly significant purchasing group, accounting for about one-quarter of all feed and farm machinery sales.

If the market is defined by the number of acres farmed, operators with 100 acres or less become even more significant, accounting for 64% of all U.S. farms.

If the definition lies in the operator's involvement in his or her farm, very few farm operators fit the picture of the traditional farmer. In the 1982 Census of Agriculture, 88% of farm operators reported working off the farm at least one day a year. But almost 71% of those worked 200 days *or more* off the farm—more than half a year.

But regardless of how the market is defined, many agri-marketers agree that it is significant.

Steady cash flow is what part-time farmers offer agri-marketers that full-time farmers can't, says Howard "Bud" Kerr, program director for USDA's Office of Small-Scale Agriculture. "The beautiful thing about the part-time farmer is that he has full-time off-farm income," Kerr says. As a result, part-time farmers are often a better financial bet than farmers who are dependent solely upon agricultural production for their income.

Nothing unusual

Jack Odle, editor of *Progressive Farmer,* Birmingham, Ala., says the South has always had a high percentage of producers with off-farm income. "I doubt there's a farmer out there without some source of outside income anymore," he explains. "What's changed in the past few years is that outside income has become more and more important to stay in farming."

He says a significant number of part-time farmers are concentrated in

the coastal area formed by the Atlantic Ocean, Gulf of Mexico and Pacific Ocean. The moderate climate there allows for farming diversity, while the large number of urban centers offers off-farm employment and market proximity, factors which have inhibited the proliferation of part-time producers in the Midwest.

According to the Census Bureau's definition of the part-time farmer, 55% of the South's farmers are part-timers. The bureau defines a part-time farmer as a farm operator who spends 50% or more of his or her work time in an off-the-farm job.

At 35%, the Midwest has the smallest number of part-time farmers; while 43% of the Northeast's farmers are part-timers and 47% of the West's are part-timers.

"There is no typical geography or crop when you look at the (southern) part-time farmer," Odle says. "In one area with cow-calf operations, the husband works the 'other job' while the wife farms. In a row-crop area, if the producer is under 35, he farms and the wife works full-time off-farm."

From Odle's perspective, the only thing southern part-time farmers have in common is a desire to live in the country and plenty of income. "Typically these folks are looking for a place to go to get away from the city," he says. "They don't usually figure on making any money."

Ties that bind

"All we know for sure is that there are more today than yesterday," says the research director of a prominent agricultural advertising agency.

Based on research done for the agency's clients, this researcher thinks the part-time farmer probably lives within 50 miles of a small city where he works; needs off-farm income of about $40,000 to play the game; and typically spends about $7,000 annually on expenses—except land, which he may own or rent cheaply, probably from a family member. He hopes to make a small profit, prays to break even and usually gets out to cut his losses if neither happens.

He probably comes from a farm background—in which case there usually is a family connection of some kind to get a break on the purchase of farm inputs—and sticks to conventional agriculture.

This researcher also thinks the part-time farmer who doesn't have a farm background and wants to make money is more likely to explore alternatives such as growing produce for a roadside stand or a pick-your-own operation. After failing with inorganic farming methods, this part-timer tends to use pesticides at a high rate.

Because they operate on a small scale and are often employed full time at another job, part-time farmers often require a different set of services from their suppliers than do full-time farmers. Given the difficulty in defining the market, then, servicing the part-time farmer presents a challenge for agri-marketers.

Special needs

While many part-time farmers have already discovered that it is too expensive to buy fertilizer, seed and chemicals at the local hardware store, garden supply store or nursery, they don't purchase enough to buy in the quantities supplied by the conventional farm supplier. For that reason, some suppliers are beginning to look at alternative packaging and distribution systems to serve the part-time farmer.

This includes doing more private-labeling and packaging supplies in intermediate sizes (more than a quart, less than a 5-gallon can), to be available in suburban Sears or Walmart stores.

Results from a study conducted by Doane Marketing Research back up the idea of offering part-time farmers different services than the full-time farmer receives.

Doane Research Director Joy Block says sundowners are not "casual farmers"; they are in business for a profit. In addition, she says, "they don't have the luxury of time." They conduct much of their business on the telephone, and "tend to depend upon those things they can be sure of." For example, she says, "they are very serious about the servicing and maintenance of their equipment."

The bottom line

In addition to developing different services for the part-time farmer, agri-marketers also have the challenge of reaching this audience with an advertising message.

Deere's Van Hook, for example, says the company's smaller tractors sell best in the Southeast and West and around major metropolitan areas. So far, the company has attempted to reach the part-time farmer by advertising in national farm publications and publishing an edition of its 150-year-old publication, *The Furrow,* for farmers with less than $42,000 yearly gross income.

Next spring, however, Deere will run ads for the first time in *American Fruit Grower* and *American Vegetable Grower.* "We've considered other publications and media, but we just don't think there is anything out there yet that is really cost-effective." Van Hook says, "We're still looking."

Hungry Heifer Family Restaurants

▬ INTRODUCTION

During the 1980s the Hungry Heifer Family Restaurants (HHFR) had grown from a single outlet in an Atlanta, Georgia, suburb to a chain of 228 outlets reaching from Florida to Maryland. The secret to their success was to (1) provide lunches and dinners in an atmosphere that was a definite cut above the fast-food outlets at prices only slightly higher, and (2) good cost controls.

▬ MARKET APPROACH

The management of HHFR prides itself on staying on top of their customer needs and wants. To help ensure their success, they often perform very detailed market research before entering a new market. They know from past experience that their target audience are young families in which the adults are 25 to 50 years of age and have above-average incomes. By catering to children with a child's menu and other promotions, they feel they gain market share. For a few dollars more than a trip to a fast-food outlet, a family can go to dinner, sit at a table, be waited on, and eat in a pleasant environment.

▬ THE SITUATION

HHFR is contemplating expanding into Pennsylvania. Three counties have been selected for further analysis as possible locations for a new restaurant. Centre County is located in the middle of the state. It is somewhat isolated from the rest of the state but contains a large university. Pike County is located in a resort area in the eastern side of Pennsylvania on the Delaware

---

This case was prepared by James G. Beierlein, Associate Professor of Agricultural Economics, Department of Agricultural Economics and Rural Sociology, Pennsylvania State University, as a basis for classroom discussion rather than to illustrate either effective or ineffective handling of a business situation.

River. Bucks County is located just north of Philadelphia in a rapidly expanding area.

You have been given the job of deciding which of these counties should be selected for a future restaurant opening. Once a county has been chosen, a separate siting study will be conducted to determine the exact location of the new outlet.

To assist you with your task you have been given the following information:

1. The market research statistics in Exhibits 1 to 7
2. Company policy is to sell:
   a. Dinner (adult) for $7.00
   b. Dinner (child) for $3.50
   c. Lunches (adult and child) for $4.00
3. The standard income statement of HHFR is as follows:

Sales	100%
Cost of goods sold	– 46
Gross margin	54
Operating expenses	– 49
Operational profit	5
Other expenses	– 2
Profit before tax	3%

▬▬ QUESTIONS

1. Analyze the market situation for restaurants in the three counties.
2. Analyze the demographic situation in the three counties.
3. Select one county with the brightest prospect for further analysis and determine its unmet need.
4. Determine the market share, number of meals, and sales per day needed to break even.
5. Would you open a restaurant in any of these counties? Explain why or why not in a brief report.

EXHIBIT 1 Market research statistics: Population and number of households.

COUNTY	POPULATION	AVERAGE AGE	PERCENT OF POPULATION						NUMBER OF HOUSEHOLDS
			0–17	18–24	25–34	35–49	50+		
Centre	116,000	25.7	20.3	28.5	17.1	15.4	18.7		38,900
Pike	21,000	40.3	22.2	7.3	13.7	17.8	39.0		8,400
Bucks	511,300	31.3	27.7	11.2	17.5	20.4	23.2		176,500
PA	11,965,400	33.6	24.5	11.6	16.1	17.8	30.0		4,451,800

Source: Sales and Marketing Management.

EXHIBIT 2 Market research statistics: Income.

COUNTY	EFFECTIVE BUYING INCOME	MEDIAN HOUSEHOLD INCOME	PERCENT OF HOUSEHOLDS WITH INCOME OF:					
			$0– 10,000	$10,000– 20,000	$20,000– 35,000	$35,000– 50,000	$50,000+	
Centre	$1,045,378,000	$22,388	19.2	25.2	31.2	15.6	8.8	
Pike	204,886,000	21,133	18.3	28.6	32.2	13.8	7.1	
Bucks	6,048,149,000	32,242	9.3	15.6	31.3	26.3	17.5	
PA	$126,497,923,000	$25,213	16.6	21.9	31.7	18.9	10.9	

Source: Sales and Marketing Management.

EXHIBIT 3 Market research statistics: Retail sales.

COUNTY	TOTAL RETAIL	FOOD	EATING AND DRINKING	GENERAL MERCHANDISE	FURNITURE FURNISHINGS APPLIANCES	AUTOS	DRUGS
Centre	$548,575,000	$110,889,000	$56,808,000	$59,548,000	$25,142,000	$99,751,000	$19,049,000
Pike	54,258,000	11,522,000	7,671,000	981,000	1,204,000	8,047,000	1,314,000
Bucks	3,222,956,000	615,405,000	233,161,000	380,237,000	114,612,000	877,623,000	74,647,000
PA	$60,483,693,000	$12,897,648,000	$5,327,320,000	$7,618,943,000	$2,645,306,000	$12,055,434,000	$2,108,585,000

Source: Sales and Marketing Management.

EXHIBIT 4 Market research statistics: Number of establishments.

COUNTY	TOTAL RETAIL	FOOD	EATING AND DRINKING	GENERAL MERCHANDISE	FURNITURE FURNISHINGS APPLIANCES	AUTOS	DRUGS
Centre	593	76	127	18	43	99	18
Pike	93	15	30	NA	NA	19	NA
Bucks	2,415	318	537	57	152	409	99
PA	60,567	8,210	14,834	1,662	3,920	9,685	2,524

Source: U.S. Department of Commerce, Bureau of the Census, County Business Patterns.

EXHIBIT 5 Market research statistics: Retail sales per establishment.[a, b]

COUNTY	TOTAL RETAIL	FOOD	EATING AND DRINKING	GENERAL MERCHANDISE	FURNITURE FURNISHINGS APPLIANCES	AUTOS	DRUGS
Centre	$925,084	$1,459,000	$447,307	$3,308,222	$584,698	$1,007,586	$1,058,278
Pike	583,419	768,133	255,700	NA	NA	423,526	NA
Bucks	1,334,557	1,935,236	434,192	6,670,824	754,763	2,145,777	754,010
PA	$998,624	$1,570,968	$359,129	$4,584,202	$674,823	$1,244,753	$834,622

[a]Exhibit 3 values divided by Exhibit 4 values.
[b]NA, not available.

EXHIBIT 6 Market research statistics: Per person sales.[a]

COUNTY	TOTAL RETAIL	FOOD	EATING AND DRINKING	GENERAL MERCHANDISE	FURNITURE FURNISHINGS APPLIANCES	AUTOS	DRUGS
Centre	$4,729	$ 955	$489	$513	$216	$860	$164
Pike	2,584	548	365	46	57	383	62
Bucks	6,303	1,204	456	744	224	1,716	146
PA	$5,054	$1,077	$445	$637	$221	$1,007	$176

[a]Exhibit 3 values divided by Exhibit 1 values.

EXHIBIT 7 Market research statistics: Average number of people per establishment.[a, b]

COUNTY	POPULATION	TOTAL RETAIL	FOOD	EATING AND DRINKING	GENERAL MERCHANDISE	FURNITURE FURNISHINGS APPLIANCES	AUTOS	DRUGS
Centre	116,000	$196	$1,526	$913	$6,444	$2,698	$1,172	$6,444
Pike	21,000	226	1,400	700	NA	NA	1,105	NA
Bucks	511,300	212	1,608	952	8,970	3,364	1,250	5,165
PA	11,965,400	$198	$1,457	$807	$7,199	$3,052	$1,235	$4,741

[a]Exhibit 1 values divided by Exhibit 4 values.
[b]NA, not available.

Dorset Crop Service

■■■ INTRODUCTION

Bill Wallace leaned back in his chair and stared out his office window toward the fertilizer storage buildings of Dorset Crop Service, Inc. (DCS). His mind was clearly not on the trucks moving past the window. Instead, after a successful spring and a reasonably good fall season, he was wrestling with a question that was sure to affect the future of his firm: How could he profitably meet the needs of the growing number of large farmers—those who buy more than 100 tons of fertilizer a year—in Dorset's market area.

Bill read the trade press religiously and knew that this issue had been critical in other areas for some time. But the unique area of northeastern Ohio and northwestern Pennsylvania that DCS served had not kept pace with those trends—at least not until recently. Farmers around Dorset, which is near Lake Erie and the Pennsylvania border, traditionally worked smaller acreages than those in the Midwest. Crop farmers were the minority in this locale. In general, production practices were less intense than those in many regions of the country, and most fertilizer still moved in bagged form. Farmers had not adopted dry bulk and fluid fertilizers as quickly in this area.

DCS had met the needs of these farmers effectively and currently enjoyed a high market share within a 15-mile radius of the plant. During the past 10 years, however, retirements, financial problems, and farm consolidations had begun to reshape the DCS market area, and an important group of larger operators was slowly emerging. These farmers were progressive and monitored agronomic advances, adopting them when profitable. They were increasingly buying dry bulk material and fluid fertilizers and would

This case was prepared by Linda D. Whipker, Senior Marketing Analyst with Agribusiness Group, Inc., Indianapolis, Indiana; Jay T. Akridge, Associate Director of the Purdue Center for Agricultural Business (CAB) and an Associate Professor in the Department of Agricultural Economics; and W. David Downey, Director of CAB and Professor in the Department of Agricultural Economics at Purdue University as a basis for classroom discussion rather than to illustrate either effective or ineffective handling of a business situation.

listen to a presentation on complete fertilizer/pest management programs. They pushed pencils when making input purchase decisions. In short, this emerging group of high-tech, larger operators was a different breed and was beginning to be an important part of the market that demanded special attention.

Dorset Crop Service had been monitoring this trend and, since new ownership took control of the plant in 1986, had made significant changes in its business to meet the needs of this group. DCS added bulk-blending and fluid-handling capabilities, began custom applying material, and marketed other agronomic services. Although these changes had apparently been successful, Bill had the nagging feeling that current efforts were not adequate to meet the needs of this segment of the market—a segment that seemed to be increasingly price conscious. In fact, a number of outlying competitors had recently initiated no-frills, direct-selling programs aimed specifically at larger farmers in DCS's market, and DCS was beginning to feel the effects. Bill wanted to maintain the market share that DCS enjoyed in the immediate market area. The question was, how?

Defensive marketing strategies were not the only thing running through Bill's mind. Because DCS had virtually saturated the market near its plant, Bill knew he would need to expand beyond his traditional market boundaries to attain any significant growth. And to do so, he had to deal with the large farmer issue from a slightly different perspective, that is, how to wrestle the large farmer business away from competitors.

Complicating matters further was that DCS was a wholesale distributor of fertilizer in northeastern Ohio and western Pennsylvania. The fertilizer plant in Dorset had a few wholesale accounts even in the late 1970s. This wholesale business had grown significantly over time and now included several dealers in Pennsylvania. Many were smaller mom-and-pop general farm stores and feed dealers. In most cases these firms were not geared to handle the agronomic needs of the emerging large farmer segment. This established dealer network, however, meant that Bill would have to carefully examine the impact on his dealer business of any direct sales to large farmers. He had made a point of not selling directly to any farmers in areas served by his wholesale customers. On the occasions when farmers had approached him about direct sales, he referred them to the DCS dealer in the area.

Since taking over as general manager in January 1994, Bill had spent a lot of time collecting detailed information about both his retail and wholesale fertilizer markets. Now it was time to start analyzing this information and decide which action, if any, was most appropriate. Bill knew that it was time to make a decision—he had to finalize his strategy within the next two weeks if he was going to implement the plans in time for the upcoming season.

■■ THE MARKET AREA

Dorset Crop Service is in the northeastern corner of Ohio, 30 miles south of Lake Erie and two miles from the Pennsylvania border (Exhibit 1). Agriculture in this area is characterized by dairy farms and small, part-time farmers. The typical full-time dairy farmer milks 50 head of cows and has 200 to 400 acres of forages and corn. Part-time farmers own 30 to 50 acres of land and grow corn or soybeans. A few large, full-time crop farmers have 500 to 600 acres of soybeans and corn. Specialty crops such as grapes, nursery stock, and orchard crops are grown in an area along Lake Erie on farms ranging from 5 to 80 acres.

Much of the soil in the area is silty and poorly drained. This type of soil, coupled with the lake effect of large snowfalls, creates a shorter effective growing season due to wet field conditions. Few farmers can get on the fields to apply fertilizer in the fall or before planting in the spring, so most of the fertilizer is applied at planting time or is side-dressed.

Several farmers in the area buy fertilizer in the fall, in either bagged or bulk form, and store it until spring to apply through their planter. Because

EXHIBIT 1   Northeastern Ohio and western Pennsylvania.

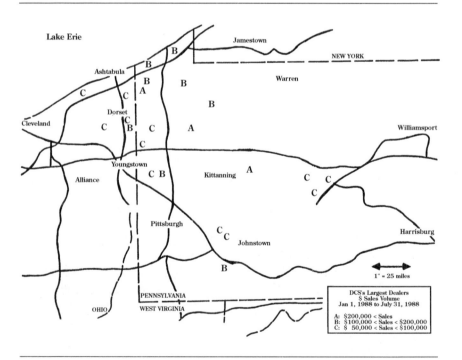

of the large number of part-time farmers in the area and the specialty crop acreage, 60 percent of DCS's dry fertilizer is sold in bagged form. Some large farmers who buy bulk fertilizer lay a concrete pad or construct a storage bin and install a front-end loader on a tractor to handle bulk fertilizer material.

■ DORSET CROP SERVICE'S HISTORY

Dorset Crop Service was established in the mid 1960s as the westernmost plant of a small regional fertilizer company. The plant sold bagged fertilizer to local farmers and to a few small dealers in the area. No bulk fertilizer was sold, and little service was provided to customers. In 1986, Dick Hanks, the owner of a nearby fluid fertilizer plant, together with the owners of Northern Ohio Chemical (NOC), a large independent fertilizer company with several outlets in Ohio, bought the plant. NOC sells a full agronomic line of fertilizers, seed, and pesticides. Last year the company sold nearly 250,000 tons of fertilizer.

Dick merged the newly acquired plant with his own fluid operation and became manager of the new Dorset Crop Service, Inc. The new corporation made several important changes immediately. First, it took advantage of NOC's buying power and was able to become more competitive with its material prices. It purchased additional equipment, began offering custom application services, and also hired a full-time salesperson and began making on-farm sales calls. The aggressive new strategy was effective. Within five years, the combined retail/wholesale fertilizer sales at DCS increased from 3,500 tons to 25,000 tons. In 1993, DCS had sales of more than $7 million and little long-term debt. During the 1986–93 period, DCS never suffered an unprofitable year. In fact, DCS consistently had posted an operating return on sales (pre-tax) that met or exceeded that of the industry's most profitable firms (typically 5–7 percent).

In December 1993, Hanks retired, selling his share of the company back to the owners of Northern Ohio Chemical (not to the NOC corporation). Bill Wallace, who had been assistant manager at DCS for several years, took over as the general manager.

■ DORSET CROP SERVICE TODAY

Today, DCS is a Sub-Chapter S corporation owned by the same group that owns NOC. DCS continues to use Northern Ohio Chemical's brand name and still enjoys the purchasing power of the parent company. DCS also takes advantage of the group training seminars and sales training meetings offered by NOC. Although Bill does discuss major decisions and strategy with the owners, NOC allows him complete freedom in managing day-to-day operations.

DCS sells dry fertilizer, liquid fertilizer (anhydrous ammonia and nitrogen solutions), pesticides, seed, a few farm supplies, lime, water tanks, and some lawn and garden products (Exhibit 2). All products are sold both retail to farmers in the four counties surrounding the fertilizer plant and wholesale to dealers in northeastern Ohio and western Pennsylvania. One-third of the total sales dollars is derived from retail sales. Dry fertilizer accounts for the largest proportion of sales volume for both the retail and the wholesale businesses.

In the Dorset area, DCS has two plants which are spread over some 10 acres. The primary location is in the town of Dorset, where the head office, blending and bagging facilities, and dry fertilizer warehouses are located. This location has 4,500 tons of dry storage capacity.

The second plant is south of Dorset and is the site of Dick Hanks's original plant. This location has storage for 15,000 gallons of liquid fertilizer and 30,000 gallons of anhydrous ammonia. Thirty miles north of Dorset on Lake Erie, DCS leases a warehouse that is used primarily for storing pesticides for application on fruit and vegetable crops. DCS also leases a fertilizer storage dome at the Ashtabula dock on Lake Erie for storing potash shipped in from Canada on lake vessels (Exhibit 3).

Most of DCS's other raw materials, such as phosphorus and urea, are unloaded from river barges on the Ohio River 85 miles south of Dorset at East Liverpool and then trucked to the DCS blending plant and warehouses. Until February 1, 1994, a rail line ran through Dorset. The rail facilities could handle three or four cars each day. Rail transportation can still be

EXHIBIT 2   Percentage of wholesale and retail sales dollars.

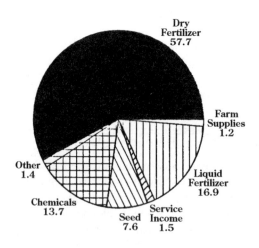

used for products from California or from other supply points, but now the cars must be unloaded in Jefferson and the materials trucked 15 miles to Dorset.

DCS's equipment includes two tender trucks for liquid fertilizer and two floater trucks for dry fertilizer. It has 12 pull-type dry fertilizer spreaders, four tool bars, eight ammonia applicators, and a 4×4 pickup sprayer. Custom application of anhydrous ammonia is not a large part of its custom application business, but it does own a tractor for custom ammonia application. DCS does not own delivery trucks but contracts with several trucking firms in the area to provide this service. DCS has been satisfied with this arrangement.

DCS employs 12 people, including Bill. The staff consists of two office and bookkeeping personnel, several warehouse and custom application personnel, and two outside sales representatives. Both sales reps have been with DCS since 1988. One salesperson, John Kepler, sells wholesale to dealers throughout western Pennsylvania and has built up a strong loyalty with many of these individuals. John previously worked as a sales representative for Ciba-Geigy in the area and so had extensive sales experience and agronomic expertise for the Pennsylvania market. Harvey Anderson calls on farmers and dealers in northeastern Ohio. He has a two-year agricultural degree from Ohio Technical Institute and a strong agronomic background. Bill is in the process of hiring another sales representative to take over retail sales in Ohio so that Harvey can concentrate on wholesale selling to the Ohio dealers and to the specialty crop market along Lake Erie.

■■■ THE RETAIL MARKET

One-third of DCS's total sales dollars is derived from retail sales. Its retail market is concentrated in a 15-mile radius around Dorset (Exhibit 3). Of DCS's 400 to 500 retail customers, 70 percent are part-time farmers who buy approximately 30 percent of the total retail fertilizer tonnage moved by DCS. The majority of the part-time farmers rent equipment to apply fertilizer and pesticides. The typical full-time farmer who buys from DCS is a dairy farmer with 200 to 400 acres of forages and corn; however, three of DCS's largest customers have 1,000 to 1,500 acres of soybeans and corn.

Along Lake Erie are several orchards and nurseries. A number of specialty crops are grown in this area. Bill estimates that DCS sells pesticides and fertilizers to 60 or 70 percent of the specialty crop farmers in Ashtabula County, either directly or through two of its retail dealers in the area. This market is difficult to service because the pesticide and fertilizer requirements are specific for each crop. On top of that, these farmers represent a variety of ethnic groups and cultural differences, which makes selling more difficult. Few competitors have the technical knowledge required to serve this market effectively. DCS's sales representatives, however, are very knowledgeable and often recommend fertilizers and pesticides for the specialty crop farmers.

Forty-five percent of DCS's 1993 retail sales dollars were derived from the sale of dry fertilizer (Exhibit 4). Last year, DCS sold 7,000 tons of dry fertilizer in the four counties around Dorset, with 80 percent of the retail bulk fertilizer and 60 percent of the retail bagged fertilizer being sold within a 15-mile radius of the plant. Because of the small farm sizes and the specialty crop requirements, approximately 50 percent of the dry fertilizer was sold in bagged form. DCS charges a flat $15 a ton premium for bagged fertilizer over bulk fertilizer of the same kind.

Pesticides account for 32 percent of DCS's retail sales. Although the margins on pesticides are much lower than those on fertilizer, Bill tries to offer a full line of agronomic products. He believes that if he can sell pesticides to a farmer, the farmer will often buy fertilizer from him as well. Approximately one-third of the pesticides sold are custom applied, and DCS offers more extensive service with regards to pesticide recommendations than most of its competitors.

DCS's market penetration in the 15-mile radius around Dorset is very

EXHIBIT 3 Retail market area showing the 15-mile radius of Dorset.

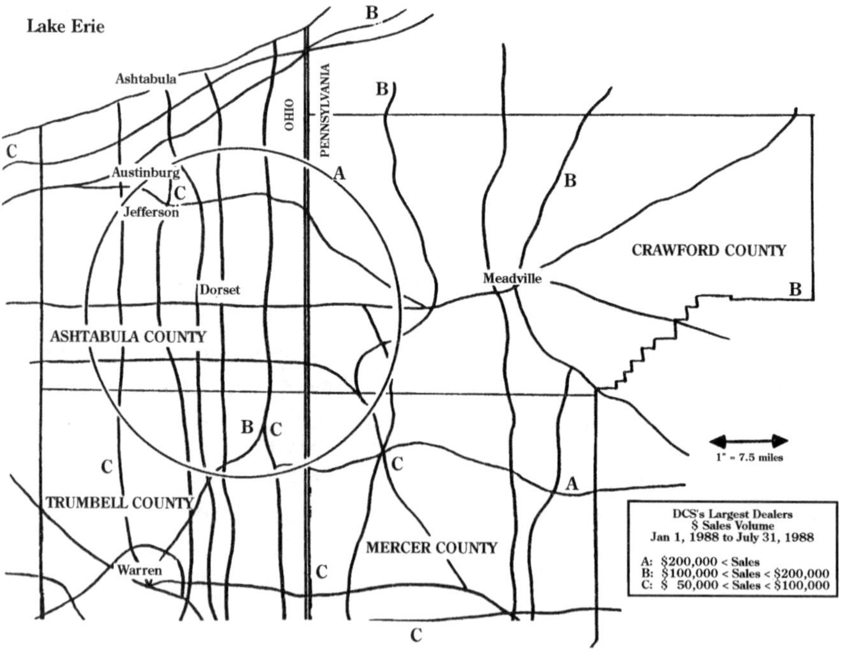

high. Bill feels less vulnerable selling in the retail market relative to the wholesale market because he knows he can provide the services necessary to keep the retail customers happy, whereas many of his dealers can't. Exhibit 5 shows DCS's total market share (including both retail and whole-sale sales) in the four counties (a 50-mile square) surrounding Dorset.

■■ SERVICES OFFERED

Besides selling fertilizers, seed, and lime at the retail level, DCS delivers fertilizer, custom applies fertilizer, pesticides, and lime, and rents equipment to customers. Only 20 percent of the retail customers require delivery and those who do are typically the larger farmers who buy more than 50 tons of fertilizer each year (Exhibit 6). Most of DCS's custom application customers are the larger farmers who buy more than 100 tons of fertilizer a year. Some of the part-time farmers use custom application as well, but more often these customers will rent spreaders and apply the material themselves. Ninety-eight percent of those customers who buy less than 20 tons a year will rent application equipment from DCS.

DCS also offers a fertility program that is becoming popular. It tests soil for its customers and bills only for the cost of the soil test (plus 50 cents an acre if DCS takes the sample). Using a computer program, it then graphs the soil types for each field and recommends the appropriate fertilizers and pesticides. All this information is entered into a computer. In subsequent years, if customers request recommendations or fertilizer delivery for a specific field, DCS has all the information readily available. And, as long as the

EXHIBIT 4   Percentage of retail sales dollars.

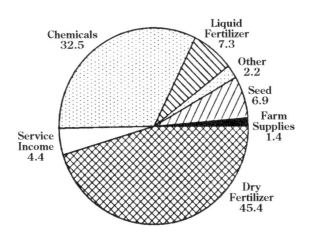

EXHIBIT 5   Market share for fertilizer sales.

COUNTY	TOTAL CONSUMPTION tons	DCS WHOLESALE tons	%
Ashtabula, OH	12,000	441	4
Trumbell, OH	9,000	1,340	15
Crawford, PA	14,000	2,607	19
Mercer, PA	13,000	9,232	71
Total	48,000	13,620	28

COUNTY	DCS RETAIL tons	%	DCS TOTAL tons	%
Ashtabula, OH	2,309	19	2,750	23
Trumbell, OH	1,170	13	2,510	28
Crawford, PA	3,224	23	5,831	42
Mercer, PA	300	2	9,532	73
Total	7,003	15	20,623	43

EXHIBIT 6   Retail customer characteristics by size in a 15-mile radius.

	CUSTOMER SIZE			
	Large	Medium	Small	Very Small
Tons of fertilizer purchased each year	>100	50 to 100	20 to 50	<20
Number of customers	10	50	100	300
Customers with bulk storage facilities	10%	5%	0%	0%
Customers who buy some fertilizer in bulk	100%	75%	60%	25%
Customers who own their application equipment	50%	25%	10%	2%
Customers who rent equipment from DCS	50%	75%	90%	98%
Customers who buy custom application:				
Fertilizer	25%	25%	25%	10%
Pesticides	50%	50%	25%	15%
Lime	25%	40%	25%	10%
Two or more services	75%	75%	60%	20%
Customers who want DCS to deliver the materials	50%	50%	25%	10%

customer buys from DCS, these services are provided at no charge. The number of customers using this service has greatly increased in the past five years. Now more than 50 percent of the farmers buying more than 20 tons a year utilize the record service. DCS is in the process of putting together a brochure promoting these agronomic services and its comprehensive fertility program.

Advertising and Promotion Program

Because DES has such a large market share in its immediate market area (Bill estimates as much as 90 percent in the 10 to 15-mile radius around Dorset, but cannot document this), DCS targets anyone who is interested in buying fertilizer and has money to spend. Besides advertising in the local papers, in magazines, and on the radio, DCS has one sales representative who calls on larger current or prospective customers. This year, in an attempt to reach more of his part-time and smaller customers, Bill also tried a direct mailing promotion to all customers about the services and special products DCS offers. He is unsure yet how effective this promotion was, but will try it again next year.

For several years DCS has held three or four meetings a year to tell invited customers about new products or to let them talk with some chemical sales representatives. Customers are chosen on the basis of which crops they grow, the size of their operation, and whether they are likely to buy the new product.

Pricing Policies

Bill prices retail fertilizer higher than the wholesale price he charges the dealers. Generally, DCS's retail price for dry fertilizer is $7 to $10 per ton higher than the dealer's wholesale price. Large farmers could be charged as little as $3 per ton above the dealer price, but this price is negotiable. Fertilizer delivery is usually $10 to $50 per truckload, depending on the distance of the haul.

The issue of how to price fertilizer for large farmers versus dealers concerns Bill. He is seeing a trend toward more direct selling to farmers. Currently, some of DCS's larger customers buy significantly more from DCS than its smaller dealers. Several wholesale competitors will sell truckloads of fertilizer to anyone at the dealer price. Last year, DCS lost a few of its largest farmer customers to this type of competition. Bill is concerned, however, that if he aggressively pursues this business he will seriously damage the relationships he has developed over the years with his dealers.

For the most part, Bill has managed to avoid selling fertilizer directly to farmers at wholesale prices. He has sold phosphorus and urea to two or three of his retail customers at the dealer price because the customers picked up truckloads of the materials directly from the dock at East Liverpool. Bill knows that if doesn't offer the dealer price to these farmers, they will buy from a competitor, and, in fact, last year they did. (A large competitor with similar facilities at the Lake Erie dock will sell at dealer prices to anyone who picks up the fertilizer at the dock.)

Retail Competition

There are only two major competitors in the four counties around Dorset: Jefferson Countrymark, 15 miles to the north of Dorset, and an independent dealer supplied by the Andersons out of Maumee, Ohio, 25 miles to the south in Trumbell County.

Jefferson Countrymark is a well-run cooperative that is a full-service farm supplier. It sells approximately 5,000 tons of fertilizer each year. In addition to fertilizer and feed, the cooperative is the only grain marketer in the county and will often trade grain for fertilizer with farmers. It rents equipment and offers some fertility programs but does not provide the level of agronomic consulting that DCS does.

The independent Anderson dealer has six bulk storage bins and no blender. He sells only on a cash basis and usually holds margins very tight. He rents a little equipment and is estimated to sell about 3,000 tons of fertilizer a year.

■■■ WHOLESALE MARKET

Two-thirds of DCS's total sales dollars comes from its wholesale business. Most of its 128 dealers are in western Pennsylvania; two are in the southwest corner of New York, and the remainder are in Ohio. Approximately 30 percent of DCS's wholesale volume comes from 5 of the 128 dealers; the top 20 dealers account for 64 percent of its wholesale sales dollars (Exhibit 7).

The dealers vary widely in their characteristics. A few of DCS's larger dealers are truckers who call on customers and deliver fertilizer to them without offering any services. A couple of other large dealers specialize in nursery crops or other specialty crops. The typical dealer, however, is a feed dealer who sells fertilizer as a sideline and has neither agronomic technical knowledge nor an interest in selling fertilizer.

Dry fertilizer sales generate 57.7 percent of the wholesale sales dollars (Exhibit 2). Because of the many small dealers, more than 60 percent of the dry fertilizer is sold in bagged and blended form. The number of dealers with facilities to handle bulk fertilizer is slowly increasing throughout the area, and Bill expects this trend to continue. Large farmers throughout Pennsylvania, however, are gearing up to handle bulk fertilizer faster than

EXHIBIT 7   Percentage of wholesale sales by number of dealers.

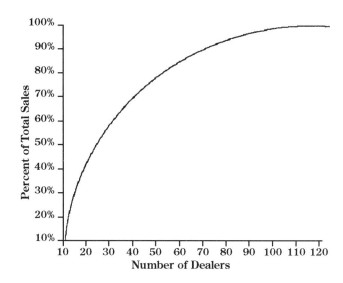

dealers are, and Bill is concerned that his dealers will not be able to meet the needs of this group.

Pricing Policies

DCS prices blended fertilizer at $20 to $26 per ton above the cost of material transported to the Dorset plant. If the dealer will pick up unblended material directly from a barge at East Liverpool or from the fertilizer storage dome on Lake Erie without any handling by DCS, the dealer is charged $5 to $7 above the cost of the material. Bagged fertilizer costs the dealer $15 per ton more than bulk fertilizer, regardless of the type. All prices are based on the dealer's picking the fertilizer up at the dome, barge, or plant. DCS rarely arranges transportation for the dealers.

Marketing

One salesman calls on the dealers in Pennsylvania and over the years has built up strong loyalty between DCS and the dealers through his visits and on-farm sales calls with them. These relationships are important to Bill, and he doesn't want DCS's future plans to jeopardize them.

Although no formal services are offered to the dealers with respect to fertility programs, dealers are encouraged to call DCS at any time with questions. DCS will also advise them on how to set up computerized record-keeping for their customers. And, as a distributor for SuperCrost seed, Bill is encouraging the more progressive dealers to use both the seed and the recommendations included in the SuperCrost Agri-Match program.

Wholesale Competition

At the wholesale level, DCS has four major competitors, who are spread throughout Ohio and Pennsylvania. These include the Andersons near Toledo, Ohio; D.W. Dickey in East Liverpool, Ohio; Agway Cooperative throughout Pennsylvania; and CPS in Alliance, Ohio. Of these, D.W. Dickey and the Andersons appear to represent the biggest threats to DCS's wholesale dealer relationships.

D.W. Dickey is a large firm that deals in several products other than fertilizer. Currently, they unload barges for DCS in East Liverpool. Dickey has a blending and bagging plant in East Liverpool and will sell fertilizer at dealer prices to anyone who buys a truckload. No services are offered with the sale. Until early this year, Dickey had only one salesman, who sold over the phone to customers in Ohio and Pennsylvania. Since the salesman's retirement six months ago, three salesmen have been hired—two for Ohio and one for Pennsylvania. Bill is not sure how aggressive Dickey will be with its new sales force or who it will target.

Agway Cooperative has several wholly-owned cooperatives throughout Pennsylvania. As a rule, these cooperatives buy all their products from Agway. Agway has more blend plants throughout western Pennsylvania than any other company. During the last two years, Agway has offered the lowest prices for fertilizer of all the competitors. This is partially because of the construction of an unloading dock for barges on the Ohio River, approximately 75 miles northeast of East Liverpool at Kitanning. The lower transportation costs that resulted had a major impact on the market in that area. Other than at the Kitanning dock, Agway sales reps do not sell directly to the farmer, but Bill feels that this may not always be the case. Agway also offers good training programs for their sales reps, and these individuals are often better trained than those from independent companies. Agway seems to target the large farmer who has money to spend and wants to buy fertilizer early in the season.

Andersons is another aggressive competitor in the Ohio and Pennsylvania wholesale market. It supplies dealers with both fertilizer and seed. Although Andersons' trucking costs from Toledo are much higher than those for DCS from eastern Ohio, it makes up the difference with backhauls of grain. During the last two years, Andersons has offered a program through its dealers for farmers who want to lock in a price for fertilizer. For a $5 per ton deposit in December, the customer can get delivery in March at the December price. This program has been well received and is very effective.

CPS in Alliance, Ohio, is similar to DCS in that it sells fertilizer to a retail market in a 20-mile radius of Alliance and to a wholesale market in Pennsylvania and other parts of Ohio. It has a blending and bagging plant but offers no other services to its customers. Its supply point is also East Liverpool. Bill isn't sure how aggressive CPS will be during the coming season because its only salesman is retiring at the end of next month.

■■ THE DILEMMA

After mulling over all this information, Bill knew that something had to be done. How was he going to handle the growing threat of direct sales to large customers while maintaining his dealer business? DCS must be competitive to get the dealer's business, but if a farmer bypassed the dealer and wanted more fertilizer than the dealer would sell in a year, should the farmer get the dealer price? What would that do to his relationship with the dealers? Although these relationships were very important to him, he certainly wanted to see the retail division of DCS continue to grow. Bill had a lot of questions, a lot of data, and little time . . .

AgMan SeedCo

Jim Lenox was again seriously thinking about retirement. He had almost retired two years ago from the business he and his father started many years ago. Jim felt that it was about time to turn the reins over to someone else. Before he died, Jim's father wrote a history of the hybrid seed corn industry, and looking at it now, Jim realized how far AgMan had come (see Attachment A).

It all started when Jim's father decided to try the new hybrids being developed at Iowa State College. Jim joined his father in the depths of the Great Depression after obtaining a degree in agriculture from Iowa State College. Together they raised hybrid seed corn. Most of their production was under contract to Pioneer, an Iowa company that grew into a major multinational seed company.

After his father's death, Jim pursued his interest in corn breeding. He developed some hybrid varieties particularly suited to the soil and climate of southwestern Iowa. He sold the seed to neighbors, who were satisfied with the growth results, and word spread about his hybrids. Over the years, Jim developed hybrids for different areas of Iowa and adjacent states.

As the business grew, Jim tried to maintain close contact with customers. He felt one of the advantages AgMan SeedCo had over the other major companies was personal knowledge of growing conditions. Because Jim had direct contact with the farmer, he could explain to the farmer how to choose the right hybrid and how to adjust cropping practices to optimize yields. Year after year, AgMan varieties outyielded other hybrids. It was easy to show customers the benefits of the AgMan program.

Eventually, Jim hired salespeople. He traveled with them as often as he could. They seemed to have more success when he was with them. The

This case was prepared by Michael W. Woolverton, Continental Grain Professor of Agribusiness at the American Graduate School of International Management; and George J. Seperich, Associate Professor in the School of Agribusiness and Environmental Resources at Arizona State University, as a basis for classroom discussion rather than to illustrate either effective or ineffective handling of a business situation. The authors would like to acknowledge the assistance of Audra Singinani, who helped update the case.

salespeople claimed that Jim's personal reputation helped them to sell seed.

Sales continued to grow until finally, two years ago, Jim just couldn't take the heavy work load any more. He told Sarah, his wife, he was going to retire. Sarah knew that he was just tired and would enjoy the business again if he had more help. She suggested he hire someone to help run the business. Sarah was concerned about Jim's health but knew he would be bored if he retired.

Jim found who he hoped would be just the right person. Rhonda Elliot had been a district manager for one of the large pesticide companies. Rhonda had an undergraduate degree in agronomy and an agribusiness master's degree. She was considered very knowledgeable in the area of corn production. "The product will sell itself" was one of Rhonda's favorite expressions.

Jim made Rhonda sales manager for the company. Rhonda hired several more salespeople and instituted a sales training program that included training on product knowledge, selling skills, and communications skills. She planned to increase sales by placing the new salespeople in territories carved out of territories of the more experienced sales personnel. The new salespeople then would have established customers to call on and could build up new customers gradually. The established salespeople would retain part of their old territories, but would expand selling activities into surrounding states.

Part of Rhonda's plan, which Jim agreed with, was to make AgMan SeedCo a regional seed corn company rather than just an Iowa company. Based on a quick market evaluation, Rhonda had projected a 20 percent increase in sales for 1993. But sales had not increased. In fact, after the farmers return seed corn they did not plant, sales may show a decline. Although southwest Iowa escaped serious flooding, some of AgMan's customers couldn't plant corn at all because of wet fields. Jim asked Rhonda to meet with him this morning to discuss the situation.

Rhonda briskly walked into his office. Before Jim had a chance even to say good morning, Rhonda handed him a paper with *AgMan SeedCo Marketing Philosophy* typed across the top of the page (see Attachment B).

"Here is the marketing philosophy paper I mentioned to you a few days ago. I want to give it to our salespeople next month at the sales meeting. Look on the second sheet. I've made up a series of questions and answers that explain the marketing philosophy in more depth. Look it over to see if you think it's okay."

Jim glanced at the paper, but before he had a chance to comment, Rhonda said, "I want to use this to kick off the sales meeting. Even though they have heard all this before from both you and me, this is the first time it has been put on paper. I want to be sure our salespeople understand what this company is all about. After we've had a chance to discuss this—you'll be there to answer questions, won't you?"

Jim nodded yes.

Rhonda continued, "We'll talk about our early order sales program for next year. I've got it about ready for the typist, but I wanted to talk with you about some of the specifics."

His patience wearing thin, Jim said brusquely, "Rhonda, shut the door and have a seat. We've got some problems we need to talk about."

Rhonda shut the door and sat down with an apprehensive look on her face.

"I've gone over your sales report for the year [see Attachment C]. Frankly, the results are disappointing. We had floods and wet fields, and farmers didn't take all the seed they ordered. I know we have to expect things like that once in a while, but our people just have to work harder. With the returns that are still going to come back to us, it looks like we are going to lose about $100,000 this year. This cannot go on for very many years. I know I'm going to die sometime, but I sure as hell don't want to die broke." With that, Jim could see Rhonda draw her breath.

"Rhonda, we've got to turn this thing around. My future depends on it. So does yours. I've been thinking about some alternatives. We'll go over them, and then we'll decide what we are going to do."

Attachment A

Average corn yields have tripled since 1930. This has been the result of:

- the change from open-pollinated varieties to hybrid varieties
- production practices that promote high yield, primarily the increased use of nitrogen fertilizer but also the use of insecticides and herbicides

Hybrids are more productive than open-pollinated corn because of "hybrid vigor" and because the technique of inbred parent lines enables plant breeders to select for more productive types.

Plant breeders have improved corn performance by selecting genetic types that:

- make better use of moisture, light, fertilizer, and so on
- produce high plant populations: open-pollinated corn varieties were planted at about 12,000 plants per acre, but modern hybrids produce the highest yields at 24,000 or more plants per acre
- resist insect and disease damage
- adapt to different geographic (length-of-day) locations

Hybrids have been developed that have the yield potential for more than 300 bushels per acre. Some farmers are able to approach this level of production in small test plots, but yearly average corn yield in the United States is about 120 bushels per acre.

The methods used to market hybrid seed corn have gradually evolved. Hybrid seed corn was first offered to the market as "open pedigree" hybrids. The parent lines were developed by the U.S. Department of Agriculture (USDA) and the state agricultural experiment stations. Nonprofit foundation seed corn companies were formed for the purpose of increasing the supply of the lines produced by the state agricultural experiment stations and distributing to seed corn producers. Small seed corn producers made the final cross, cleaned, treated, bagged, and sold the seed to local farmers. At one time, more than 300 seed producers were at work in Iowa. These early seed producers were trained by state university specialists in the techniques of hybrid seed corn production and use.

The first hybrids were sold as certified. Before a hybrid could be certified, it had to meet minimum performance standards as determined by a variety release committee. State experiment stations conducted tests at several locations in each state to determine how the hybrids compared. The pedigree was printed on the tag. The state experiment station, before releasing the variety, assigned the hybrid a number. A particular pedigree could be sold only as the number originally assigned regardless of where or by whom it was sold.

This method of marketing made it very difficult to develop a following for one company's brand. Certified Iowa C64, for example, was known to have the same pedigree, regardless of who offered it for sale.

Seed corn was soon in surplus supply. Individual producers, in an attempt to capture a larger share of the market, placed their seed on consignment with local grain elevators and farm supply stores. Because two or more producers generally served the same area, an elevator would often stock seed of the same pedigree for several seed producers.

Severe price competition and lack of brand identity encouraged the more aggressive marketers to discontinue producing and marketing certified seed. They began to market their own company brands. Initially, these branded hybrids were produced using the same inbred lines used to produce the certified hybrids. All this caused confusion for corn growers. They now had the problem of trying to decide which brand was best. The local elevator dealer was of little help. He did not understand seed corn and, because of the press of other business activities, had little interest in learning about it.

By the middle of the 1940s, several national seed corn companies began to emerge. Initially they marketed their branded seed through local elevators and farm supply stores. It became apparent, however, that this would not give them the representation and aggressive selling effort they needed.

Dekalb found a solution to this problem. It appointed farmer/dealer representatives. A substantial dealer training program and a very aggressive national brand advertising and promotion program set the marketing pattern for the industry.

The early dealers were effective. They were selling an idea as well as seed corn. They were proud to be part of a fast-growing, successful company marketing a new product. A popular selling approach was to explain to farmers/customers that a large corporation could develop and produce hybrids superior to those developed by the university experiment stations. The major-brand national companies devoted their major marketing effort to building strong, respected brand images. They were successful. Dekalb once was able to advertise that "more farmers plant Dekalb seed than all other brands combined."

Today 80 percent to 90 percent of all seed corn is marketed by three or four major companies. Pioneer is the industry leader with near 50 percent market share. Most companies used the Dekalb approach of farmers/dealers. Aside from Dekalb, Pioneer, and Funks G, most of these efforts were relatively ineffective. The smaller companies could not compete with the larger companies in establishing a strong corporate brand image. They advertised their research and testing program as though they were responsible for the breeding and development of the hybrids they were selling. This caused a credibility problem. The corn grower could not understand how the small seed-corn producer could possibly produce hybrids that were equal to those of the major national brand companies.

Most of the farmers/dealers for the smaller companies made little effort to sell seed. They accepted the dealership because of cost savings to themselves. In many cases, farmers/dealers did not have much confidence in the seed offered by the smaller company. Even though they were dealers, the farmers continued to use mostly major brand seed on their own farms.

The large national brand company did not necessarily have better seed. The state agricultural experiment stations and the USDA continued to do most of the basic research. The foundation seed companies expanded their programs of applied research and hybrid testing. This made it possible, for any seed producer, large or small, to have good parent line seed.

This is generally not understood by the corn grower. Each company represents its hybrids as unique. There are slight differences, but that may or may not make them better.

Corn growers confronted with the task of deciding which hybrid to plant are in a quandary. They have literally hundreds of choices. In self-protection, most growers limit their purchases from any one supplier. Farmers usually plant several hybrids each year, hoping that low-yielding hybrids will be more than offset by the high-yielding hybrids.

Average yields are much less than 300 bushels per acre (bpa), which emphasizes the relationship between genetics and the environment. The stress of high plant population, soil moisture, fertility, disease, insects, weeds, and so on may result in very low yields. The potential for high yields will be realized only if a favorable environment is provided.

Genetic types susceptible to insect and disease damage may escape damage when moisture and temperature are unfavorable for the insects or the disease. Aphids, for example, will cause crop damage, but only if the weather is hot and dry prior to tasseling. Leaf blight requires warm, humid weather for maximum development. First-brood corn borer may be more damaging in early planted corn than in corn planted later in the season. Second-brood is usually more damaging to late planted corn.

In the past 20 years, AgMan SeedCo has tested and evaluated nearly 800 hybrid pedigrees. The results clearly demonstrate real differences among hybrids. The yield differences among brands can be 20 percent or more. The tests also show that farmers can increase profits by using the newer hybrids.

To reap the maximum benefits, a corn grower should be prepared to accept new hybrids as they are proven superior. The AgMan testing program is designed to provide information that will allow a grower to use proven hybrids with confidence.

One of the more frequently asked questions is, Why do hybrids run out?

This question is asked when it is observed that a hybrid does not yield or stand as well as previous plantings. It just seems logical that the hybrid has changed. But the hybrid has not changed. The characteristics of the seed—the genetic potential—remain fixed. The observed performance may change, however, because diseases have changed. Diseases may be caused by viruses, bacteria, or fungi, which are constantly changing. Inbred lines that at one time were very resistant to rots, mold, blight, and so on are gradually more affected as disease organisms slowly evolve over time.

Better hybrids are the result of better inbred lines. Corn breeders at public and private research stations are constantly modifying older inbred lines and developing new ones. Thousands of hybrids can be developed using the vast number of inbred lines available. Much breeding is haphazard. In many instances, there are no real reasons for what is done except the hope that a winner might be found.

In the future, the development of new corn hybrids will become more precise. The genetic code of corn is being mapped. Using biotechnology, plant breeders will be able to fine tune the genetic makeup of new lines.

AgMan SeedCo was established as a privately held corporation for the purpose of helping corn growers improve profits from growing corn. The AgMan program has three parts.

1. *Hybrid information.* Comprehensive tests determine the important performance characteristics of commercial and experimental hybrids. Then statistical analysis determines how different hybrids perform when conditions of weather, year, location, fertility, and so on vary. The purpose is to make information available that will enable corn growers to select hybrids with the characteristics they consider most important.

2. *Better corn hybrids.* Produce and offer for sale hybrids that have demonstrated superior performance in research tests and on farm trials.

3. *Personal services*

    A. *Corn specialists.* AgMan area representatives are full-time employees. They are responsible for sales and customer service in their sales territory. They assist with the hybrid tests and during the growing season, they inspect the growing crop and evaluate results. Because of their training and experience, they are qualified to interpret test results, select hybrids best suited to particular situations, arrange for agronomic tests, and provide analysis designed to help the grower improve yield and profit.

    B. *Management seminars.* A wide range of production, marketing, and business management subjects are taught by qualified professionals. The purpose is to provide an opportunity for customers to learn about new ideas and exchange experiences with one another.

Attachment B

■■■ AGMAN SEEDCO MARKETING PHILOSOPHY

Our purpose is to help our customers improve corn yield and profit. We will accomplish this by:

1. Providing information about corn hybrids.
   A. How hybrids compare in yield, maturity, and plant characteristics.
   B. How hybrids vary in response to various environmental conditions, for example, fertility, length of growing season, rainfall, temperature, insects, and disease.
2. Furnish high-quality hybrids that have the yield, maturity, and plant characteristics with the best chance of producing an optimal profit yield. The income from the sale of seed pays the entire cost of the service.
3. Professional help in developing a high-profit, corn-growing plan.
   A. Area representatives will review soil management and fertility practices. If appropriate, representatives will make suggestions relating to cost, adequacy, or risks of these programs.
   B. Area representatives will make one or more field inspections to check on crop progress and look for symptoms of insect infestation, weeds, fertility problems, or disease. If a problem is identified, representatives will provide information that can be used to reduce the severity of the problem or prevent recurrence.
   C. Area representatives will assist in developing a hybrid plan suited to customers' soil and production goals.
   D. Area representatives will discuss final results and assist in evaluating the corn-growing plan. These results will be used to develop a corn-growing proposal for the following year.
   E. AgMan SeedCo will provide crop production and marketing seminars to customers free of charge.

Questions About Our Marketing Program

How do we compete with the major companies?

AgMan SeedCo does not engage in the "claims game" with other seed corn companies. We provide customers with information and analysis that allow them to make choices in their own best interest. To compete successfully, we must demonstrate that our hybrids and services are of greater value. We know we can offer hybrids at least equal to the rest of the competition. The exact value lies in helping customers build a more profitable corn-growing program. Our expertise in testing hybrids, providing information, and personal service provides our competitive edge.

Do we raise all our own seed?

No! In fact we raise none of it. We develop the hybrids from which seeds are produced for us. All AgMan seed is produced by experienced contract seed growers. AgMan supplies the foundation seed and specifies minimum production standards. The acreage is detasseled by the contract growers. At harvest time, the growers deliver the dry, shelled seed to the plant for sizing, treatment, and bagging. All seed must meet minimum specifications for genetic purity, as determined by Florida growouts, moisture content, and germination percentage.

What about warehousing and delivery?

These operations are under direct control of AgMan SeedCo management. The processed, bagged seed is stored under protected environmental conditions at our plant. Deliveries are made early in the spring directly to each customer. Part of the seed is delivered by AgMan SeedCo personnel using company-owned vehicles. The rest is delivered by contract haulers.

How do AgMan SeedCo test results compare with university extension service test results?

It is only natural to assume that the state tests would be less biased than the tests of a business firm. Bias has nothing to do with it. It is easy to demonstrate that AgMan obtains results similar to the state test at some locations. Our challenge is not to be critical of the tests but to help customers understand how to use the tests to their advantage. The real benefit from testing is not the absolute numbers but the understanding that comes from a study and analysis of the test results. This is only possible when results are available from many locations and many different environments.

The limitation of the university tests is that they are conducted at only a few locations. Only six locational environments are studied each year, and only a few hybrids are planted in all six environments. In a few locations, yield differences due to environmental influence can be quite large. A study of test results of similar pedigrees will show yield differences of 20 to 40 bushels per acre or more. Replicated tests usually cancel these differences.

AgMan tests are conducted at 24 locations. The purpose of these tests is to collect information on selected popular commercial hybrids. Comparisons are made for yield, maturity, disease, plant and grain characteristics, and insect reaction. The performance of each hybrid is compared with one or more standard hybrids. This method provides a way to rank hybrids by various characteristics because all hybrids are directly compared with the same standards.

The services provided to corn growers are valuable. Why don't we charge a service fee?

The concept behind the AgMan marketing program is that the service becomes part of the product. A farmer who buys our seed does not pay extra for the information and professional services provided. To be a valid concept, the hybrid offered for sale must have performance characteristics at least equal to the best hybrids offered by the competition. We have demonstrated that this is a practical reality. The pedigrees we offer for sale have proven to be equal or superior to most of the commercial hybrids available. Under some conditions, a competitive hybrid may have traits superior to a similar AgMan hybrid. In that case, customers will be encouraged to include the competitive hybrid in their production plans.

Why don't we lower our price or give discounts so that customers have more incentive to buy?

Our pricing is competitive with the major seed corn companies. AgMan is not a low-priced seed company. The sale of the seed pays all the costs of operating the business. It is expected that returns will be sufficient to provide all operating expenses, personnel benefits, and cash for improving facilities and customer benefits and a fair return on shareholders' investments.

Attachment C

AgMan SeedCo personnel and sales report.

TERRITORY	NAME	AGE	DEGREE	EXPERIENCE
1	Bill Hayes	37	B.S. Ag. Engineering	Fertilizer Sales 6 yrs. AgMan 7 yrs.
2	Kim Olson	23	B.S. Agronomy	No previous work
3	James Jillison	26	B.S. Ag. Education	VoAg Teacher 2 yrs. AgMan 1 yr.
4	Michael Perry	25	B.S. Animal Science	Feed Sales 3 yrs. AgMan 1 yr.
5	Karen Ankes	24	B.S. Animal Science	No previous work AgMan 1 yr.
6	Max Williamson	39	No Degree	AgMan 15 yrs. Production then sales
7	John Duffy	38	B.S. Ag. Education	VoAg Teacher 5 yrs. AgChem Sales 7 yrs. AgMan 3 yrs.
8	Keri Arenholtz	31	B.S. Bus. Admin.	Retail Store Mgr. 3 yrs.
9	Randy Booker	25	B.S. Plant Pathology	Lab. Technician 2 yrs. AgMan 1 yr.

Sales 1992 and 1993 (estimated).

NAME	CUSTOMERS		SALES (UNITS)[a]		COMPENSATION[b]	
	1992	1993	1992	1993	1992	1993
Hayes	150	112	8,800	6,300	$48,800	$37,900
Duffy	132	104	6,950	5,200	37,850	34,600
Williamson	154	100	7,250	4,450	39,500	33,450
Arenholtz	120	73	6,500	3,200	36,500	32,200
Perry	—	81	—	3,150	——	32,150
Jillison	—	60	—	2,650	——	32,000
Booker	—	49	—	1,750	——	32,000
Ankes	—	30	—	1,000	——	32,000
Olson	—	22	—	700	——	32,000
Total	556	631	29,500	28,400	$162,650	$298,300

[a]A unit of seed corn is a bag that contains a minimum of 80,000 kernels. A unit weighs 40 to 50 pounds, depending on variety, and will plant about 3 1/2 acres, depending on desired plant population.
[b]Compensation in 1992 was based on a $30,000 base plus a commission of $1 per unit in excess of 2,000, $2 per unit in excess of 4,000, $3 per unit in excess of 6,000, and $4 per unit on sales of more than 7,500 units. In 1993, the commission schedule remained the same, but base pay was raised to $32,000.

CASE

5

The Cherrex Decision

▬ INTRODUCTION

This case introduces the U.S. tart cherry industry and a proposed export-trading company that would sell processed and semiprocessed tart cherries in Japan. Three fruit processors and the director of a federated marketing cooperative weigh the pros and cons of joining the proposed company in late 1988.

The Proposal

With the 1988 harvest behind them, rival fruit processors Bob Packer, John Minnema, Mike Anderson, and Jim Brian are each wrestling with the same decision. Each has to decide for or against joining Cherrex, a new export trading company that Dick Johnston has proposed for handling any and all of their future sales of cherry products to Japan.

Dick Johnston, executive director of the Cherry Marketing Institute (CMI), had the idea, and although he invited all of the some 40 processors in the CMI's constituent states (Michigan, Utah, and Wisconsin), he needs just enough processors to be able to supply all the Japanese demand for tart cherries that CMI was hoping to develop through a separate promotional program already underway. Cherrex would assure a standard of quality, one reliable source for all tart cherry purchases, and perhaps most important, a unified price that would hopefully be higher than that realized with the processors all bidding against one another.

The idea to put together a joint export company could trace its roots to the mid-1970s when Michigan State University agricultural economist Don Ricks proposed forming such an organization to take advantage of the

This case was prepared by James M. Hagen, Doctoral Student in Business Administration and Food and Agribusiness Management Fellow; and Assistant Professor Michael A. Mazzocco, Associate Director of the Food and Agribusiness Management Program at the University of Illinois at Urbana-Champaign, as a basis for classroom discussion rather than to illustrate either effective or ineffective handling of a business situation.

Webb-Pomerene Act, which permitted the operation of cartels for price fixing in the export market. The Export Trading Act of 1982 greatly enhanced the appeal of joint export trading companies, in part by giving participants greater assurance that they wouldn't be charged with antitrust violations for price fixing under the law's guidelines (Exhibit 1).

CMI had already made its commitment to promote tart cherries in Japan. With canned cherry exports to Japan actually declining for the past five years to a current level of 700,000 pounds (raw product equivalent), CMI hoped to reverse the trend and drive annual exports to Japan up to about 40 million pounds in 20 years. Now it wanted to organize a means to facilitate the hoped for sales and take advantage of the promotional effort. Without a selling organization, CMI cautioned that its own promotional efforts could result in sales by West Coast growers rather than CMI's own grower/constituents in Michigan, Utah, and Wisconsin. Freight to Japan, after all, was about six cents a pound more from Michigan than from Oregon.

EXHIBIT 1   The Export Trading Company Act of 1982.

On October 8, 1982, President Reagan signed into law the Export Trading Company Act of 1982 (P.L. 97-290,96 Stat. 1233). The ETC Act is intended to increase U.S. exports of goods and services, primarily by removing two impediments: (1) restrictions on trade financing and (2) uncertainty about the application of U.S. antitrust laws to export trade. The changes that the ETC Act makes in banking and antitrust laws are reflected in four titles, which, for the most part are independent of each other.

- Title I sets forth the overall purpose of the legislation, establishes the Office of Export Trading Company Affairs (OETCA) in the Department of Commerce (DOC) to promote the formation of ETCs, and creates a service to facilitate contact between producers of exportable goods and services and firms offering export trade services.

- Title II, the Bank Export Services Act, amends the Bank Holding Company Act to permit bank holding companies and other specified banking entities to invest in ETCs, establishes a program for working capital loan guarantees by the Export-Import Bank of the United States (Eximbank), and amends the Federal Reserve Act by increasing significantly the amount of bankers' acceptances a bank may have outstanding at any time.

- Title III provides for the issuance of export trade certificates of review by the Secretary of Commerce (with the concurrence of the Department of Justice) under which the export conduct of any person may receive specific antitrust protection.

- Title IV clarifies the jurisdictional reach of the Sherman Act and the Federal Trade Commission Act with respect to export-related commerce.

Source: U.S. Department of Commerce, *Export Trading Company Guidebook* (Revised August 1987), p. 5.

As proposed, Cherrex would (1) sell its members' tart cherry products under a Cherrex or other joint label, (2) negotiate on behalf of members for transportation, storage, and promotion, (3) establish prices and terms for the sale of products in Asia, and enter into sales agreements on behalf of members, (4) establish exclusive distributorship agents in specific markets, (5) advise the U.S. government and negotiate with foreign governments in relation to trade conditions, and (6) develop new product applications and technologies, with the option of licensing some of those technologies in export markets.

Members would make annual investments (ranging from several hundred to several thousand dollars per member per year) according to their proportionate share of the product being promoted for export. Those joining after 1988 would have to pay their share of prior years' developmental expense. In addition, Cherrex would retain a commission of approximately 5 percent of any tart cherry sales it arranged. Cherrex hoped, within five years or so, to be self-supporting and require no further investment from members. Cherrex expected that the same Japanese agent hired by CMI to promote cherries would serve (at additional expense) as agent for Cherrex sales, with the agent's expense divided in some fashion between CMI and Cherrex. CMI would serve as business agent for Cherrex, and CMI executive director Dick Johnston would also serve as Cherrex managing director. Lots of ideas for helping the cherry industry have been floated over the years only to be sunk by protest, lack of interest, or changed circumstances. Without members, Cherrex would be another idea that died. Bob, John, Mike, and Jim have individual factors to consider before deciding whether to join.

▰ BACKGROUND

Growing Cherries

Cherries are a perennial tree fruit. The many varieties of cherries can be divided into two classifications: *sweet cherries* (used primarily for fresh fruit, maraschino cherries, and glacé) and *tart cherries* (used in pies and related sugar-added products). Cherries grow best in sandy soils in moderate climates. Major cherry-producing countries in order of tonnage grown are Russia, Yugoslavia, the U.S., and Chile. Within the U.S., the Great Lakes area provides excellent growing conditions. Major producing states and their percentages of total production of tart cherries are Michigan (72%), New York (9%), Utah (8%), Wisconsin, Oregon, and Washington (3% each), and Pennsylvania (2%). About 75 percent of Michigan's production is concentrated in the Grand Traverse area, where hilly peninsulas jutting into Lake Michigan provide excellent climatic and soil conditions.

In 1988, the U.S. total bearing tart cherry acreage was 49,280 acres. With pounds harvested per acre that year of 4,790, the total U.S. production was 233.5 million pounds. Tart cherry trees are planted at about 125 trees per acre, with an average harvest per mature tree of about 45 pounds of cherries per once-a-year season.

Cherry trees must be about 8 years old before their first harvest, and their total life expectancy is about 20 years. Prospective planters are challenged with estimating the market for cherries 8 to 20 years into the future. History has shown that more trees are planted when prices are high, and this results in long-term cycles in cherry production. Cherries are very sensitive to climatic conditions. A frost after budding can destroy an orchard's crop; heavy rains can swell the cherries to the point of splitting; strong wind can cause them to beat against each other, leaving brown blemishes. This susceptibility to loss or damage on the tree along with geographic concentration results in severe year-to-year fluctuations of production (see Exhibit 2). Because they are extremely perishable upon harvest, tart cherries are put in cooling tanks of cold water in the orchard immediately upon harvest, and within hours they are delivered for same-day processing.

Processing and Marketing Tart Cherries

As commercial plantings of cherries took root around the turn of the century along Lake Michigan, the first crops were actually shipped fresh to Chicago and other urban markets. Refrigerator cars (once they became available) were used until 1912 when the first canning factory brought fresh shipments to a near end. In 1922 a packing plant in northern Michigan froze cherries at the point of production for the first time. Their pack of 25 pounds of cherries with five pounds of sugar (as a preservative and to

EXHIBIT 2   Tart cherry production and price.

	1980	1981	1982	1983	1984
Quantity[a]	218.0	133.0	311.0	155.0	271.0
Price[b]	20.2	46.4	13.5	49.1	24.8

	1985	1986	1987	1988
Quantity[a]	286.0	224.0	359.0	236.0
Price[b]	21.7	129.7	7.4	17.8

[a]Total U.S. production in millions of pounds (raw equivalent)
[b]Cents per pound (raw equivalent) paid to growers
Source: R. T. Boehm. *Red Tart Cherries: Crop Statistics and Market Analysis.* Red Tart Cherry Growers Marketing Committee and the Michigan Agricultural Cooperative Marketing Association, Inc. 1992.

enhance color and flavor) became the standard frozen cherry pack and is referred to as 5+1. The industry grew, and by 1950, Michigan had more than 2 million trees in production, and the Great Lakes states produced about 285 million pounds of tart cherries out of a total U.S. production of about 315 million pounds.

Early processing was by proprietary enterprises, but with the financial and legislative incentives behind the cooperative movement of the 1920s, a number of cherry grower cooperatives organized, in some cases establishing their own processing plants. Competition between processors was (and is) stiff, primarily focusing on price. The biggest cooperative, Cherry Growers, was organized in the 1930s and has hundreds of grower members with ownership of the largest cherry-packing plant in the world.

In the early 1970s tart cherry processing changed in some major ways. Most processing was still being done by proprietary operators, with most operations located adjacent to Lake Michigan or area rivers for the easy discharge of wastes. Federally mandated water quality standards forced these plants off the water, and in the process several large processors simply went out of business. For example, Morgan Packing Company, a large processor that had recently merged with a competitor, F&M Packing Co., ceased operations in December 1972. With the help of a federal grant, Traverse City offered to buy Morgan's large waterfront plant for recreational use, and the owners (by inheritance) of the company liquidated the entire operation.

Other canners had financial difficulties. Traverse City Canning Company was a major canner that struggled until its final bankruptcy in 1981. The Cherry Growers processing plant, at the time owned by Duffy Mott, was put up for sale in 1972. Realizing they may have no place to take their fruit, area tart cherry growers nervously approached the year's harvest with the prospect of no place to sell their fruit. Several things happened quickly. Cherry Growers, which was then just a delivery co-op, bought the Duffy Mott plant, and membership grew. Dozens of growers established their own small processing plants, often forming cooperatives in the process.

Cooperatives came to account for about 80 percent of the tart cherry pack, but some growers did not view this as cause for celebration. Cooperatives (often the only buyers for cherries) would pay their growers whatever money was left after the processed cherries were actually sold, shifting all price risk from processor to the grower. With a mandate of processing nearly all that their members produced, the processing cooperatives would be forced to negotiate prices downward to make sales.

To put a break on the downward price spirals in high production years (which 1974 and 1975 were), a federal marketing order provided for cherry set-asides (with the grower processing, but not selling, his own fruit) as an alternative to fruit abandonment. Those growers who did custom process and held on to their fruit until prices were up had such positive results that planting surged in Michigan, as well as in Utah, Oregon, and Washington (which were exempt from the order), exacerbating an over-supply problem when those plantings began to bear about eight years later. The successes of 1974 and 1975 were followed by successive years of low prices. Growers, angry at being unable to recover their costs in processing and storing the set-aside fruit, voted the marketing order down. Wild year-to-year fluctuations in prices to growers continue to characterize this indus-try (Exhibit 2).

As the structure of the cherry-processing industry shifted in the early 1970s, some marketing channels were disrupted. With encouragement from Dr. Donald Ricks, a Michigan State University agricultural economist, and George McManus, the Grand Traverse County Extension Agent (and a grower himself), a group of processing cooperatives got together and formed a federated marketing cooperative, exempted from certain antitrust restrictions by the Capper-Volstead Act. Called Cherry Central Co-opera-tive, it resembled a marketing cooperative called Citrus Central that had earlier been established in Florida.

In 1973, its first year, it had about four processing members (the biggest being Cherry Growers) and a general manager who had been working for the National Red Tart Cherry Institute. Helped by a short crop, Cherry Central succeeded in selling all its product. Cherry Central met with considerably less marketing success in the high surplus years of 1974 and 1975, and some of its members wanted to quit the organization. In the turmoil, a grower named John Minnema became general manager, and under his leadership, Cherry Central grew to the point that it could count 16 members in four states (and about half the nation's tart cherry sales) at the time of the Cherrex discussions. Total sales (including apples and other products) were approaching $100 million in 1988. Cherry Growers Cooperative accounts for about 30 percent of Cherry Central's sales, and Cherry Central is the biggest marketer of tart cherry products in the country.

Sociological and technological changes have also had an impact on the cherry industry. Harvesting had traditionally been done primarily by migrant Hispanic laborers based in Texas and Florida, who came to the orchards by the tens of thousands for the several weeks of harvest each July. In the late 1960s, government attention turned to the migrants' living conditions, and growers were required to provide them with a higher stan-dard of housing and sanitation facilities. At the same time that migrants were becoming a more expensive labor source, Michigan State University was developing mechanical harvesting equipment to shake cherries from the trees, thus manual harvesting gave way to mechanical. The cost of that equipment raised the minimum efficient scale, and orchard size increased while the number of orchards decreased.

The Basic Tart Cherry Pack

The 1988 tart cherry pack, as others in preceding years, consisted of the three main types of pack: industrial, food service, and retail. Dried cherries, though discussed more than in the past, were still a minuscule part of the market. Frozen and water pack cherries must be packed within about 20 hours of harvest. Pie fill can be made from fresh, individually quick frozen (IQF), 5+1, or even previously canned cherries. Dried cherries can be made from frozen cherries. Exhibit 3 gives fresh weight equivalents of major packs.

Industrial (for example, for confectionery companies): Individually quick frozen (IQF) cherries are packed like marbles in plastic bag-lined 30-pound boxes. The alternative 5+1 pack is 25 pounds of cherries topped with 5 pounds of sugar in buckets and then frozen. Because of labeling technology, labels must be affixed at the time of processing rather than as orders come in after the pack.

Food Service (for restaurants): These cherries are canned in water, in a light syrup, or with starches and sweeteners in the form of pie filling. The #10 can is standard for this.

Retail: Frozen cherries were a market failure at the retail level several years earlier. In 1988, the basic retail pack was cherries canned in water, in a light syrup, or as a pie filling. Water pack (including with light syrup) can sizes are primarily a #303 size (16 ounces). Pie fill generally goes in a #303 or an A size (20 ounce) can.

Cherry Consumption

Per capita movement (Exhibit 4) of processed tart cherries in the U.S. has dropped over the past several decades from an average of 1.43 pounds (1955–64) to 0.84 pounds (1975–84). Price uncertainty and supply unreliability have been major handicaps in expanding the markets for

EXHIBIT 3   Processed to fresh weight conversion factors for tart cherries.

PROCESSED WEIGHT	FRESH WEIGHT
One pound frozen	1.11 pounds fresh
One pound juice	1.47 pounds fresh
One case (24 cans of #303 size)	26.15 pounds fresh
One case (6 cans of #10 size)	42.20 pounds fresh
One case (24 cans of #2.5 size)	45.87 pounds fresh
One case (12 cans of #2 size)	12.00 pounds fresh

Source: R. T. Boehm. *Red Tart Cherries: Crop Statistics and Market Analysis,* Red Tart Cherry Growers Marketing Committee and the Michigan Agricultural Cooperative Marketing Association, Inc. 1992.

cherries. Some manufacturers even dropped cherries from their product lines in the 1970s and early 1980s. Increasing promotional expenditures in oversupply years has generally been unsuccessful at expanding demand for tart cherries in the short run.

Efforts aimed at long-term demand expansion have also been less than successful. Some possible reasons are:

1. Cherries contain hard pits that can damage teeth if bitten on unexpectedly, and at this time, the state of the art of cherry processing is such that no processor is willing to guarantee a pitless product. USDA standards for grade A cherries allow one pit per 40 ounces.
2. The supply is unstable, with production fluctuating from year to year.
3. Consumer preference has shifted toward fresh produce and away from sweetened desserts. In the U.S. at least, tart cherries have not been eaten except when sweetened.

Industry and Government Efforts to Improve Tart Cherry Marketing

Industry organizations have come and gone over the years. In 1988, the Cherry Marketing Institute (CMI) was launched as the main marketing organization for the industry. In the midst of organizational turmoil in the mid '80s, a marketing instructor at Northwestern Michigan Community College, Dick Johnston, put together a plan for an organization that came to life in 1988 as the Cherry Marketing Institute. Soon after, Dick (a dynamic promoter whose college position was meant to wind down a marketing career that

EXHIBIT 4   Processed tart cherries: U.S. movement (millions of pounds—raw product equivalent).

YEAR	FROZEN	CONSUMER SIZES (Canned)	NO. 10 (Canned)	TOTAL Canned	OTHER	TOTAL APPARENT MVMT	PER CAPITA MVMT
1980–81	124.3	8.1	17.2	25.3	49.5	199.1	0.87
1981–82	96.6	7.6	5.2	12.8	31.5	140.9	0.61
1982–83	168.5	8.7	11.6	20.3	55.1	243.9	1.05
1983–84	111.0	6.5	3.9	10.4	34.3	155.7	0.67
1984–85	135.0	8.5	5.4	13.9	63.0	211.9	0.90
1985–86	147.1	12.0	7.4	19.4	47.3	213.8	0.90
1986–87	186.3	8.3	4.4	12.7	41.8	240.8	1.00
1987–88	179.5	13.4	8.3	21.7	42.4	243.6	1.00

Source: R. T. Boehm. *Red Tart Cherries: Crop Statistics and Market Analysis.* Red Tart Cherry Growers Marketing Committee and the Michigan Agricultural Cooperative Marketing Association, Inc. 1992.

included a vice presidency at Winnebago) became CMI's director. With an office in Okemos, Michigan, and a staff of about four, the CMI is funded largely by tart cherry growers in Michigan, Utah, and Wisconsin, with each state requiring its growers to pay dues. Michigan growers, for example, must pay a promotion surcharge of $10.00 per ton of production, with most of that money going to the CMI. Although they produce about 10 percent of the nation's tart cherries, New York growers have opted to not join CMI.

The CMI funds university research for the development of improved cherry varieties and cherry products and for improvements to processing, production, and pest management. In advocating the creation of the CMI, Dick Johnston envisioned tapping some of the USDA funds administered by the Foreign Agriculture Service (FAS) for market promotion. So far these funds have not been used for cherries or for any other commodity in Michigan. Called TEA (Trade and Export Assistance) funds, this financial aid could be used for either generic commodity promotion or branded products promotion on a dollar-for-dollar matching basis. For branded product promotion, a Chicago-based organization called Mid-America Trade Council (MIATCO) distributed federal funds to specific businesses in a 12-state region for promotion in export markets on a dollar-for-dollar match with private funds. Generic commodities would be funded as commodity councils applied for it. More than a few growers and processors are philosophically opposed to using government money to support free enterprise. Also, some think the return from promotion would be greater if directed domestically rather than internationally.

For market promotion, the CMI aimed its sights on Japan, with a goal of dramatically increasing tart cherry sales from the U.S. to Japan. With a population of 125 million and a prosperity receiving almost daily newspaper coverage, Japan seemed ideal. Although tart cherries were virtually unknown (and not grown) in Japan, cherry trees and blossoms are revered in literature and in art, and locally grown sweet cherries are a well-liked but expensive dessert fruit. With Japan as a beachhead, the other newly industrialized countries of Asia could be on deck for further market expansion. In its first year of market promotion in Japan, CMI anticipated using about $350,000 of the federal funds, 26 percent of which CMI would have to match with funds from other sources.

■ FOUR DECISION MAKERS

Bob Packer, Packer Canning Company

Packer Canning Company is a three-generation family business that specializes in canning cherries, plums, blueberries, and asparagus. Its one plant is along the road heading south out of the small town of Lawton and into the gently rolling orchard and grape land of southwestern Michigan. Bob Packer, president and son of the founder, lives just across the road. Eight-by-ten photos of Packer-sponsored Little League teams are the main front office decor, but another feature is a few color ad sheets—in Japanese—for canned cherries. Packer is not a huge operation (about $12 million in annual sales), but it is the biggest retail canner of cherries in the U.S., and the biggest exporter of retail pack cherries to Japan.

Packer has been in the Japan market since an early linkup with a Japanese trading company more than 15 years ago. These days the business is helped by having a Japanese employee on staff in Lawton. More than an employee, Isao Asakura is a friend of the family, a relationship that goes back to a visit Isao's sister made to Lawton as an exchange student. Isao, who has various responsibilities, is Packer's contact person with MIATCO, a source for some of Packer's promotion expenses in Japan.

Packer specializes in the traditional water pack and does not make a pie fill. In addition to its well-known Michigan Maid brand name, Packer has 50 private labels. The company has probably the highest volume of the half-dozen plants packing tart cherries for the retail trade. Packer is not the dominant player in the institutional trade, but more than half its tart cherry production is generally institutional. Although about 30 percent to 50 percent of Packer's cherry sales are overseas (mostly in Europe and Japan), cherries exported to Japan account for less than 10 percent of Packer's total revenues from all commodities. Packer has been sending one of its semis, loaded mostly with canned cherries, off to its Japanese trader in Portland about once a week. A semi load of the retail size #303 cans is 1,500 cases.

Bob had reason to be skeptical about Dick's proposition. Why should he share any sales with his competitors, most of whom hadn't invested a dime in trying to enter the Japan market? But what if the processors formed a company that he wasn't part of and proceeded to dominate the Japan market? Dick was not short on reasons for prospective members to join, and one was the chance to fix prices higher than if the tart cherry packers all bid against one another. In any event, Bob has long been active in industry associations, and he knows the cherry industry is not in good shape. He's not about to dismiss any idea without careful consideration.

John Minnema, Cherry Central Cooperative

As a federated marketing cooperative handling well over half the tart cherry harvest in recent years, with a staff of 30 and a track record in export sales, Cherry Central might well question the value of ceding a potentially major market to a new organization that would be promoting Cherry Central *and* its competitors.

Rather than buying fruit *from* its growers, Cherry Central sells fruit *for* the growers. As such, it sells whatever is grown, meaning it has to move widely fluctuating supplies of fruit regardless of market demand. As the trend has been toward oversupply, any new market for cherries is very much in Cherry Central's interest. The more U.S. cherries that are sold in Japan, the better it may be for Cherry Central, even if those sales are by competitors.

In effect buying an outlet for its fruit, Cherry Central bought Wilderness Foods (facilities and name) in 1979. This bold advance in the retail arena drew negative responses from some of the retail packers that Cherry Central had been selling to on an industrial basis. In 1986, Cherry Central sold Wilderness to the Curtice Burns/Pro-Fac alliance, becoming a major stockholder with delivery rights to Pro-Fac of more than 15 million pounds of cherries. Since then, Cherry Central's niche has remained in the institutional and industrial markets.

As an example of upstream integration, Cherry Central also bought Dunkley International, the nation's primary source of cherry-processing equipment. This afforded some protection against the possibility of Dunkley failing to be a reliable provider and innovator of state-of-the-art equipment. Also, with Dunkley's worldwide market and other product lines, the acquisition was a step toward diversification.

John Minnema knew what a threat the processor/marketing failures of the early 1970s were to the cherry growers, and to assure against that happening again, he sees a dose of diversification as very healthy.

To solidify its relationship with its members, Cherry Central began taking other crops from members besides cherries. Now apples are the co-op's biggest product in tonnage (though not value). Blueberries, peaches, plums, and asparagus are also important, with fresh produce a growing part of the business. To have a strong enough presence to get the attention of an increasingly concentrated community of supermarket buyers, Cherry Central needed to expand its list of offerings and find multiple sources for its products. Cherry Central is now a significant trader of such diverse crops as mangos and sugar snaps, with contracts throughout the hemisphere.

In about 1984, Cherry Central bought West Bay, a canned cherry brand name (without processing facilities) in the bankruptcy sale of Traverse City Canning Company, a former cherry processor. Traverse City Canning had established the West Bay label in the 1970s and sold as many as 10 shipping containers a year to Japan through the Kanematsu Trading Company.

During the couple years that lapsed between the demise of Traverse City Canning and the sale of the West Bay label, Anderson Foods supplied Kanematsu under a new label, W&B, which strongly resembled the West Bay label. Although no longer using the West Bay name, Cherry Central continues to do business with Kanematsu. Total annual Cherry Central sales to Japan average about $300,000, or 24 containers worth, mostly in industrial packs. Cherry Central has been sending representatives to Japan at least every other year and feels comfortable with its efforts in Japan. It also appreciates the frustration and the demand for patience that accompany trading in Japan.

As John considers what Cherrex could do for Cherry Central and vice versa, many things come to mind. Cherry Central, a $100 million (annual sales) company with a 17-year history, is responsible for marketing over half the tart cherries in the U.S. Considering its relatively large size, it would probably have to pay at least 40 percent of the Cherrex expenses. CMI (the proposed manager of Cherrex) is a small organization with no track record. CMI, however, has promotion money (from growers and federal market promotion funds) that it will spend in Japan, apparently with or without Cherrex. If CMI is going to promote cherries, it must have a coherent means of selling and delivering them. Active promotion in Japan is admittedly too expensive for even Cherry Central.

Cherry Central is a cooperative of processors, and those processors are in turn cooperatives of individual growers. Most of those same growers form the constituency for CMI. Although CMI and Cherry Central are completely independent, any clashes between them could present a politically awkward situation. John Minnema has to consider what's best for his company in the short and long run, for his industry and for the many growers that he works for indirectly.

Mike Anderson, Anderson Foods

During the past 12 years, the Andersons developed their family orchard into one of the biggest retail canning companies in Michigan. Operating under the name Anderson Foods, the operation has annual sales of about $25 million. Finding success in others' failures, the Andersons acquired three plants serving more than 150 miles of Michigan's coastal fruit belt. Mike primarily works out of the Acme plant, which is close to the true center of the nation's tart cherry industry, Traverse City, Michigan. Anderson Foods specializes in retail packs and has a diversified product line including more than 20 fruits and vegetables. About half the company's sales are of tart cherries, and they are all packed in cans at the Acme plant. A large proportion of its pack is as pie fill, and it commands about a 20 percent share of the cherry pie fill market.

Anderson Foods is very much a family business, but it sources cherries by contracting with a cherry growing cooperative to buy all of that co-op's cherries. Anderson and some other processors use this arrangement because it helps to insulate the processor from price risk. Growers get a down payment at delivery, and the final price to the grower often comes months later and is based on the processor's sales success. This method of payment has proven more workable when carried out in conjunction with a co-op.

Mike has long been aware of Japan as a market for cherries. In the several years between Traverse City Canning Company's 1981 bankruptcy and the sale of the company's West Bay label to Cherry Central, Anderson took over the sales account with a label (W&B) reminiscent of the West Bay label. Those sales amounted to about 15–20 containers a year. Kanematsu, the Japanese broker for the West Bay account, called Anderson in 1988 with a request for a very specialized pack of 15,000 cases of #10 cans of light sweet cherries. Cherry Central, with whom Kanematsu regularly deals, had turned down the job because it did not fit with the company's processing capabilities. The pack was a significant interruption from the normal flow of business for Anderson Foods too, as the buyers physically monitored every step of it on site, including exactly which cherries from which trees were to be used. The buyers provided their own flavors and colors. In Japan, the cherries were used for individually packaged dessert cups containing five cherries each in gelatin. Although the return to Anderson was high, so was the tedium and expense, and Mike declined further contracts of this type.

Except for that special order, Anderson's sales to Japan have been largely nonexistent since the demise of the W&B label. Like most canners, Anderson does a fair amount of private label packing without necessarily knowing where the product is finally consumed. Some of Anderson's production has even ended up under a competitor's label.

Anderson packs more apples (by weight) than cherries, but cherries are definitely its biggest product in value terms. It finds it valuable to have a line of products to compete in a market. Part of Anderson Foods' success in selling to big chain stores is its ability to deliver a truck with 20 canned products. The Cherrex proposal represents an opposite philosophy. Cherrex plans to specialize in one product, cherries, in all forms from frozen to canned. Anderson specializes in one form, canned, but offers a range of products. Mike Anderson is as eager as anybody to develop new markets for tart cherries, but when he hears all the excitement about the great potential Japan has, his own arduous experience with the Japanese comes to mind and makes him skeptical.

Jim Brian, Smeltzer Orchard Company

Jim hates putting on a tie and going to meetings, but as an active leader of the industry, there's no question about his taking the time to hear out Dick's proposal. Smeltzer Orchard Company is a family farming business started by Jim Brian's grandfather in the late 1800s. Smeltzer got into the processing business after some serious dissatisfaction with its membership in Cherry Growers Cooperative in 1942. Today, Smeltzer is putting out sales in the range of $12 to $14 million a year, 35 to 45 percent of that being tart cherries. Strictly an industrial freezing operation, Smeltzer packs IQF and 5+1. Although Smeltzer feels some commitment to its growers, Jim takes pride in his company being sales, rather than supply, driven.

Smeltzer has sold product to Europe over the years, but that has always been a hit-or-miss proposition. The variability of both production in Europe and exchange rates means that sometimes the market is there and sometimes it isn't. Smeltzer has not sold any product to Asia yet. If the CMI has any luck expanding the now minuscule market in Japan for cherries, that may change. Like a lot of northern Michigan farmers who stand to benefit from government funds, Jim suffers some discomfort at the thought of using taxpayers' money to promote cherries, but he's living with that discomfort as the promotion campaign gets underway.

The real key to improved sales, Jim says, is improved quality. Although the conventional wisdom says the decline in demand for pie fill is due to changing consumer preferences, Jim says at least some of the blame must be assigned to low quality (for example, too much starch and not enough fruit). Demand for pie fill is important to him in that much of the market for his 5+1 product is pie fill manufacturers. He'd like to see some USDA standards in the pie fill industry.

One big advantage that Cherrex could give its members in the Japan market would be standards of quality. If the few Japanese people who are already buying tart cherry products in Japan (retail, institutional, or industrial) are anything like American buyers, they must be getting fed up with the struggle to get decent quality. Cherrex could offer one name and one standard—a high one—of quality. When Jim ran the Cherrex idea past his fellow members on Smeltzer's board of directors, they simply said it was Jim's decision. With a cost in dues of a couple of thousand dollars a year, he figures he'd need to sell a 100 thousand pounds a year or so through Cherrex to come close to breaking even on the proposition. Furthermore, Japan has yet to buy any U.S. frozen tart cherries. Smeltzer's main competition is Cherry Central. One advantage of the Cherrex plan is that for at least the Japan market, Smeltzer and Cherry Central could not be played off against each other in a price-bidding war.

■■■ THE DECISION

With the Michigan fruit harvest behind them this crisp autumn day, Bob, John, Mike, and Jim are all in their separate cars headed for a meeting that Dick Johnston has called in central Michigan. With drives ranging from two to four hours, each has time for some final thoughts on the question they know Dick is going to ask: Will you join Cherrex as a founding member? Although none of them relishes these trips from their homes in the rolling hills and lakes of fruit country to the flatter, if more convenient, center of the state, they all know how precarious their business is with its too frequent oversupply problems and dramatic volatility. They're open to ideas.

Although Bob, John, Mike, and Jim must each decide whether to join Cherrex, they don't have to reach an agreement. To fly, the Cherrex proposal hardly needs *every* tart cherry processor to join. However, as the idea is to capture the advantages of joining forces, the proposal does depend on enough forces joining to make it worthwhile. Although competitors, Bob, John, Mike, and Jim do know one another, and they're free to discuss the proposal with one another and with any other prospective Cherrex members before making their decisions. Ultimately, though, each must make his own decision, and the time for that is now.

Disco Foods

Disco Foods, Inc., a regional food processor located in the upper Midwest, undertook an empirical estimation of the demand relationships for its frozen fruit pies. The firm was attempting to formulate its pricing and promotional plans for the following year, and management was interested in learning how certain decisions would affect sales of the frozen pies.

An analysis of earlier demand studies for its other prepared foods led Disco to the hypothesis that demand for fruit pies was a linear function of the price charged, advertising and promotional activities, the price of a competing brand of frozen pies, per capita income, and population in the market area. It was decided that a trend term should also be included in the hypothesized demand function to account for the continuing shift to prepared foods and for the growth in sales resulting from increased consumer awareness of the product.

Disco had been processing frozen pies for about three years, and the market research department had two years of quarterly data for six regions on sales quantities, the retail price charged for its pies, local advertising and promotional expenditures, and the pace charged for the major competing brand of frozen pies.

Statistical data published by *Sales Management* magazine on population and disposable incomes in each of the six locations was also available for the analysis; it was thus possible to include all the hypothesized demand determinants in the empirical estimation.

The following regression equation was fitted to the data:

$$Q_{it} = a + bP_{it} + cA_{it} + dPX_{it} + eY_{it} + fPop_{it} + gTF_{it} + U_{it}$$

Here Q is the quantity of pies sold during the tth quarter; P is the retail price in cents of Disco's frozen pies; A represents the dollar amount spent for advertising and promotional activities; PX is the price, measured in cents,

---

This case was prepared by James G. Beierlein, Associate Professor of Agricultural Economics, Department of Agricultural Economics and Rural Sociology, Pennsylvania State University, as a basis for classroom discussion rather than to illustrate either correct or incorrect handling of an administrative situation.

charged for competing pies; Y is dollars of per capita, real disposable income measured on an annual basis; Pop is the population of the market area; and TF is the trend factor. The subscript i indicates the regional market from which the observation was taken, and the subscript t represents the quarter during which the observation occurred, that is, TF = 1, 2, 3, 4, 5, 6, 7, 8.

Least-squares estimation of the regression equation on the basis of 48 data observations (eight quarters of data for each of the six areas) resulted in the estimated regression parameters and statistics given in Exhibit 1.

The terms in parentheses are the standard errors of the coefficients. An analysis of the error terms, or residuals, indicated that all the required assumptions regarding their distribution were met; hence the least-squares regression procedure is a valid technique for estimating the parameters of this demand function.

EXHIBIT 1   Estimated demand function for frozen pies.

$$Q = -500 - 275P_{it} + 5A_{it} + 150P_{it} + 7.25Y_{it} + 0.25Pop_{it} + 875TF_{it}$$
$$(52)\quad (1.1)\quad\quad (66)\quad\quad (3.2)\quad (0.09)\quad\quad (230)$$

Coefficient of determination (R^2) = 0.92
Standard error of the estimate = 775.38
F-value = 13.05
Prob $F > 13.05$ = 0.03284

▬ QUESTIONS

1. Evaluate this model statistically and economically.

2. How many pies can Disco expect to sell in one market with a 95 percent confidence level where price is $1.50, promotional activities are $1,000, price of competing pies are $1.40, population is 50,000, per capita real disposable income is $5,000, and the quarter being forecast is the ninth?

3. What is the price elasticity and cross-price elasticity for Disco pies? What sorts of recommendations could you make regarding their pricing policy?

4. What is the advertising elasticity (percent change in quantity divided by the change in A) for Disco pies? The advertising manager feels that a major effort in this area will yield greater sales. What do you think of his recommendation, and why?

5. What happens to sales if the firm does nothing the next year?

FINANCE

CASES

Portland County Co-op

■ OVERVIEW

Portland County Co-op (PCC) is in Portland County, Ohio. It is a local cooperative that provides farm supplies and grain-marketing facilities for its farmer members. The central facility for PCC is in Portland, with two branches in Richmond and Oak Hill. PCC is the end product of a merger that combined three co-ops four years ago. Two were nearly insolvent at the time of the merger; the other was in satisfactory financial condition. PCC has improved its financial condition during the past three years. An effort has been made to increase profitability and to recapitalize the firm. These efforts have paid dividends, but additional steps must be taken to ensure the long-term viability of the co-op.

The primary elements of PCC's business are feed, grain, and the crops division, which includes fertilizer, spray materials, and seeds. Annual sales are approximately $22.5 million. The co-op assumes ownership of the grain in the marketing process. Thus, the grain division accounts for approximately 90 percent of the total dollar sales. Supply sales and services contribute the remaining 10 percent.

Grain storage capacity is an important element for PCC's grain-marketing business. The primary storage facility is in Portland and has a capacity of approximately 100,000 bushels; the Richmond branch has a capacity of approximately 68,000 bushels. Grain storage at the other branches is in conjunction with the feed business.

Marketing Area

The primary marketing area for PCC is Portland County. This county currently contains 1,180 farms with approximately 230,000 acres, which is

This case was prepared by James R. Dayton, Research Associate, Department of Agricultural Economics and Rural Sociology, Ohio State University; and David E. Hahn, Professor, Department of Agricultural Economics and Rural Sociology, The Ohio State University, as a basis for classroom discussion rather than to illustrate either correct or incorrect handling of a business situation.

approximately 90 percent cropland (Exhibit 1). The area contains three kinds of farmers: The part-time farmer, the traditional farmer, and the large farmer. The part-time farmer (approximately 300) operates 200 to 500 acres of owned or rented ground. Off-farm part-time employment, readily available in the area, nurtures the part-time farmer. The traditional farmer (approximately 750) works 500 to 1,000 acres. These farmers typically are strong co-op supporters and need the competitive services provided by the co-op. The large farmer (approximately 130) operates more than 1,000 acres and buys inputs at wholesale prices. Frequently, this is the same price that PCC pays when stocking these items for resale. These farmers typically have considerable on-farm grain storage and therefore market their grain directly in the Toledo market, which permits access to the St. Lawrence Seaway.

PCC, like many co-ops, is confronted with changes occurring on several fronts. These changes directly involve co-op membership and their willingness to continue participating in PCC.

1. Many current members are older farmers. It is not clear who will replace these farmers when they retire.
2. The most important enterprise in this area is grain production. Weather conditions have decreased yields in several areas of the county in recent years.
3. The percentage of business done by the co-op with members has been shrinking over the past several years. Farmers are basing business decisions on who has the best price, not on membership in the co-op. Thus, the co-op must be very competitive in pricing goods and services.

Feed Division

The feed division typically accounts for about $1.4 million in annual sales. PCC controls about 25 percent of the market for feed. The volume mix in terms of market shares of animal groups is as follows: 90 percent of sheep feed sales, 20 percent of swine feed sales, 40 percent of dairy feed sales, and 20 percent of beef cattle feed sales. The competitive environment for feed marketing is keen. PCC has seven competitors in the area, of which

EXHIBIT 1   Number of farms and acreage.

	1984	1985	1989	1990
Number of Farms	1,270	1,250	1,210	1,180
Average Size (acres)	177	180	190	195
Land in Farms (acres)	225,000	225,000	230,000	230,000

three are very aggressive. Exhibit 2 shows the livestock population of Portland County.

Grain

The grain market served by this firm is extremely competitive. The large Toledo grain terminals are within 75 miles of PCC's marketing area. These terminals siphon off approximately 50 percent of the grain that is produced in the area. PCC has approximately 25 percent of the remainder, or 12.5 percent of the total grain produced in the area. Its elevator volume mix is as follows: 70 percent corn, 25 percent soybeans, and 5 percent wheat. PCC has three competitors in the area for its grain business, all extremely aggressive. PCC's strength in grain marketing is its grain storage capacity at the Portland facility, coupled with a 10-car rail capacity. It focuses on using three-car train units in shipping grain. Its competitive advantage is in shipping corn to the East Coast, serving primarily the southeastern market. It does not have a good outlet for soybeans, and therefore many soybeans in the area go directly to the Toledo terminals. Exhibit 3 shows the crop production in Portland County.

Crops

The crops division includes fertilizer, chemicals for spray materials, and seeds. PCC has 15 percent of the market share. Approximately 50 percent of its fertilizer and chemical sales is custom applied. PCC is a major custom applicator, covering 40,000 acres per year. It has a full line of application equipment and a strong reputation for good custom application work. An additional 35 percent of the business is directed toward farmers who rent equipment from PCC and apply fertilizer and chemicals on their own farms. Another 15 percent of the fertilizer and chemical business is accounted for in direct shipments to large farmers.

The greatest competition PCC faces is in direct sales of anhydrous

EXHIBIT 2   Livestock population.

	1984	1985	1989	1990	1991
Hogs & Pigs[a]	44,000	47,000	51,000	49,000	
Sheep & Lambs[b]	3,000	2,500		2,550	2,750
Cattle & Calves[b]	35,000	25,000		28,600	27,000
Milk Cows[b]	10,000	10,200		9,700	8,900

[a] As of December 1.
[b] As of January 1.

ammonia to large customers. PCC has 12 competitors in the fertilizer-pesticide division, with 8 rated as very aggressive.

Seed

PCC has only 2 percent of the seed business in the county. It has not seriously tried to compete. Many farmer dealers in the area are members of PCC. In addition, many of the seed company brands of its competitors have good reputations. The seed market is very fragmented for PCC.

■ PROPOSED NEW BUSINESS LINE: PETROLEUM

The trade area would be Portland County and one-third of Lincoln County, which borders Portland on the east. The volume mix would be approximately 75 percent farm fuel (40 percent diesel and 60 percent gasoline) and 25 percent heating oil. The petroleum division would contribute approximately $1.5 million in total annual sales. An investment of $5.8 million in facilities, equipment, and stock would be required. Some board members would like to apply for a loan from the National Bank for Cooperatives for the necessary capital for this investment. The terms specify a variable interest rate loan. The current rate is 6.5 percent, and the loan must be repaid over five years.

PCC currently does not handle petroleum products. Several members want PCC to offer diesel fuel and gasoline.

EXHIBIT 3   Crop production.

	1984	1985	1989	1990
Corn				
Acres	59,000.0	60,100.0	49,200.0	56,300.0
Bushels per acre	131.0	128.7	127.4	124.2
Thousands of bushels	7,729.0	7,735.0	6,267.0	6,995.0
Soybeans				
Acres	70,800.0	74,400.0	81,300.0	71,400.0
Bushels per acre	38.0	41.1	33.6	41.0
Thousands of bushels	2,690.0	3,057.0	2,733.0	2,929.0
Wheat				
Acres	24,000.0	21,300.0	34,300.0	39,100.0
Bushels per acre	46.0	66.4	51.7	62.9
Thousands of bushels	1,104.0	1,415.0	1,774.0	2,460.0
Hay				
Acres	15,000.0	14,700.0	16,400.0	14,800.0
Bushels per acre	4.0	3.93	3.55	4.97
Thousands of bushels	60.0	57.8	58.2	73.5

■ FINANCIAL STATEMENTS[1]

Typically, a cooperative's accounting system provides a monthly operating statement and a monthly balance sheet. Both statements are used by the general manager and the board of directors to evaluate current operations and business trends and, if necessary, to take corrective action. A third statement, although not usually prepared monthly, is the statement of cash flows.

The use of these three basic financial statements reveals the cooperative's financial position, its performance, and its ability to meet its obligations. Often, supplemental statements, schedules, and footnotes accompany these financial statements to provide more detailed information and greater meaning.

Operating Statement

The operating statement, sometimes called the statement of operations or profit and loss statement, reflects the cooperative's business activity over a period of time. Much like a report card a student gets from school, the operating statement tells what progress the cooperative has made for a certain period of time. Frequently, the operating statement shows business activity for the month just ended as well as the year-to-date activity, which covers the period of time from the beginning of the fiscal year. In addition to these two reporting periods, the operating statement will generally compare the current year-to-date information with the same period of a year earlier and with the budget. An operating statement without comparative information is substantially less valuable to a manager or a board of directors.

Three major sections make up the operating statement: income, expenses, and savings. The following simple equation is used to prepare the operating statement:

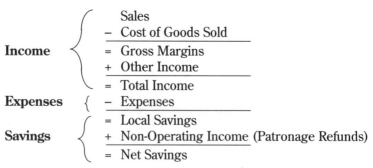

$$
\begin{array}{ll}
\textbf{Income} & \left\{ \begin{array}{l} \text{Sales} \\ -\ \text{Cost of Goods Sold} \\ \hline =\ \text{Gross Margins} \\ +\ \text{Other Income} \\ \hline =\ \text{Total Income} \end{array} \right. \\[1em]
\textbf{Expenses} & \left\{ \begin{array}{l} -\ \text{Expenses} \\ \hline \end{array} \right. \\[0.5em]
\textbf{Savings} & \left\{ \begin{array}{l} =\ \text{Local Savings} \\ +\ \text{Non-Operating Income (Patronage Refunds)} \\ \hline =\ \text{Net Savings} \end{array} \right.
\end{array}
$$

[1]*Analyzing a Cooperative Business,* National Bank of Cooperatives, 1990.

Income

The income portion of the operating statement summarizes all revenues received by the cooperative during the accounting period. The cooperative's sales, or the total revenue from all goods sold (the transfer of inventory to customers), are listed first. The cost of goods sold, or what the cooperative paid for the goods it sold, is subtracted from sales, resulting in gross margins, or the portion of the sales dollar the cooperative keeps. In other words, gross margin is the profit on the sale before any expense associated with the sale (other than cost of goods sold) is deducted.

Other income, such as storage, drying, fertilizer application, and finance charges, is added to gross margins, resulting in gross revenue or gross income. This is the total revenue the cooperative received from providing goods and services to patrons.

Expenses

Expenses are then subtracted from gross revenue. Expenses are what the cooperative paid to do business and are generally divided into three broad categories: personnel expenses, fixed expenses, and variable expenses.

Personnel expenses obviously have to do with people. These expenses include not only employees' salaries but the benefits the cooperative pays on behalf of the employees, such as Social Security, retirement, and medical insurance.

Fixed expenses are those expenses over which management has little control. Fixed expenses are those costs incurred whether the cooperative does business or not and include long-term loan interest, depreciation, property taxes, and insurance.

Variable expenses are costs that management can control to some extent. These expenses are affected by day-to-day operations. The amount of business, as well as whether the business is open, impacts the amount of variable expenses. They include repairs and maintenance, utilities, bad debts, advertising, data processing, and supplies, to name a few.

Savings

Subtracting total expenses from gross revenue results in local savings for the period examined. This figure is also sometimes referred to as operating savings, net operating gain, local earnings, or operating profit. This figure reflects the earnings (or loss) to the cooperative on the products and services provided for members during the accounting period. Local savings is key in determining a cooperative's profitability. Local savings plus patronage refunds from the cooperative's regional affiliations equals net savings. Net savings is also referred to as net earnings or net profit.

Most cooperatives prepare both a monthly and a year-to-date operating statement. The monthly statement shows the local savings and net savings for the month; the year-to-date statement shows the cumulative net savings generated since the beginning of the fiscal period. Many cooperatives now also prepare departmental and location operating statements to show the profitability of the various branches or departments within the organization. This procedure is highly recommended to help the management team focus on what needs the most assistance.

■■■ BALANCE SHEET

The balance sheet is a financial picture of the cooperative at a specific time. It is reported as if all activity stopped and a complete inventory taken of the entire business. It is usually prepared at the end of each month and at the end of the fiscal year. A balance sheet can, however, be prepared at any time.

The balance sheet is devised from a basic accounting equation:

Assets = Liabilities + Members' Equity

Assets are what the cooperative owns; liabilities are what the cooperative owes; and members' equity is what the members have provided through capital stock and deferred patronage refunds. Customarily, the cooperative's assets are listed on the left side of the statement, and liabilities and members' equity are on the right. Occasionally, assets are shown at the top of the page with the section of liabilities, and members' equity is shown at the bottom.

Assets

Assets are categorized into sections according to the amount of time it is expected that the asset will be converted to cash. The assets of a cooperatively organized business are normally classified into three types: current assets, fixed assets, and other assets.

Current assets are those that are expected to be converted into cash within the next 12 months. Typically, current assets include cash, accounts receivable, inventories, grain in transit, and margin deposits. Current assets are usually listed at their expected, reasonable cash value. For example, accounts receivable are listed in total and then decreased by an amount (a reserve) estimated to be nonrecoverable resulting in net accounts receivable. Likewise, inventories are valued at an amount that reasonably reflects their near cash value.

Most accounting textbooks suggest inventories be valued at "lower of cost or market," which means that if the present market for a commodity is less than the cost of the product, it should be valued on the balance sheet at market value. On the other hand, if the market for the product is substantially higher than the cost of the product, the value used would still be the lesser amount or the cost. Because accounts receivable and inventory make up the lion's share of current assets, it is extremely important that they be valued properly.

Fixed assets are the bricks and mortar of the cooperative. They include elevators, service stations, fertilizer and feed plants, office buildings, and warehouses as well as vehicles, machinery, and land. These assets are used continuously in the business and are not intended for sale. Therefore, fixed assets are listed on the balance sheet at net book value rather than at market value. Net book value is determined by subtracting the allowance for depreciation from the original cost.

With the exception of land, all of a cooperative's fixed assets are subject to depreciation. Depreciation is the decline in a fixed asset's useful value due to wear and tear and the passage of time. When a fixed asset is purchased, a useful life expectancy is assigned to that asset. Depreciation recovers the asset's cost over the expected life. In recent years, however, the Internal Revenue Service has allowed businesses to assign an accelerated depreciation rate to some assets that results in the asset depreciating at a much faster pace than normal life expectancy.

The allowance for depreciation is the amount that has been charged off the cost of all fixed assets the cooperative has purchased. On the balance sheet, this depreciation allowance is subtracted from the acquisition cost of the assets, resulting in net fixed assets.

Other assets are assets that do not fit in the category of current assets because they are not expected or planned to be converted to cash within 12 months, and they are not fixed assets. For a cooperative, these normally include investments in regional cooperatives, such as the CoBank and regional farm supply or grain cooperatives. Other assets also include the noncash portion of patronage refunds received by the local cooperative. Other assets may also include accounts receivable that no longer fit the definition "convertible to cash in 12 months" and other miscellaneous types of assets.

Current assets, fixed assets, and other assets make up total assets, or everything the cooperative owns at a particular time. These assets are financed by liabilities and members' equity—the other side of the balance sheet.

Liabilities

Like assets, liabilities are classified by time. Obligations that are due within one year are called current liabilities; those that are due beyond 12 months are called long-term liabilities.

Current liabilities, or those liabilities due within the next 12 months, include trade accounts payable, deferred grain payables, seasonal operating loans, cash patronage refunds payable to members, accrued taxes and insurance, and any payments on long-term notes that are due within the next 12 months. Current liabilities can be considered as all debts the association must pay during the next 12-month period.

Long-term liabilities are those debts or portions of debts due beyond the next 12 months. These normally include the loans from banks that finance major fixed assets, member building notes, and long-term contracts. These kinds of liabilities are usually set up with a specific repayment schedule that includes monthly, quarterly, semiannual, or annual payments.

Deferred or other liabilities are those obligations of the cooperative that do not meet a test as to the exact timing of payment: They are not due in the next 12 months, nor do they have a fixed time for payment. Normally, this category includes deferred income tax liabilities (due to differences in tax depreciation rates versus financial reporting depreciation rates) or deferred compensation for employees.

Members' Equity

Members' equity, or the difference between assets and liabilities, is the members' investment in the cooperative. It is sometimes called net worth or owners' equity because it records the portion of a cooperative's assets directly owned by the members. It is risk capital.

The equity section of the balance sheet usually lists the following classifications:

- capital stock (voting stock)
- deferred patronage refunds
- retained earnings

Capital stock in a cooperative is often classified into two types: voting and nonvoting. Most cooperatives issue voting common stock (often called "A" stock) only to agricultural producers. Nonvoting common stock (also called certificates of interest, "B" stock, or certificates of participation) is usually issued to nonproducers. Holders of either type of common stock are entitled to patronage refunds; only holders of "A" stock are normally entitled to vote.

Stock credits represent partial ownership of a share of common stock. Many cooperatives allow a member to earn a full share of common stock through patronage. Until the full value of the common share is earned, the funds are classified as a stock credit.

Deferred patronage refunds represent the portion of the allocation of net savings that has been retained for a period of time by the cooperative for capitalization purposes. Each year the cooperative closes its books and divides up the savings (if any). The major portion of savings is allocated to members according to the business done with the cooperative. At least 20 percent of that allocation is paid in cash to members, and the remaining portion goes into deferred patronage refunds. This section is usually by far the largest part of members' equity because it represents several years of the deferred portion of allocated savings. Some cooperatives in recent times have reclassified deferred patronage refunds as a preferred stock class.

Regardless of the title used for deferring allocated patronage refunds, it is extremely important that the cooperative develop a policy on deferred patronage revolvement that results in the ownership of the cooperative staying in the hands of current users of the cooperative. Many cooperatives pay out a portion of deferred patronage to all members each year. Others pay out the deferred patronage in its entirety to members who have retired from farming. Some cooperatives do both. The ability to pay out equity is heavily dependent on consistently generating adequate levels of local savings.

Retained earnings, also known as surplus, undistributed savings, or unallocated equity, is the portion of prior years' earnings retained by the cooperative and on which federal income taxes were paid. These earnings, however, may or may not have been allocated to the cooperative's members. In the event of a loss, the amount of the loss is usually deducted from this category. Some cooperatives, however, allocate a loss to members, which has income tax benefits to the member. Most cooperatives' articles of incorporation specify the amount of annual savings that is to be placed in retained earnings. State statutes may limit the amount in this classification.

Because of the increasing size and complexity of cooperatives and usage of nonqualified distributions of net savings, numerous other members' equity accounts are placed in this section. Directors should be familiar with various categories of equity on their cooperative's balance sheet.

The dollars represented by members' equity have been invested in the assets of the cooperative. Members' equity is not cash or money in a checking or savings account. Equity lists the dollars invested directly by members and the dollars members have earned through patronage of their cooperative and have allowed the cooperative to use. These dollars, along with current and term liabilities, finance vehicles, elevators, inventories, accounts receivable, and all other assets the cooperative owns.

A balance sheet, composed of assets, liabilities, and members' equity, can be prepared at any time. Most cooperatives prepare a balance sheet at the end of each month and at the end of their accounting or fiscal year. The balance sheet shows what the cooperative owns on the date the statement is prepared, what it owes to others on that date, and what the members have invested in the cooperative.

◼◼◼ ANALYSIS OF FINANCIAL STATEMENTS

Simply knowing the construction and makeup of operating statements, balance sheets, and statements of changes in financial position is not enough to make informed decisions about a business. These statements must be analyzed, interpreted, and evaluated before any real use can be made of them. Analysis includes examination and testing; interpretation simply means understanding what you see; and evaluation is making judgments and decisions about possible courses of action based on analysis and interpretation.

The desired results must be identified to analyze financial statements effectively. To do that, financial statements must be reduced to data that can be compared with historical results or with similar kinds of businesses or industry standards.

Because entities differ in size and volume, ratios are frequently used when comparing one cooperative association with another, with itself, and with a desired goal. Ratios are simply relationships. Ratios, stated in accounting terminology, compare similar amounts within a balance sheet, one with another; or they describe the relationship of operating statement amounts to each other; or they describe any combination of two things to one another. Ratios allow easy comparison from one time to another in the same business or from one business to another. They eliminate size differences when comparing a company that has $10 million in sales with one that has $50 million in sales if, and only if, the companies have a similar mix of sales (grain, petroleum, fertilizer, feed, and so on). Successful, financially strong grain marketing cooperatives have ratios that are different from those of successful, financially strong petroleum cooperatives.

Ratios are generally expressed as "something to something"; for example, "term debt to fixed assets." In a ratio, a colon (:) substitutes for the word to. The "term debt to fixed assets" ratio asks, What is the relationship between term debt and fixed assets? or, How many dollars (or parts of a dollar) of term debt are there for every dollar in fixed assets? The mathematical calculation, then, is to consider the colon (:) a division sign; so we would divide the dollar amount of term debt by the dollar amount of net fixed assets. For example, "total term liabilities" of $832,000 would be divided by "net fixed assets" of $2,630,200. The result is 0.32 or, expressed as a ratio, 0.32:1. In other words, the cooperative has 32 cents of long-term debt for each $1 in net fixed assets. For last year, the ratio was 0.36:1.

Financial Ratios

Financial statements of cooperatives are usually analyzed according to four kinds of ratios: profitability, liquidity, efficiency, and solvency. Profitability has to do with overall ability to generate savings; liquidity measures short-term cash flow ability; efficiency suggests how well things are done; and solvency indicates long-term financial health and stability. Some financial indicators are traditionally displayed as true ratios (1:1, for example); others are traditionally shown as percentages. In the context of the information that will follow, the word *ratio* will include some indicators that will be expressed as percentages. In the example above, the ratio 0.32:1 could also be expressed as 32 percent.

Eight financial indicators are discussed in Attachment A. Hundreds could be analyzed, but it is important to select just a few financial ratios and then use them. The ratios are categorized by the statement used to get the information to calculate the ratio. Some are calculated from information found only on the operating statement, some are calculated from information found only on the balance sheet, and some are calculated from information found on both the operating statement and the balance sheet. Each ratio, however, is identified as a profitability, liquidity, efficiency, or solvency measurement.

No one financial indicator by itself provides adequate information by which to judge a cooperative's financial health. Therefore, it is important to look at the financial ratios in groups and over a period of time.

■■■ QUESTIONS

Copies of the balance sheet and the statement of operations for three years are shown in Exhibits 4, 5, and 6.

1. Calculate the financial ratios shown in the Exhibits.
2. Analyze the current situation. Explain what you learned from the ratios, and list any other information you can glean from the data.
3. Provide the board with a reasoned set of alternatives for remedying any problems in the analysis. State any assumptions you must make in producing the analysis and the recommended business strategy.
4. Evaluate the possible addition of the petroleum division, and provide the board with a recommendation. Include in your reasoning any assumptions you must make in this analysis.
5. Recommend a course of action for the board, and produce a pro forma balance sheet and statement of operations depicting the result of your plan of action. Calculate the ratios for these pro forma statements.
6. Prepare a 30-minute presentation to the board in which you present your recommendations. A written report containing details of your analysis and an executive summary should accompany the oral report.

EXHIBIT 4   Balance sheet: Assets (December 31, 1991).

	DECEMBER 1991	DECEMBER 1990	DECEMBER 1987
Current Assets			
Cash on Hand in Bank	$ 64,000	$ 15,458	$ 5,736
Notes Receivable—Current	42,776	36,360	24,962
Accounts Receivable—Patrons	312,080	260,868	218,456
Less Allowance for Doubtful Accounts	(88,174)	(33,765)	736
Net Accounts Receivable—Patrons	223,906	227,103	219,192
Accounts Receivable			
Grain Firms	834,742	698,817	218,456
Advances	21,291	19,162	736
Hedging	74,595	67,136	52,217
Feed	138,613	106,732	97,029
Other	95,151	72,315	66,606
Accrued Storage Receivable	77,686	69,917	54,380
Inventories	1,814,079	1,698,819	1,069,881
Prepaid Insurance	489	440	342
Prepaid Pension	970	873	679
Total Current Assets	3,612,204	3,240,235	2,029,408
Investments—at Cost			
Stock and Deferred Patronage Refunds Allocated			
Countrymark Cooperative, Inc.	1,074,435	1,066,992	913,270
National Bank for Cooperatives	109,814	98,833	85,655
Farmers Commodities Service, Inc.	19,190	17,271	13,433
Midstates Terminals, Inc.	1,000	900	700
Ohio Power Company	360	324	252
Southern States Cooperative, Inc.	221	199	155
Rural Serv, Inc.	10	9	7
Mutual Service Cooperative	10	9	7
Total Investments	1,205,040	1,184,536	1,013,478
Property, Plant, and Equipment—at Cost			
Land	68,937	62,043	48,256
Land Improvements	2,423	2,181	1,696
Buildings	1,143,430	1,104,087	785,490
Machinery and Equipment	1,669,522	1,527,750	1,135,189
Furniture and Fixtures	69,879	62,890	48,915
Trucks and Equipment	96,341	86,707	67,439
Total Equipment	2,981,595	2,783,434	2,038,729
Accumulated Depreciation	1,194,763	1,075,286	836,334
Less Accumulated Depreciation	1,786,832	1,708,148	1,202,395
Net Property, Plant and Equipment	1,855,769	1,770,191	1,250,651
TOTAL ASSETS	$6,673,013	$6,194,961	$4,293,538

EXHIBIT 5   Balance sheet: Liabilities and stockholders' equity (December 31, 1991).

	DECEMBER 1991	DECEMBER 1990	DECEMBER 1987
Current Notes Payable			
Seasonal Loan			
National Bank for Cooperatives	$ 627,880	$ 946,566	$1,205,754
Old Fort Banking Co.	1	1	1
Current Installments on Long-Term Debt			
National Bank for Cooperatives	85,800	59,400	66,000
Total Current Notes Payable	713,681	1,005,967	1,271,755
Current Liabilities			
Bank Overdraft	11,234	10,111	7,864
Accounts Payable			
Trade	91,363	109,636	63,954
Grain	1,034,498	1,193,123	699,149
Net Contracts	7,215	6,494	5,051
Customer Advances	139,056	125,150	97,339
Grain Advances	560,204	454,183	327,143
Federal Income Tax Payable	1,910	1,719	1,337
Marketing Fees Withheld	13,761	12,385	9,633
Accrued			
Salaries and Wages	14,046	12,641	9,832
Directors' Fees	2,520	2,268	1,764
Interest	11,938	10,744	8,357
Property Taxes	18,712	16,841	13,098
Unemployment Taxes	304	274	213
Industrial Insurance	2,703	2,433	1,892
Sales Tax	438	394	307
Total Current Liabilities	2,623,583	2,964,362	2,518,686
Long-Term Liabilities			
Notes Payable, Excl. Current Installments			
National Bank for Cooperatives	738,200	632,383	119,995
Registered Debentures	431,800	388,620	317,030
Total Long-Term Liabilities	1,190,003	1,021,003	437,025
Total Liabilities	3,813,586	3,985,365	2,955,711
Stockholders' and Patrons' Equity			
Capital Stock			
Preferred	1,212,960	727,776	185,300
Common	15,175	13,658	10,623
Total Equity Outstanding	1,228,135	741,434	195,923
Revolving Capital Credits			
Qualified	719,420	647,478	503,594
Nonqualified	42,041	37,837	29,429
Retained Earnings	869,832	782,848	608,882
Total Capital Stock Outstanding	1,631,293	1,468,163	1,141,905
Total Stockholders' Equity	2,859,428	2,209,597	1,337,828
Total Liabilities and Stockholders' Equity	$6,673,013	$6,194,961	$4,293,538

EXHIBIT 6   Statement of operations (December 31, 1991).

	DECEMBER 1991	DECEMBER 1990	DECEMBER 1987
Total Revenue			
Sales—Net	$19,362,601	$17,261,759	$14,602,352
Cost of Commodities Sold	18,337,536	16,503,782	13,558,357
Gross Selling Margin	1,025,066	757,977	1,043,995
Other Revenue			
Grinding, Cleaning, and Treating	34,603	31,143	18,567
Storage and Handling—Net	188,726	169,853	95,108
Drying	165,309	148,778	85,716
Trucking and Delivery	6,794	6,115	3,765
Sales of Feed and Supplement	1,442,035	1,297,832	869,547
Fertilizer, Chemicals, and Seed	1,533,753	1,380,378	782,674
Gain on Disposal of Fixed Assets	0	0	10,332
Applicator Service and Spreader Rental	142,692	128,423	71,522
Interest, Finance Charges Earned, and Discounts	73,075	65,768	45,153
Total Revenue	3,586,987	3,228,288	1,982,384
Gross Revenue	4,612,053	3,986,265	3,026,380
Non-Operating Income			
Patronage Refunds Earned	27,436	24,692	15,205
Dividends Earned	18	16	13
Total Non-Operating Income	27,454	24,709	15,218
Expenses			
Salaries and Wages	445,237	498,665	534,284
Directors' Fees	2,340	2,106	1,638
Advertising and Annual Meeting	27,390	24,651	23,282
Bank Charges	931	838	652
Depreciation	150,276	135,248	105,193
Doubtful Accounts	4,318	3,886	5,398
Dues and Subscriptions	3,310	2,979	2,317
Heat, Power, and Light	122,148	109,933	85,504
General and Workers' Compensation Insurance	40,827	36,744	32,662
Group Insurance	43,858	39,472	30,701
Interest	215,124	193,612	182,855
Legal and Professional	37,083	33,375	55,625
Office Supplies	27,370	24,633	19,159
Uniforms and Laundry	2,411	2,170	1,688
News Service	2,732	2,459	1,912
Pension Plan	15,385	13,847	10,770
Floater Expense	31,242	28,118	21,869
Plant Repairs, Maintenance, and Supplies	115,201	103,681	80,641
Rent and Lease	16,129	14,516	11,290
Property and Other Taxes	50,970	45,873	35,679
Payroll Taxes	39,519	35,567	27,663
Telephone	15,767	14,190	11,037
Traveling and Meeting	6,554	5,899	4,588
Truck Expense	27,734	24,961	19,414
Feed and Supplement	1,250,677	1,063,075	744,153
Fertilizer, Chemicals, and Seed	1,624,795	1,299,836	909,885
Miscellaneous	900	810	630
Total Expenses	4,320,228	3,761,144	2,960,487
Total Expenses + Cost of Commodities Sold	22,657,763	20,264,926	16,518,844
Local Savings	291,825	225,121	65,893
Net Savings	$ 319,279	$ 249,830	$ 81,110

Attachment A

▰ OPERATING STATEMENT RATIOS

1. *Local Return on Sales—Profitability Ratio*

   Formula: Local savings divided by total sales.

   Meaning: Measurement of profit (local savings) based on total sales.

   Guideline: 2% (at least 2 cents of local savings for each $1 in sales). High % of grain sales = 1–3%; no grain sales = 4–8%.

   Improve by: Improve margins, increase service fees, or reduce expenses.

2. *Interest Coverage Ratio—Liquidity Ratio*

   Formula: Local savings before interest expense (local savings + interest expense) divided by interest expense.

   Meaning: Measurement of the adequacy of local savings to pay interest and still provide funds for other uses, such as principal payments on long-term debt.

   Guideline: 3:1 (at least $3 of local savings before interest for each $1 of interest expense).

   Improve by: Reduce interest expense by collecting old receivables, improving inventory turnover, disposing of assets and reducing debt with proceeds, or reducing debt with working capital. Improve local savings by increasing sales without increasing expenses, improving margins and other income, or reducing expenses.

▰ BALANCE SHEET RATIOS

3. *Current Ratio—Liquidity Ratio*

   Formula: Current assets divided by current liabilities.

   Meaning: Measurement of the ability to meet current obligations in a timely manner.

Guideline: 1.80:1 (at least $1.80 in current assets for each $1 in current liabilities). High % grain sales = 1.2 to 1.5:1; no grain sales = 2.0:1.

Improve by: Increase current assets by increasing local savings, selling additional capital stock, borrowing additional long-term debt, or disposing of unproductive fixed assets and retaining proceeds. Reduce current liabilities by retaining a greater portion of allocated savings (reducing the cash portion).

4. *Local Leverage Ratio—Solvency Ratio*

Formula: Total long-term debt divided by total members' equity minus regional investments.

Meaning: Measurement of the relationship between long-term debt and members' equity adjusted for regional investments. Measures debt capital in relationship to risk capital.

Guideline: 0.50:1 (not more than 50 cents of long-term debt for each $1 in local members' equity).

Improve by: Reduce long-term debt by disposing of unproductive assets using proceeds to liquidate debt, accelerating payments on long-term loan. Improve local equity by generating higher levels of local savings, slowing down equity retirement programs, selling additional capital stock or retaining a greater portion of allocated savings.

5. *Term Debt to Fixed Assets—Solvency Ratio*

Formula: Total long-term debt divided by net fixed assets.

Meaning: Measurement of the relationship between long-term debt and fixed assets. Indicates whether term debt is used to finance fixed assets or other assets (working capital) and if long-term debt has been repaid in accordance with the expected life of fixed assets.

Guideline: 0.50:1 (not more than 50 cents of long-term debt for each $1 in net fixed assets).

Improve by: Reduce long-term debt (see #4) or increase savings, financing a greater portion of fixed assets with working capital.

6. *Ownership Ratio—Solvency Ratio*

Formula: Total members' equity divided by total assets.

Meaning: Measurement of the degree to which members own the business. Influenced by seasonal swings in accounts receivable and inventory levels, however.

Guideline: 0.50:1 (at least 50 cents of members' equity for every $1 in total assets; members should own at least half the assets).

Improve by: Increase equity by improving local savings, selling additional capital stock or slowing down equity retirement programs. Reduce total assets by disposing of unproductive assets (old accounts receivable, obsolete inventory, obsolete fixed assets).

▬ OPERATING STATEMENT AND BALANCE SHEET RATIOS

7. *Return on Local Assets—Profitability Ratio*

Formula: Local savings divided by the sum of current assets and net fixed assets

Meaning: Measurement of the relationship between local savings and assets utilized locally. Indicates if local assets are assisting in the generation of total savings.

Guideline: 0.08:1 (at least 8 cents of local savings for each $1 in local assets).

Improve by: Improve local savings or reduce unproductive local assets.

8. *Working Capital to Sales—Liquidity Ratio*

Formula: Working capital (current assets minus current liabilities) divided by total sales.

Meaning: Measurement of the degree that working capital should meet daily obligations in relation to business volume.

Guideline: 0.07:1 (at least 7 cents of working capital for each $1 in sales or, 10% of non-grain sales + 2% of grain sales).

Improve by: Improve working capital (see #3), or reduce unprofitable sales while maintaining working capital.

Crider Crop Service

■■■ INTRODUCTION

Jim Riley was stunned. He stood behind his army surplus desk holding the phone even though the accountant for Crider Crop Service (CCS) had long since hung up. It was a hot August day in central Illinois, but the sweat on Jim's forehead was almost cold. Jim knew that he and his brother Frank had tried a few new things last spring, mainly adopting a more aggressive pricing policy, but sales had been up. They had almost hit their volume goal of 5,000 tons. He also knew that CCS had not yet paid off the $60,000 balance remaining on their $150,000 line of credit from the Farmers Bank of Madisonville. For the first time in its 25 years of operation, CCS had been forced to carry seasonal financing after August 1. Jim, however, was in no way prepared for the bomb the accountant had dropped on him—CCS had lost more than $80,000 in fiscal 1994 on sales of $1.4 million.

Jim was wondering how to break the news to Frank. Frank, who farmed 600 acres in addition to helping Jim run CCS, was taking care of some farm errands that morning. Jim finally hung up the phone. His mind drifted to the job offer from a major agrichemical manufacturer that he had turned down last winter. Should he have taken the job? His thoughts didn't dwell there long. Jim was extremely proud of his family-owned firm, and he again focused his attention on the future of CCS. Could the retail fertilizer operation recover from such a devastating loss? What were the prospects for the business? Should he and Frank get out now or try to turn it around next year? Clearly, Jim and Frank Riley had a lot of tough choices to make before the fall application season got into full swing.

This case was prepared by Jay T. Akridge, Associate Director of the Purdue University Center for Agricultural Business (CAB) and an Associate Professor in the Purdue Department of Agricultural Economics; Steven P. Erickson, Professor in the Department of Agricultural Economics at Purdue University; and Linda D. Whipker, USDA National Needs Graduate Fellow in Agribusiness and Ph.D. student in the Purdue Department of Agricultural Economics, as a basis for classroom discussion rather than to illustrate either correct or incorrect handling of a business situation.

■ HISTORY

Crider Crop Service was formed in 1969 by Jim and Frank's father, David Riley. David was raising corn and soybeans on about 300 acres of prime central Illinois ground when he literally slipped into the retail fertilizer business. In 1967, David Riley had begun buying some of his fertilizer and chemicals directly from wholesale suppliers that he met through a farmer friend in southern Illinois—an unusual step at the time. Soon, his neighbors learned that David was making some direct purchases and asked him to purchase their fertilizer as well. David decided that the need existed for another source of fertilizer materials in the Caldwell County area, and Crider Crop Service was born.

During the first three years of operation, CCS had virtually no storage capacity or blending facilities. CCS was simply a purchasing agent for Caldwell County farmers. Frank, who was 16 when CCS opened for business, continued to handle many of the farm responsibilities, working with his father when needed. Jim, 11 when the company was formed, pulled his share of the farm jobs, but it was clear then that he didn't like the farm as much as Frank did. When an old warehouse in Crider, Illinois, was put on the auction block in 1972, David and Frank saw the opportunity to expand their business by adding bulk blending capabilities. The next spring they added agrichemicals to their product line and started selling some seed. They also purchased a used dry spinner-type spreader truck and began custom application of their products.

By 1975, CCS had two dry spreaders and a full line of agrichemicals and was selling three types of seed corn—one national brand and two locals—as well as a full line of field seed. In addition to David and Frank, Jim spent time after school in the plant. David's wife, Elizabeth, kept the books. They had one full-time employee and picked up seasonal help as needed to get them through peak periods.

The business continued a pattern of slow, steady growth during the 1970s. Frank had decided to stay with the family business. He just "wasn't the college type." Jim enrolled at the University of Illinois and majored in agricultural economics, but took a number of agronomy courses. When he graduated in 1981, he decided not to return to the family farm and fertilizer operation, choosing instead to pursue a career with Monsanto. After an initial training period, Jim moved to northeast Ohio, where he was the district sales representative for the company. Two years later, however, the urge to be his own boss was too strong, and he left Monsanto to return to the family business.

When Jim returned in 1983, Frank had assumed most of the responsibility for day-to-day management of the operation. David was still active at this time, but tended to act more as a consultant, a sounding board for Frank's ideas. Frank had begun to establish a solid reputation for making reliable, accurate fertilizer and agrichemical recommendations. And, because David and Frank were farmers, they had an edge in the market. Each year they tried to put out a few test plots demonstrating new materials, application techniques, and chemicals. Their customer base, however, was largely restricted to the farmers that the father-son team knew personally. CCS did little actual selling and almost never made an on-the-farm sales call, relying instead on word of mouth for new customers.

Jim's experience complemented the pair nicely. He knew his agronomics, and his formal training in agricultural economics included courses in management and business computer applications. Jim quickly took over the selling role and started making some on-farm sales calls. He also started keeping limited field records on a computer. By 1989, Jim had CCS using the computer for all the bookkeeping functions, including generating monthly statements.

CCS continued to concentrate on the service area of the business during this period. It had virtually no rental equipment, choosing instead to custom apply all the dry bulk material it sold, except for the small amount that was picked up at the plant by a few farmers. In 1989, CCS leased an Air-Flow dry fertilizer applicator, the first in its market area to do so. Farmers immediately liked the job this applicator did, to the point that the spinner-type spreader they owned was little used.

David gradually turned all phases of the operation over to his two sons. By 1990, David only showed up to help out during the spring or to visit with customers at meetings. Frank, in turn, handed over the majority of his responsibilities to Jim so that he could spend more time on his expanding farming operation. Frank was farming nearly 500 acres in 1990, but continued to help out in the plant whenever possible. Then, in late 1993, David died at the age of 66, leaving the business and the farm to his wife and two sons.

■■■ MARKET AREA: CUSTOMERS AND COMPETITION

Crider Crop Service is in central Illinois, just outside the city limits of Crider, a town of about 500. The nearest city of significant size is Madisonville, with a population of 60,000. Madisonville is about five miles from Crider. Farmers in the area grow primarily corn and soybeans. Several large hog operations are also in the area. A small river runs northeast to southwest through the CCS market area. Farmers to the southeast of the river farm some of the finest land in central Illinois. These individuals are large, progressive operators who have experienced few financial problems.

To the northwest of the river however, the ground is not as good. Farm size is slightly smaller, and more operators have struggled with finances over the past five years. "We don't go after much business on the northwest side of the river," said Jim. "Farmers on that side have had more trouble paying bills than those on the southeast side." In general, farmers have aggressively participated in the government programs. Only to the northwest side of the river, however, has any ground been enrolled in the 10-year Conservation Reserve Program.

Competition in the area is as intensive as the agriculture. Five competitor plants are within five miles of CCS and eight more are within 15 miles. Of those within 15 miles of CCS, four are cooperative plants, four are outlets for corporations operating nationally, two are multiplant independents operating only in Illinois, and the remaining two are single-location independents. Overall, the dealers in the area are progressive. Four of the 12 CCS direct competitors now operate Air-Flow dry applicators.

■ ORGANIZATION: STRUCTURE AND PERSONNEL

Crider Crop Service is organized as a Subchapter-S Corporation with all stock held by Jim and Frank Riley and their mother, Elizabeth. Jim works full time at the firm. He handles selling, does all buying, keeps the records on the computer, and even drives the front-end loader during season. "We run a pretty tight ship and just don't have a lot of employees," said Jim. "And I usually find that it is easier for me to go ahead and do things rather than try and explain how they should be done to someone else." Jim is paid $30,000 a year for managing the plant.

Frank farms 600 acres—150 of it rented—in addition to working in the plant. Frank also began doing some custom harvesting in 1989. In 1993 he custom-harvested more than 500 acres. He has a full-time hired hand to help him with the farm work. At the plant, Frank drives a loader in season, oversees maintenance and repair work, does some selling, and consults with Jim on all decisions of any consequence. "Running a farm and helping run the plant really pushes me in the spring," said Frank. "But there's no way that I would pull out on Jim, especially now."

Frank is the firefighter around here," said Jim. "He comes in about two and a half days a week in season and takes care of whatever crisis is most pressing." Frank and Jim use a two-way radio to stay in close touch during the season when Frank is working on the farm. Frank is paid $24,000 as assistant plant manager.

Crider Crop Service employs two full-time people for custom application, hauling, maintenance, and general plant work. One has been with Jim and Frank for 15 years, the other 10. "We have always taken care of our employees and have never fired anyone," said Jim. These two full-timers make $8.00 per hour with no overtime paid. In 1992, they were paid $6 per hour plus a bonus. "Just changing it to $8 per hour made life easier for everyone," said Jim. In addition, CCS pays a full-time bookkeeper $6.50 per hour to handle clerical tasks. Again, no overtime is paid, but she usually works between 37 and 45 hours per week. During 1994, this woman had some severe personal problems, and her job performance slipped dramatically. Frank and Jim's mother, Elizabeth, comes in from time to time in season to run the scales and help with the bookkeeping.

Frank and Jim pick up part-time and seasonal people as needed to meet peak labor demands and keep one part-timer around most of the year to handle odd jobs such as equipment clean-up and routine maintenance. Generally they pick up two additional people during the peak season to drive a tender truck and help unload material, among other tasks. In 1993, they employed several part-timers to help out with painting and remodeling their main storage building. A local hog farmer drives their semi from time to time, picking up material at a river terminal. The part-timer and two seasonal people make $5 per hour, and the farmer/trucker is paid by the trip. Any extra seasonal help—such as the crew used to remodel the plant—makes minimum wage.

▄▄ FACILITIES

The CCS facility is just outside the city limits of Crider. The main plant and storage area is a remodeled building that once housed an implement dealership. The building, 150' × 50', will hold 1,700 tons of dry material. CCS has one eight-ton rotary blender/mixer in the north end of the building. Although more than 40 years old, the building is in reasonably good shape. It was reroofed in 1992 and some spot work was done on the exterior in 1993. "It needs a coat of paint now, but otherwise the building is sound," said Frank. CCS has long taken pride in the overall appearance of its facilities, viewing this as an important contribution to the community. A 50' × 50' concrete block building is used to store some pesticides and the small amount of bagged fertilizer material that CCS sells. The building also houses the shop. CCS has a machinery shed, enclosed on three sides, to keep equipment out of the weather. An area in the rear of the 25' × 50' office is heated for storage of other pesticides. The office, with a set of scales adjacent, houses the computer. CCS handles no other farm supplies and hence has no retail showroom space.

CCS leases a 1992 Air-Flow dry fertilizer applicator and owns a 1985 Ford spinner applicator equipped with floater tires, two nurse trucks, and a Bobcat loader. CCS does not own any spreader buggies for rental purposes. It owns two 20,000-gallon anhydrous storage tanks, 24 two-ton anhydrous ammonia wagons, and six anhydrous tool bars. One heavy-duty 42-foot bar is almost new; two of the remaining five are nearly ready for the scrap heap. A 1976 Ford pickup is used to pull the anhydrous wagons to the field. Three 5,000-gallon tanks store 28 percent nitrogen solution, and two 2,500-gallon tanks store 10-34-0. A 1983 International tractor owned by the firm is used to pull three trailers—one for hauling anhydrous, one for hauling dry material, and one for hauling fluid material.

■ MARKETING

CCS has focused on selling to the large, profitable corn-soybean operations in the western portions of its market area. These are sophisticated, innovative operators—people who can use the equipment and expertise of CCS. The eastern part of the market area is not actively pursued. "People in that part of our market are smaller operators, farming lower quality soils, and, in general, have a much higher potential for credit problems," said Jim. CCS will not sell to a customer who appears to be a poor credit risk. It offers liberal terms, however, to customers considered good risks. Credit terms to smaller customers involve a 10 percent cash discount, net due in 30 days. It does not apply a service charge to delinquent accounts, choosing instead to reduce the level of the discount by 1 percent per month as the account due date is passed. To large, well-capitalized operations, CCS will grant fall terms with no collateral. For these farmers' convenience, CCS does not bill until the farmer's fall fertilizer application is complete, permitting the farmer to write one check for the full year's bill. If Jim and Frank feel one of these large operators is a credit risk, they will still extend fall terms, but insist on a crop lien as collateral.

Over time, CCS has pursued an aggressive price policy in the marketplace. Margins have been held below those of most competitors. No formal volume discount policy is in place, but in certain instances price concessions are made. "Since we were farmers ourselves, we always wanted to offer a fair price to the farmer," said Frank. In 1994, CCS set a volume goal of 5,000 tons and priced at a level that they thought would help them meet that goal. "Dad always thought that the company could be considered successful if we sold 5,000 tons of material," said Jim. The volume goal meant cutting margins on all products well below their standard target margin.

Dry bulk fertilizer sales account for more than 60 percent of the firm's total sales dollars. Roughly half of the 4,900 tons sold in 1994 were impregnated with pesticides. Although CCS does some pre- and post-emerge spraying, most of its agrichemicals are sold over the counter. It does not rent spreader buggies, choosing instead to custom apply all the dry material it sells. (A very small amount of dry fertilizer material is picked up at the plant.)

Advertising is minimal—the standard classifieds and an occasional co-op ad with a pesticide manufacturer. CCS sponsors an award in the corn-growing contest at the Caldwell County Fair. In addition, it gets a lot of mileage out of dealer meetings. Jim screens the speakers carefully for these meetings. "I'm really tough when it comes to dealer meetings. I want a speaker who knows what he is talking about, and I want one who will let me have a good chunk of the program. I know my agronomics, and I like to use these meetings to continue to build my credibility," said Jim. CCS discontinued the test plots on the family farm in 1992 because they were too labor intensive.

The firm does not employ an outside salesperson, although they are considering doing so. Jim does almost all the selling and, in his opinion, can outsell anyone in the market area. He just hasn't had time in the past couple of years to get out much, however, other than to handle complaints and make a few follow-up visits after a customer's crop is up. Frank pushes CCS when he gets the chance—usually in informal conversations at the coffee shop or at county social events.

Both brothers feel their customers are very loyal, and many have been buying with CCS for 15 or more years. Many of these customers are family friends and acquaintances—15 of their 35 largest customers live within a mile of the Rileys' homes. Most competitors in the area have outside salespersons making on-farm calls at least part of the year. Their quality and effectiveness vary, but Frank and Jim are both concerned with the implications of these outside salespeople for their business.

■ FINANCING

Crider Crop Service has traditionally been financed through retained earnings and a loan from family members. The firm has maintained an unspoken goal of 100 percent internal financing. Borrowing was frowned upon by David and both sons have the same attitude toward outside financing. Until 1990, CCS had been able to use these internal sources along with short-term supplier credit to handle even peak seasonal capital requirements.

In 1990, CCS obtained a $150,000 line of credit with the Farmers Bank of Madisonville. Until 1994, CCS was able to pay off this line of credit by August 1 and not borrow against it again until after December 1. By late May 1994, however, CCS was using almost all of the line and was not able to pay it off by August 1. Jim would like to reduce dependence on the line of credit, returning the operation to 100 percent internal financing as soon as possible. In anticipation of 1995 credit requirements, however, Jim has applied for a $200,000 line of credit from the Farmers Bank.

■ PURCHASING

CCS purchases fertilizer material from three main suppliers, using a couple of others when conditions make it profitable to do so. Most agrichemicals are purchased from a wholesaler in southern Illinois, although CCS regularly buys from four others. Over the past few years, Frank and Jim have typically trucked in material. They haul their own material and sometimes haul for competitors. CCS is located on a rail spur, however, and lately bringing in material by rail has been cheaper than trucking.

Jim feels that he is an astute buyer, leaning hard on suppliers for the best price. "I really enjoy buying," he said. He has focused on purchasing quality materials, choosing quality over price in many instances. He has little patience with suppliers who don't deliver on promises and has dropped two key suppliers in the past five years. One of the two requested a set of financial statements from CCS in late 1993. The supplier indicated that the statements were needed before a decision could be made about extending credit for CCS's spring purchases. Jim promptly stopped doing business with the supplier. Most CCS purchases are for the business only; however, on some occasions—if the money is right—Jim will pool orders with some of the other independents in the area.

■■ THREATS AND OPPORTUNITIES

CCS faces many challenges in the immediate future. Jim and Frank are taking stock of their operation and trying to make the decisions that will be most profitable for their families over the longer term. They are considering several alternatives that must be acted on quickly.

Of most pressing concern is a determination of just what went wrong in 1994. Jim is concerned with the CCS pricing policy and tonnage goal. He is now wondering just what type of pricing policy he should pursue and what policy is financially feasible. Along these same lines, Jim is concerned that their hard line on credit has cost them sales. His accountant told him that they should extend credit to the point where 1 percent of net sales would be written off as bad debts. "Our father would roll over in his grave if he knew we were paying for that kind of advice," Jim said.

CCS has never had any type of formal marketing plan. Jim has toyed with the idea of putting one together for some time. As part of this expanded marketing effort, Jim and Frank have kicked around the idea of hiring an outside salesperson. The salesperson might also help alleviate another problem: both feel their hours are much too long. An outside salesperson would take some of the load off both of them.

Crider Crop Service has provided a comfortable living to the Riley family for nearly 25 years. The verdict is still out on whether the firm can continue to serve the needs of Caldwell County farmers profitably. Jim and Frank have a long winter ahead.

■■ GENERAL FINANCIAL ANALYSIS

Attachments A, B, and C present the income statements and balance sheets for CCS for the 1989–1994 period. In addition, these attachments present some comparative financial information from the Fertilizer Industry Analysis Project (FIAP). As you complete your analysis, note that chemicals account for a large portion of CCS's total sales relative to the average plant in the industry. Chemical sales and costs are included in the per ton and percentage data. Therefore, give appropriate consideration to this difference in product mix as you review the financial information.

▄▄ HIRING A SALESPERSON

After taking a hard look at the financial situation of the firm, Frank and Jim began to think about their long-term plans for Crider Crop Service. One area they are particularly concerned about is the company's organizational structure and personnel resources. Frank and Jim aren't totally satisfied with the way job responsibilities are currently defined. In addition, they really aren't sure if their current group of employees is what they need for long-term survival and growth.

Jim wants to continue at the helm, directing the firm's buying, hiring, and selling decisions. After considering his alternatives, Jim has decided that his future is with CCS—at least for the foreseeable future. Frank admits, however, "I haven't taken a vacation with my family for over three years." He clearly has become concerned about the pressures the business has put on his family as well as the financial well-being of his farming operation. To ease some of this personal pressure and to get the operation back on track, Frank has suggested that CCS look for an outside salesperson who would take over some of the miscellaneous duties Frank has handled for the firm. He feels this will free him to spend more time managing his farming operation and enjoying his family. He would still help as needed, especially during rush periods in the spring of the year, and would maintain his ownership interest, consulting with Jim on all major decisions.

Jim agrees with his brother. He realizes that Frank has been pushed hard the last few years and has even wondered himself at times if things weren't getting a bit out of hand for his brother. Frank has indicated that, because of the current financial condition of the firm, he would give up half of his $24,000 annual salary to help defray the costs of hiring this new outside salesperson. If they can hire the right person, both Jim and Frank believe that the firm should be able to increase revenues enough that the salesperson's salary would be covered by the increased sales.

▄▄ EVALUATING CREDIT POLICY

"Over time, we've taken a hard line on credit," said Jim. "If we don't feel good about a customer, we just don't fool around with that customer," he added. CCS has no formal written credit policy. "We use a lot of different tricks in the credit area," said Frank. The decision to extend credit is made solely on Frank and Jim's evaluation of the individual's financial situation. Here they rely on the "grapevine" and their own experience. No formal credit limits are established. In general, customers fall into one of three classes: small operators; large, well capitalized operators; and large, potentially risky operators. The terms for each class are outlined below.

Small operators, representing approximately 25 percent of fiscal 1994 sales, receive a 10 percent discount if they pay cash for their purchases. Statements are mailed the 15th of the month with the balance due on the 30th. As long as the bill is paid by the 30th, the customer will still receive the 10 percent discount. If statements go out after the 15th, as sometimes happens during the peak season, the balance is not due until the following 15th. The same discount policy remains in effect. If the bill is not paid by the due date, the 10 percent discount is reduced by 1 percent per month until the bill is paid. Since virtually all of CCS's smaller customers pay by the due date, this provision is rarely invoked.

Large, well capitalized operators currently account for 60 percent of total CCS volume. CCS grants very liberal terms to these operators. They are billed once a year after all fall material has been applied. This permits the farmer to write one check for his entire fertilizer bill. The balance is not due until January 15th, which gives farmers some flexibility in tax planning. Farmers in this class receive the 10 percent discount regardless of when the balance is paid. In the 25 years CCS has been in operation, no farmer in this class has ever walked away from an obligation to Crider.

The final class, large potentially risky operators, accounted for about 15 percent of fiscal 1994 sales volume. These individuals are given the same terms as the other class of large farmers with one important exception— Frank and Jim obtain a lien on the growing crop as collateral from these customers. To date, losses from these customers have been minimal as well.

Although not sure, Frank and Jim feel that these terms are more generous than those offered by competitors. In addition, they are somewhat more liberal than those in place when David was around. However, the hurdle for extending credit has changed little—only the cream of the crop can purchase material on credit at CCS. And, one slip is all a farmer gets.

■■■ EVALUATING PRICING POLICY

After looking over their financial statements, both Jim and Frank have decided that it's time to attempt to determine exactly what went wrong last year. They both admit that the gross margin CCS reported for 1994 was the lowest ever and considerably lower than the target they kicked around at the beginning of the year. "We were so focused on selling 5,000 tons of product," said Jim, "that it appears we lost sight of what we were doing to our gross margin."

Jim seems to take their 1994 performance as a personal defeat because he has always taken great pride in being a tough buyer and in his ability to lay quality product into their plant at the lowest possible cost. Frank added, "We decided at the beginning of last season that we would do almost anything it took to not let a farmer out of the office without making a sale." Jim reinforced what his brother said: "We don't want our biggest and best customers taken away from us by our competitors. Our goal was to get some of our largest customers to buy all of their product from us during 1994 and not split their orders with someone else down the road. We priced product to get this business."

The pricing policy CCS employed during 1994 was fairly standard— adding a percentage markup to the cost of goods. Frank and Jim then adjusted the price as necessary, backing off a bit depending on the customer, the size of the order, and the cost of servicing that customer. In 1994, they simply made much bigger adjustments to selling price than usual. Frank and Jim have toyed with other pricing mechanisms, but feel the markup method is easy and gives a lot of flexibility in setting the final price.

The brothers have looked at their trends in gross margin over the past six years and agree that they can't survive another 1994. They agree that they must concentrate their efforts on doing things which will improve their gross margin for 1995. They have toyed with the idea of a written policy on volume discounts, but "when someone is sitting across the desk from you and you know they're about to walk out and go to a competitor, you price to keep their business—if you can make something."

■■■ QUESTIONS

1. Based on the information in the text, what are the primary strengths of CCS? Primary weaknesses?

2. Comparing the CCS figures against those from the FIAP Project, where does CCS perform better than the industry? Where does the firm lag behind the industry? When possible, explain why you think the CCS results differ from the industry averages.

3. Compute and interpret at least one financial ratio in each of the following areas: liquidity, solvency, activity, profitability, and growth. Compare your ratios to those from the FIAP project. What conclusions can you draw?

4. Construct a cash flow statement for 1994. The accountant for CCS has provided some additional information that may be helpful. He indicated that depreciation expense was $48,151 in 1994 and that the long-term debt figure shown on the 1994 CCS balance sheet includes the long-term lease obligation. In addition, he mentioned that the owners made an additional equity investment in the business in 1994.

5. Complete a Dupont profitability model for the 1994 CCS operating results. Using your profitability model and answers for 1 through 4 above, develop a general strategy for turning CCS around in 1995.

6. How should Frank and Jim analyze the decision to hire a new person? What would you suggest that Frank and Jim look for in an outside salesperson? Given their circumstances, what characteristics are important for this person? What suggestions do you have for Jim and Frank as they think about the type of compensation plan to offer this new employee?

7. Jim has talked with faculty members in the Agronomy Department at the local land-grant university and found that the going annual salary for new graduates in this type of position is about $22,000. He figures that fringes will cost him about another one-third of this person's total salary. Jim believes, however, that he might be able to furnish housing and utilities for the new salesperson since his mother owns an unoccupied house in Crider. Thus, he might be able to hire an individual for less than $22,000. What do you think about the idea of hiring a new graduate? Discuss the positive and negative aspects of this type of person.

8. Jim also knows that a local sales representative for a national chemical manufacturer is looking for a new opportunity. The person has been with the chemical company for a little over five years. Jim only knows this person casually, but he seems to be honest and a hard worker. He figures that it would take at least $33,000 to hire the sales representative, not including fringes. What are the advantages and disadvantages you see with this type of person?

9. Given their current (1994) margin and cost situation, how many additional sales (dollars) will CCS need to justify hiring a new graduate? How many sales will be required to justify hiring the more experienced sales representative? How will these figures change if CCS is able to raise their overall gross profit to that generated by the plants in the 1994 FIAP results? The accountant for CCS has provided some additional information, indicating that of the $123,789 in labor costs incurred by the firm in 1994, $1,839 was for part-time labor, $8,592 was for payroll taxes, and $890 was for employee benefits. The remaining $112,468 was for full-time labor, including Jim and Frank's salaries.

10. What specific recommendations would you make to CCS? What problems, in general, do you see with the firm hiring an outside salesperson? Are there other alternatives they should consider?

11. Evaluate CCS's current credit policy. Based on the information in the case and the comparative data presented in Attachments A, B, and C, discuss CCS's credit management performance. How does the firm's performance compare with that of other plants documented in the FIAP results?

12. Discuss the strong and weak points of CCS's credit policy from both a financial and a marketing perspective.

13. CCS's accountant suggested that Frank and Jim extend credit until 1 percent of net sales is written off as bad debts. Discuss the pros and cons of this suggestion. Jim has accumulated some additional data to help you make your recommendation. He estimates that over the long run, bad debt loss for his small customers and his low-risk large customers will run about 0.1 percent of sales. Jim's best estimate of bad debt loss on his larger, more risky customers is 2.5 percent of sales. He also did some additional analysis, calculating the days sales in receivables (DSR) ratio for each group using monthly data. His estimate of the DSR for his small customers is 15 days, for his large low-risk customers the DSR is 90 days, and for his large high-risk customers the DSR is 120 days. CCS is paying 9 percent for short term, seasonal money. In addition, Jim figures that CCS is open for business approximately 300 days per year. Jim estimates that CCS will sell $1.25 million of fertilizer and agricultural pesticides in 1995 if they don't change their selling strategy. If they aggressively pursue additional sales, these sales will come from the large high-risk customers. He can't move any more product to the smaller farmers or to the large, low-risk operators. Will it pay to aggressively pursue additional sales to the point where bad debt loss hits 1 percent? Suggest an alternative credit policy for CCS. How will CCS implement your suggested policy?

14. Discuss briefly the trends in volume and gross margin for CCS from 1989–1994 based on the data in Attachments A, B, and C.

15. What problems do you see with the current pricing policy? What dangers are inherent with the markup policy?

16. How should CCS set prices? Should it have a written volume discount policy? Discuss.

17. How much volume ($) would CCS have needed at 1994 prices to break even? How much more volume ($) would have been necessary to generate as much NIBT as the firm did in 1993?

18. Frank and Jim decide that they will use the 1994 FIAP figures for their 1995 gross margin target. What will their new break-even point be if they achieve this goal? What strategies do you have to help them boost their gross margins to this new, higher level? The information provided in question 9 may be useful.

Attachment A

Income statement 1989–1994.

| | 1989 | | | |
CATEGORY	CCS		FIAP	
F+C Product Sales	$1,264,675	100.00	$1,313,056	100.00
F+C COGS	1,023,652	80.94	1,020,350	77.71
F+C Gross Margin	241,024	19.06	292,706	22.29
		% Rcts		% Rcts
Service Income	70,027	5.25	57,367	4.19
Gross Profit	311,051	23.30	350,073	25.54
F+C Expenses				
Total Employee Costs	109,212	8.18	124,023	9.05
Local Taxes, Licenses	4,559	0.34	6,509	0.47
Insurance	18,173	1.36	18,399	1.34
Total Depr, Rent, Lease	41,495	3.11	47,051	3.43
Advertising & Promotion	3,122	0.23	7,193	0.52
Total Equip Opr Expense	12,970	0.97	19,400	1.42
Total Repair & Maintenance	23,727	1.78	24,333	1.78
Bad Debt Loss	1,737	0.13	10,903	0.80
Other Expenses	19,813	1.48	34,154	2.49
Total Operating Expenses	234,808	17.59	288,307	21.04
Net Operating Profit	76,243	5.71	61,766	4.51
Other Income	6,907	0.52	20,278	****
Interest Expense	30,511	2.29	29,806	2.17
Net Income Before Taxes	52,639	3.94	56,409	****
Less: State Tax	6,856	0.51	****	****
Federal Tax	6,758	0.51	****	****
Net Income	39,025	2.92	****	****

*Note: FIAP figures represent the average for each plant reporting each line item. Hence, individual line items will not add down.

Income statement 1989–1994, continued.

| CATEGORY | 1990 | | | |
	CCS		FIAP	
F+C Product Sales	$1,192,993	100.00	$1,128,210	100.00
F+C COGS	997,232	83.59	865,038	76.67
F+C Gross Margin	195,762	16.41	263,172	23.33
		% Rcts		% Rcts
Service Income	65,940	5.24	61,192	5.14
Gross Profit	261,702	20.79	324,365	27.27
F+C Expenses				
Total Employee Costs	82,318	6.54	125,824	10.58
Local Taxes, Licenses	5,323	0.42	6,805	0.57
Insurance	24,572	1.95	9,813	0.83
Total Depr, Rent, Lease	46,010	3.65	51,309	4.31
Advertising & Promotion	6,640	0.53	5,716	0.48
Total Equip Opr Expense	16,473	1.31	18,092	1.52
Total Repair & Maintenance	24,675	1.96	25,392	2.13
Bad Debt Loss	0	0.00	6,771	0.57
Other Expenses	16,596	1.32	48,346	4.07
Total Operating Expenses	222,607	17.68	294,385	24.76
Net Operating Profit	39,095	3.11	29,980	2.52
Other Income	8,823	0.70	42,785	****
Interest Expense	28,646	2.28	30,381	2.55
Net Income Before Taxes	19,272	1.53	51,490	****
Less: State Tax	5,807	0.46	****	****
Federal Tax	262	0.02	****	****
Net Income	13,203	1.05	****	****

*Note: FIAP figures represent the average for each plant reporting each line item. Hence, individual line items will not add down.

Income statement 1989–1994, continued.

CATEGORY	CCS		FIAP	
		1991		
F+C Product Sales	$1,420,202	100.00	$1,267,931	100.00
F+C COGS	1,189,979	83.79	984,899	77.68
F+C Gross Margin	230,224	16.21	283,032	22.32
		% Rcts		% Rcts
Service Income	87,944	5.83	55,890	4.22
Gross Profit	318,168	21.10	338,922	25.60
F+C Expenses				
Total Employee Costs	97,387	6.46	117,743	8.89
Local Taxes, Licenses	6,661	0.44	5,926	0.45
Insurance	16,001	1.06	7,299	0.55
Total Depr, Rent, Lease	70,353	4.66	41,645	3.15
Advertising & Promotion	8,368	0.55	6,052	0.46
Total Equip Opr Expense	20,756	1.38	18,632	1.41
Total Repair & Maintenance	27,812	1.84	30,496	2.30
Bad Debt Loss	2,047	0.14	4,531	0.34
Other Expenses	24,068	1.60	38,127	2.88
Total Operating Expenses	273,453	18.13	267,491	20.20
Net Operating Profit	44,715	2.96	71,431	5.40
Other Income	18,040	1.20	13,237	****
Interest Expense	41,933	2.78	23,919	1.81
Net Income Before Taxes	20,822	1.38	61,946	****
Less: State Tax	6,703	0.44	****	****
Federal Tax	–3,690	–0.24	****	****
Net Income	17,809	1.18	****	****

*Note: FIAP figures represent the average for each plant reporting each line item. Hence, individual line items will not add down.

Income statement 1989–1994, continued.

| CATEGORY | 1992 | | | |
	CCS		FIAP	
F+C Product Sales	$1,472,652	100.00	$1,258,810	100.00
F+C COGS	1,208,262	82.05	980,196	77.87
F+C Gross Margin	264,390	17.95	278,614	22.13
		% Rcts		% Rcts
Service Income	79,579	5.13	59,633	4.52
Gross Profit	343,969	22.16	338,247	25.66
F+C Expenses				
Total Employee Costs	107,603	6.93	130,975	9.93
Local Taxes, Licenses	20,402	1.31	5,496	0.42
Insurance	23,932	1.54	9,775	0.74
Total Depr, Rent, Lease	82,498	5.31	54,780	4.15
Advertising & Promotion	5,816	0.37	5,146	0.39
Total Equip Opr Expense	23,491	1.51	15,924	1.21
Total Repair & Maintenance	60,836	3.92	36,536	2.77
Bad Debt Loss	0	0.00	16,051	1.22
Other Expenses	16,515	1.06	39,908	3.03
Total Operating Expenses	341,093	21.97	306,851	23.27
Net Operating Profit	2,876	0.19	36,817	2.38
Other Income	13,943	0.90	23,610	****
Interest Expense	42,822	2.76	28,859	2.19
Net Income Before Taxes	−26,003	−1.68	19,129	****
Less: State Tax	5,503	0.35	****	****
Federal Tax	0	0.00	****	****
Net Income	−31,506	−2.03	****	****

*Note: FIAP figures represent the average for each plant reporting each line item. Hence, individual line items will not add down.

Income statement 1989–1994, continued.

	1993			
CATEGORY	CCS		FIAP	
F+C Product Sales	$1,182,046	100.00	$1,296,866	100.00
F+C COGS	931,132	78.77	1,025,612	79.08
F+C Gross Margin	250,914	21.23	271,254	20.92
		% Rcts		% Rcts
Service Income	64,219	5.15	61,473	4.54
Gross Profit	315,133	25.29	332,997	24.51
F+C Expenses				
Total Employee Costs	97,877	7.85	137,473	10.12
Local Taxes, Licenses	14,495	1.16	8,263	0.61
Insurance	28,756	2.31	10,255	0.75
Total Depr, Rent, Lease	67,819	5.44	54,501	4.01
Advertising & Promotion	3,427	0.27	5,448	0.40
Total Equip Opr Expense	18,101	1.45	12,567	0.92
Total Repair & Maintenance	34,624	2.78	35,130	2.59
Bad Debt Loss	0	0.00	12,438	0.92
Other Expenses	15,854	1.27	47,107	3.47
Total Operating Expenses	280,952	22.54	315,459	23.22
Net Operating Profit	34,181	2.74	17,538	1.29
Other Income	17,558	1.41	22,914	****
Interest Expense	24,794	1.99	20,537	1.51
Net Income Before Taxes	26,944	2.16	23,829	****
Less: State Tax	5,825	0.47	****	****
Federal Tax	0	0.00	****	****
Net Income	21,119	1.69	****	****

*Note: FIAP figures represent the average for each plant reporting each line item. Hence, individual line items will not add down.

Income statement 1989–1994, continued.

CATEGORY	1994			
	CCS		FIAP	
F+C Product Sales	$1,263,999	100.00	$1,349,590	100.00
F+C COGS	1,110,074	87.82	1,065,067	78.92
F+C Gross Margin	153,924	12.18	284,524	21.08
		% Rcts		% Rcts
Service Income	81,072	6.03	83,143	5.80
Gross Profit	234,996	17.47	367,666	25.66
F+C Expenses				
Total Employee Costs	123,789	9.20	142,422	9.94
Local Taxes, Licenses	5,757	0.43	8,982	0.63
Insurance	28,674	2.13	13,833	0.97
Total Depr, Rent, Lease	69,556	5.17	63,424	4.43
Advertising & Promotion	3,640	0.27	4,684	0.33
Total Equip Opr Expense	19,406	1.44	16,788	1.17
Total Repair & Maintenance	33,758	2.51	42,452	2.96
Bad Debt Loss	261	0.02	6,816	0.48
Other Expenses	19,590	1.46	58,666	4.09
Total Operating Expenses	304,430	22.63	375,194	26.19
Net Operating Profit	−69,434	−5.16	−7,528	−0.53
Other Income	24,498	1.82	13,330	****
Interest Expense	30,249	2.25	19,472	1.36
Net Income Before Taxes	−75,185	−5.59	23,821	****
Less: State Tax	10,136	0.75	****	****
Federal Tax	0	0.00	****	****
Net Income	−85,321	−6.34	****	****

*Note: FIAP figures represent the average for each plant reporting each line item. Hence, individual line items will not add down.

Attachment B

Balance sheet 1989–1994.

CATEGORY	1989		1990	
	CCS	FIAP	CCS	FIAP
Cash	$ 61,463	$ 23,033	$129,910	$ 41,629
Accounts Receivable	27,105	176,708	46,261	150,245
Inventory	52,154	237,274	52,667	238,528
Other Current Assets	102,000	37,317	3,888	6,184
Total Current Assets	242,722	456,392	232,726	406,130
Land	56,348	15,066	56,348	16,228
Equipment (Net of				
Depreciation)	90,475	235,641	102,048	329,367
Lease	0	N/A	0	N/A
Total Fixed Assets	146,823	250,707	158,396	345,595
Other Assets	8,169	N/A	8,169	N/A
Total Assets	$397,714	$656,957	$399,291	$652,983
Current Liabilities	13,995	383,927	2,369	430,354
Long Term Debt	275,500	150,445	275,500	130,534
Total Debt	289,495	472,827	277,869	560,888
Total Net Worth	108,219	378,399	121,422	263,995
Total Liability and				
Net Worth	$397,714	$782,426	$399,291	$749,455

*Note: FIAP figures represent the average for each plant reporting each line item. Hence, individual line items will not add down.

Balance sheet 1989–1994, continued.

CATEGORY	1991		1992	
	CCS	FIAP	CCS	FIAP
Cash	$ 69,675	$ 14,817	$ 90,756	$ 6,957
Accounts Receivable	126,125	158,999	103,327	182,997
Inventory	57,567	199,990	41,848	232,032
Other Current Assets	4,162	30,178	2,881	16,233
Total Current Assets	257,529	374,411	238,812	398,824
Land	56,348	26,713	56,348	22,025
Equipment (Net of Depreciation)	90,630	226,936	75,474	234,039
Lease	83,665	N/A	62,008	N/A
Total Fixed Assets	230,643	253,649	193,830	256,064
Other Assets	8,169	N/A	8,169	N/A
Total Assets	$496,341	$494,475	$440,811	$557,760
Current Liabilities	18,525	320,209	5,004	370,683
Long Term Debt	338,585	175,440	328,082	185,262
Total Debt	357,110	495,649	333,086	473,606
Total Net Worth	139,231	279,705	107,724	299,420
Total Liability and Net Worth	$496,341	$775,354	$440,811	$639,951

*Note: FIAP figures represent the average for each plant reporting each line item. Hence, individual line items will not add down.

Balance sheet 1989–1994, continued.

CATEGORY	1993		1994	
	CCS	FIAP	CCS	FIAP
Cash	$ 93,241	$ 27,356	$ 45,712	$ 34,104
Accounts Receivable	74,317	73,694	119,629	57,207
Inventory	106,199	187,012	88,195	118,138
Other Current Assets	2,000	85,323	21,346	69,576
Total Current Assets	275,758	323,140	274,882	232,757
Land	56,348	27,352	9,478	20,944
Equipment (Net of				
Depreciation)	52,179	257,331	116,332	221,891
Lease	41,339	N/A	117,045	N/A
Total Fixed Assets	149,866	284,683	242,855	242,835
Other Assets	8,169	N/A	8,169	N/A
Total Assets	$433,793	$529,344	$525,906	$474,063
Current Liabilities	2,818	196,255	76,833	152,635
Long Term Debt	301,867	137,067	393,027	147,176
Total Debt	304,685	305,909	469,860	263,017
Total Net Worth	129,108	228,450	56,046	211,046
Total Liability and				
Net Worth	$433,793	$511,514	$525,906	$474,063

*Note: FIAP figures represent the average for each plant reporting each line item. Hence, individual line items will not add down.

Attachment C

Financial data 1989–1994.

PER TON INFORMATION	1989		1990	
	CCS	FIAP	CCS	FIAP
Service Acres	N/A	****	13,704	****
Tonnage	N/A	4,724	3,356	4,354
Sales Dollars/Ton	N/A	277.93	355.48	259.13
COGS Dollars/Ton	N/A	215.97	297.15	198.68
Gross Margin/Ton	N/A	61.96	58.33	60.45
Service Revenue/Ton	N/A	12.14	19.65	14.05
Gross Profit/Ton	N/A	74.10	77.98	74.50
Costs/Ton	N/A	66.45	66.33	72.50
Operating Profit/Ton	N/A	7.65	11.65	2.00
Short-Term Interest Exp	****	6.31	****	6.98
Financial Ratios				
Gross Margin %	19.06	22.29	16.41	23.33
Gross Profit %	23.30	25.54	20.79	27.27
Operating Expense %	17.59	21.04	17.68	24.76
Operating Profit %	5.71	4.51	3.11	2.52
Net Income Before Taxes %	3.94	****	1.53	****
Current Ratio	17.34	1.61	98.24	1.62
Quick Ratio	13.62	0.96	76.01	0.67
Days Sales in Receivables	7.72	45.18	13.96	41.95
Inventory Turns	19.63	6.62	18.93	5.66
Asset Turns	3.36	3.24	3.15	2.39
Debt/Equity	72.79	60.94	69.59	66.56
Leverage	3.68	1.56	3.29	1.99
Return on Total Assets	13.24	8.81	4.83	7.93
Return on Net Worth	48.64	18.16	15.87	N/A

*Note: FIAP figures represent the average for each plant reporting each line item.

104

Financial data 1989–1994, continued.

PER TON INFORMATION	1991		1992	
	CCS	FIAP	CCS	FIAP
Service Acres	22,571	****	22,257	****
Tonnage	4,466	4,246	4,883	4,801
Sales Dollars/Ton	318.03	298.65	301.61	262.18
COGS Dollars/Ton	266.47	231.98	247.46	204.15
Gross Margin/Ton	51.55	66.67	54.15	58.03
Service Revenue/Ton	19.69	13.16	16.30	12.42
Gross Profit/Ton	71.25	79.83	70.45	70.45
Costs/Ton	61.23	68.36	69.86	69.32
Operating Profit/Ton	10.01	11.47	0.59	1.13
Short-Term Interest Exp	****	5.63	****	6.01
Financial Ratios				
Gross Margin %	16.21	22.32	17.95	22.13
Gross Profit %	21.10	25.60	22.16	25.66
Operating Expense %	18.13	20.20	21.97	23.27
Operating Profit %	2.96	5.40	0.19	2.38
Net Income Before Taxes %	1.38	****	−1.68	****
Current Ratio	13.90	2.21	47.72	1.13
Quick Ratio	10.79	1.49	39.36	0.72
Days Sales in Receivables	31.97	41.79	25.26	47.24
Inventory Turns	20.67	7.46	28.87	7.34
Asset Turns	3.04	4.05	3.52	3.88
Debt/Equity	71.95	63.64	75.56	78.26
Leverage	3.56	1.75	4.09	3.60
Return on Total Assets	4.20	12.95	−5.90	5.52
Return on Net Worth	14.96	13.62	−24.14	11.52

*Note: FIAP figures represent the average for each plant reporting each line item.

Financial data 1989–1994, continued.

PER TON INFORMATION	1993		1994	
	CCS	FIAP	CCS	FIAP
Service Acres	20,632	****	17,279	****
Tonnage	4,099	5,010	4,873	6,198
Sales Dollars/Ton	288.37	258.86	259.39	217.74
COGS Dollars/Ton	227.16	204.72	227.80	171.84
Gross Margin/Ton	61.21	54.14	31.59	45.90
Service Revenue/Ton	15.67	12.32	16.64	13.41
Gross Profit/Ton	76.88	66.47	48.22	59.31
Costs/Ton	68.54	66.79	62.47	60.53
Operating Profit/Ton	8.34	−0.33	−14.25	−1.21
Short-Term Interest Exp	****	4.10	****	3.14

Financial Ratios

	CCS	FIAP	CCS	FIAP
Gross Margin %	21.23	20.92	12.18	21.08
Gross Profit %	25.29	24.51	17.47	25.66
Operating Expense %	22.54	23.22	22.63	26.19
Operating Profit %	2.74	1.29	−5.16	−0.53
Net Income Before Taxes %	2.16	****	−5.59	****
Current Ratio	97.85	1.44	3.58	1.52
Quick Ratio	60.17	N/A	2.43	N/A
Days Sales in Receivables	22.63	19.54	34.07	13.86
Inventory Turns	8.77	13.23	12.59	12.58
Asset Turns	2.87	2.59	2.56	2.54
Debt/Equity	70.24	71.18	89.34	69.23
Leverage	3.36	2.47	9.38	2.25
Return on Total Assets	6.21	3.10	−14.30	4.17
Return on Net Worth	20.87	8.99	−134.15	9.36

*Note: FIAP figures represent the average for each plant reporting each line item.

Ontario Flower Growers' Cooperative (1)

In April 1984, Martin Versluis, chairman of the finance committee of the Ontario Flower Growers' Cooperative Ltd. of Mississauga, Ontario, sat down to analyze whether the co-op should renew its lease for the building where it held a biweekly auction. The lease was due to expire in December 1985 but the lessor was pressing the co-op to renew it now because other companies were interested in leasing the building. Versluis had to present a position to the board of directors that the board could present to the membership for approval at the next members' meeting in June.

■ BACKGROUND

The main business of the co-op, established in 1972 by a group of flower growers with the assistance of the Ontario government, is its auction. Grower-members sell a wide variety of floricultural products to the buyers who attend each auction. The co-op charges the seller a commission of 10 percent of the sale's value for using the auction. The co-op is nonprofit and distributes operating profits among the members at the end of each year in the same proportion as the value their sales represent of the total sales made through the co-op. This practice eliminates its income tax liability.

The need to decide about renewal of the co-op's net lease on the building it was renting was precipitated by the landlord (a net lease requires the lessee to pay taxes and maintenance of the leased property). In the fall of 1983 he offered to renew the lease at the cost of $350,000 per year for several years starting January 1985. The board of directors was shocked at

This case was prepared by Kenneth F. Harling and William M. Braithwaite, Department of Agricultural Business and Economics, University of Guelph, Guelph, Ontario, Canada, under a grant from the Small Business Secretariat of the Department of Regional Industrial Expansion, Ottawa, as a basis for classroom discussion rather than to illustrate either correct or incorrect handling of administrative problems. This case is used with permission of the authors.

both the price and duration of the lease, as the co-op paid $144,000 per year under the current lease and felt the proposed increase was exorbitant. It also felt that a long-term lease was absolutely essential because many businesses visited by users of the co-op had located in the industrial park near it. The lessor pushed the board to sign the lease. After protracted discussions he offered to charge only $250,000 per year for the first three years of the new lease. After that it would increase by 6 percent per year; but if either party felt the rent set using this formula was inappropriate, an independent arbitrator would be called upon.

■ THE DECISION

The board felt that the rental cost under the revised proposal was still much too high, so it asked the finance committee to consider whether the co-op would be better off building its own building rather than leasing. As chairman of the finance committee, Versluis had to determine what should be done about the lease.

Versluis gathered facts needed to make a decision. A building committee, set up to explore the idea of the co-op building its own structure, had found a parcel of land in a nearby industrial park for $800,000. Versluis estimated that the value of this land would increase at 6 percent per year following past trends for industrial land prices in the area. The building committee reported that the cost of erecting a suitable building on the land would be $1,800,000. Other costs associated with the building were an interest charge of $100,000 for bridge financing (financing construction of a building prior to its completion) and $50,000 for moving into the new building. The building would be depreciated for tax purposes on a diminishing balance basis at 5 percent per year.

The co-op would have to raise capital to finance the building. The co-op's banker told Versluis that a mortgage of $2 million, approximately 75 percent of the value of the building and land, could be provided, so the co-op would have to raise an additional $750,000 from its members. It has little equity because of its policy of distributing savings to members, and members have proven reluctant in the past to provide financing. Member loans of $145,000 were raised at the end of 1983 against the possible need to finance the purchase of land for a building, and the co-op had promised to pay market rates of interest on member's contributions.

Versluis decided he would have to compare the cost of a new lease with the cost of erecting a new building. He assumed for the sake of comparison that the building and land would be sold when the building was 20 years old. As he looked at his desk, he saw copies of the financial statements for the last two years (Exhibits 1 and 2). The co-op's bookkeeper had also prepared schedules for several items: the potential mortgage payments, the

EXHIBIT 1   Income statements for 1982 and 1983 (thousands of dollars).

	1983	1982
Revenue	$927	$848
Expenses		
Lease	$144	$144
Amortized leasehold improvement	11	12
Depreciation of equipment	56	28
Interest, member loan	20	0
Other	453	488
Total expenses	$684	$672
Net savings	$243	$176
Savings distributed[a]	$178	$192
Net savings after distribution	$ 65	($16)

[a]The cooperative eliminated its income tax liability each year by declaring that the savings of the previous year would be distributed over the next year.

EXHIBIT 2   Balance sheets for 1982 and 1983 (thousands of dollars).

	1983	1982
Assets		
Current		
Cash	$224	$142
Other	125	120
Total current assets	$369	$262
Long Term		
Equipment (net)	$175	$ 71
Leasehold improvement (net)	21	33
Other	4	4
Total long-term assets	$200	$108
Total assets	$569	$370
Liabilities and Equities		
Liabilities		
Current		
Member loans	$145	—
Other	32	36
Total current liabilities	$177	$ 36
Long term	—	—
Total liabilities	$177	$ 36
Equities		
Shares	$142	$145
Retained earnings	250	189
Total equities	$392	$334
Total liabilities and equities	$569	$370

depreciation schedule, and the value of the land (Exhibit 3). She had assumed that the mortgage would be for $2 million and be borrowed at 13.5 percent for 20 years, that the building would be depreciated at a 5 percent diminishing balance, and that the value of the land would increase at 6 percent per year. Versluis thought that revenues and operating costs, including insurance and tax on a building, would be the same under either alternative. Finally, as he looked at the schedule, he decided to assume that the market rate of interest of 13.5 percent would continue. With that information he began developing a course of action to recommend to the board at the next meeting.

EXHIBIT 3   Schedules of payments and receipts (thousands of dollars).

YEAR	LOAN ($2 MILLION FOR 20 YR AT 13.5%) AMORTIZED PAYMENT				BUILDING (AT 5% DIMINISHING BALANCE)			LAND AT MARKET VALUE (RISES BY 6%/YR)
	Value Present $	Future $	Interest	of Which: Principal	Book Value	Deprec. Charge	Net Value	
1	293	293	270	23	1,950	98	1,852	800
2	258	293	267	26	1,852	93	1,759	848
3	227	293	263	30	1,759	88	1,671	899
4	202	293	259	34	1,671	84	1,587	953
5	177	293	254	39	1,587	79	1,508	1,010
6	156	293	249	44	1,508	75	1,433	1,071
7	137	293	243	50	1,433	72	1,361	1,135
8	121	293	237	56	1,361	68	1,293	1,203
9	106	293	229	64	1,293	65	1,228	1,275
10	94	293	220	73	1,228	61	1,167	1,352
11	83	293	211	83	1,167	58	1,109	1,433
12	73	293	199	94	1,109	55	1,054	1,519
13	64	293	187	106	1,054	53	1,001	1,610
14	56	293	172	121	1,001	50	951	1,706
15	50	293	156	137	951	48	903	1,809
16	44	293	137	156	903	45	858	1,917
17	39	293	116	177	858	43	815	2,032
18	34	293	93	200	815	41	774	2,154
19	30	293	65	228	774	39	735	2,283
20	26	293	35	258	735	37	698	2,420
21					698	35	663	2,565

Booneville Farm Supply

■■■ INTRODUCTION

Thomas Logan climbed into his Jeep pickup and turned the key. As he eased the truck onto U.S. 41, he began to mentally review his conversation with Dave Merz, the Indiana sales representative for the Melroe Company, a North Dakota manufacturer of agricultural equipment. Logan was the owner-manager of Booneville Farm Supply (BFS), a retailer of agricultural inputs in southwestern Indiana. Logan had spent the morning discussing the Melroe Spra-Coupe 220 agricultural sprayer with Merz. Logan had listened intently to the description of the specs for the high-clearance pesticide applicator and had asked his usual bushel-load of questions. His yellow legal pad was filled with figures Merz had given him. In addition, the pad also had a score of questions scribbled in the margins, questions that Logan would need to answer himself before making any decisions.

Although the potential market for post-emerge custom application of pesticides certainly looked promising, the Spra-Coupe's $38,000 price tag was not to be taken lightly. Already this year, Logan was looking at $23,000 for a new computer system and another $15,000 for major repairs to the roof of one of his warehouses. Still, he thought this decision deserved some careful pencil pushing.

■■■ BOONEVILLE FARM SUPPLY

Booneville Farm Supply is a midsized (1994 annual sales of $2.5 million) agribusiness near Evansville, Indiana. It is an independent operation that

---

This case was prepared by Jay T. Akridge, Associate Director of the Purdue University Center for Agricultural Business and Associate Professor in the Purdue Department of Agricultural Economics; Steven P. Erickson, a Professor in the Department of Agricultural Economics at Purdue University; and Linda D. Whipker, a USDA National Needs Fellow in Agribusiness and a Ph.D. student in the Department of Agricultural Economics at Purdue University, as a basis for classroom discussion rather than to illustrate either correct or incorrect handling of a business situation. Spra-Coupe is a registered trademark of the Melroe Company.

supplies a range of inputs, including feed, seed, pesticides, bagged fertilizer, farm fence, gates, and building materials, to farmers in the southwest corner of Indiana. In addition, BFS also carries a large inventory of hardware items for both farmers and do-it-yourselfers. The firm currently has no facility for handling bulk fertilizer or pesticides. Instead, BFS sells a limited amount of bagged fertilizer to smaller farmers in the area. It does, however, move a substantial quantity of packaged pesticides over the counter to farmers who own pesticide application equipment. Despite its lack of bulk fertilizer and pesticide-handling capabilities, BFS is well respected in the area for its agronomic expertise. Pesticide volume has grown over time, and in 1994 packaged pesticides accounted for nearly 20 percent of its total sales volume.

Logan was well aware of the growing number of post-emerge herbicides on the market. Farmers in southwestern Indiana were certainly increasing their use of these products every year. Clearly, this trend was both a threat and an opportunity for BFS. In many cases, the post-emerge applications were rescue operations. The price of the pesticide was of less concern—farmers didn't shop around as much when "the field had to be sprayed today." In addition, farmers relied on BFS to recommend the appropriate tank mix to eliminate their post-emerge weed problems. On the other hand, farmers in the area tended to look first to one of BFS's competitors who was equipped with high-clearance application equipment or to the helicopter-spraying service in nearby Evansville, because BFS could not apply the pesticides for the farmer. Logan wasn't eager for competitors to take away the pesticide part of his business.

As a temporary solution, Logan had supplied pesticides to the helicopter application service on a few occasions last year. But this didn't appear to be a longer term answer to his problem. At a sales meeting sponsored by Ohio River Chemicals, Inc., his main supplier of pesticides, Logan had attended a session on the Melroe Spra-Coupe. The information presented and the discussion that followed led Logan to give some thought to the value a Spra-Coupe sprayer might have for BFS. Logan had no desire to move into bulk fertilizer at the moment, and he certainly wasn't willing to make a heavy commitment in the custom application business. The Spra-Coupe sprayer seemed to offer a reasonable alternative. BFS could focus on selling pesticides without worrying about bulk fertilizer. This type of custom application service seemed to complement the firm's agronomic reputation. The investment appeared reasonable, and the labor requirements were relatively low. Clearly, there was enough potential here to justify a more careful look.

■ THE MELROE SPRA-COUPE 220 SPRAYER

The Melroe Spra-Coupe 220 is a high-clearance, low-volume applicator especially suited for application of pesticides to growing crops. The Spra-Coupe, powered by a Volkswagen industrial water-cooled engine, can cover as much as 60 acres per hour when a two-person team is used—one to drive the Spra-Coupe and one to handle the nurse unit. In most cases, however, one person handles both the Spra-Coupe and the nurse unit. The Spra-Coupe is towed to the field by a 1½- or 2-ton truck equipped with a stainless steel or polyethylene water tank. One person can typically cover 40 acres per hour with the unit, counting both fill-up and tow time. Even at 40 acres per hour, the machine has the potential to cover a large number of acres in a season. Some firms report covering as many as 15,000 acres in a single season with the Spra-Coupe sprayer.

The four-cylinder Volkswagen engine is easy on fuel, and the machine uses about 1.5 gallons (regular gasoline) per hour. Logan budgeted about $1 per gallon for fuel. Although maintenance varies with use, Merz had indicated that most of his customers spend about $1,000 per year to repair and maintain the machine when it is used to spray from 4,500 to 7,000 acres. Merz also pointed out that insurance costs vary from dealer to dealer. Logan had obtained an estimate of $350 per year from his insurance agent. Taxes, licenses, and other fees were expected to run another $450 per year. Logan knew he would need to talk with his accountant to determine the depreciation schedule for the machine. For purposes of his budget, he decided to depreciate the Spra-Coupe sprayer on a straight-line basis (zero salvage value) over a seven-year period. Logan reasoned that this was a conservative approach because he knew he could write it off more quickly using the accelerated depreciation guidelines.

By talking with Merz and several fertilizer dealers who already owned a Spra-Coupe, Logan learned that the machine was durable. Annual maintenance was enough to keep the machine in reasonably good shape. In addition, a $3,000 overhaul and a paint job after the fifth season would put the machine back in like-new condition. Even after 10 years of use under typical conditions, the Spra-Coupe still had several useful years left. Currently, such well-used machines were bringing about $16,000. Although acquiring a used machine was a possibility, Logan decided that if he got into the custom application business, it would be with a new Spra-Coupe. He was nervous, however, about the $16,000 figure—the market for Spra-Coupes (new and used) was currently hot. Logan figured that 10 years down the road the secondary market might not be as good. He decided that $14,000 was all he could safely assume that the used Spra-Coupe would bring after 10 years.

Logan had given the nurse vehicle considerable thought. BFS had a 1980 Ford two-ton truck that was in pretty good shape. It used the truck for a variety of hauling jobs—both to deliver merchandise to customers and to pick up purchases from distributors. Logan decided that he could get the truck freed up during the post-emerge application season without causing any great inconvenience. Since insurance, taxes, license, and depreciation were all sunk costs for the truck, Logan knew he didn't need to worry about them in his analysis. He figured, however, that it would cost another $188 in fuel and $150 in repairs to put the truck on the road for the extra 1,500 miles (at eight miles per gallon) it would take to service the Spra-Coupe over the course of the application season.

Although Logan had a usable truck, he would need to buy a tank and a pump for hauling water and refilling the sprayer. Logan had priced a 2,100-gallon (83" diameter) polyethylene tank at a local spray equipment supply firm at $800. He figured the tank would last about 10 years. It would cost another $700 for a pump, hoses, and fittings to equip the nurse rig. At best, Logan figured he would get five years out of this equipment. Since this was relatively minor equipment, Logan decided that he would apply these purchases toward his Section 179 exemption. This exemption allows small businesses to deduct as much as $17,500 in depreciable property during the year of acquisition, effectively treating the acquisition as an expense. After giving it some thought, he decided that the $3,000 overhaul would likely be treated in the same fashion. Hence, none of these items would be depreciated; all would be expensed during the year of purchase.

Logan also knew that he would need a driver who was dependable and had the skills and ability to run the applicator, handle the tank mixes, and stay on schedule with little supervision. Although it wasn't the best solution, Logan had decided that Paul Wayne could handle the job. BFS had hired Paul from an area contractor five years ago to manage the warehouses. He had a farm background, and Logan was sure he could run the Spra-Coupe—and do a good job—with little supervision. He wasn't eager to have Paul away from the warehouse during the application season, but he just didn't have anyone else who could handle it. When all taxes and benefits were included, Logan figured that he would be out $14 per hour when Paul was running the Spra-Coupe.

■ REVENUE ESTIMATES

Logan assembled the data presented in Exhibit 1 from his 1994 records. BFS sold pesticides for post-emerge application on three crops—soybeans, wheat, and alfalfa. (In the case of alfalfa, the problem was weevils and not weeds.) Although a number of products were available to handle pest and weed problems for each crop, Logan decided to choose his best seller in each area to prepare his budget. For soybeans, BFS's best selling product was Fusilade, for wheat it was Harmony, and for alfalfa it was Ambush.

Based on this information, Logan decided that he should be able to generate 4,000 acres of custom application business for the Spra-Coupe sprayer during the first year. Although this might be a bit optimistic for a first-year projection, Logan reasoned that this part of his business would grow over time. It was Logan's belief that more and more farmers would be turning to custom application as they became more sensitive to the potential hazards of agricultural pesticides. And, he knew there would be swings from year to year in the number of acres BFS would be able to cover with the Spra-Coupe because of all the other factors that affect agriculture, such as weather, government programs, and so on. So, balancing all these things, Logan decided that his 4,000-acre estimate should be reasonable. With most of the applicators charging between $4.00 and $4.50 per acre for post-emerge application service, Logan decided that he would price his Spra-Coupe service at $4.25 per acre.

In addition to revenue generated directly by the application of pesticides, Logan expected some increase in the volume of post-emerge pesticides sold. Some survey data presented at the seminar he had attended on the sprayer showed that the average dealer increases its volume of pesticides sales 20 percent once the dealer begins running the machine. Logan thought this number was plausible in his situation. He assembled the data in Exhibit 2 to help him determine how much the extra 20 percent of pesticide sales would mean to his firm.

Logan thought the Spra-Coupe would create other benefits for BFS, including enhancing the firm's reputation for agronomic service as well as its reputation for high-quality customer service. And he thought that this move could be a stepping-stone for getting into the bulk fertilizer business. Logan didn't know, however, how to put a price on these factors so he left them out of his calculations.

EXHIBIT 1   Post-emerge pesticide sales history and projections.

CROP UNIT	PROJECTED 1994 SALES		PROJECTED 1995 SALES		1995 SPRAYER VOLUME[a]	
	Units	Acres	Units	Acres	Units	Acres
Soybeans (gal)	516	3,300	625	4,000	347	2,500
Wheat (oz)	1,058	1,410	1,275	1,700	750	1,000
Alfalfa (gal)	84	1,080	101	1,300	35	500
Total		5,790		7,000		4,000

[a]Note: The projected 1995 Spra-Coupe volume figures are included in the projected total 1995 sales estimates.

EXHIBIT 2   Post-emerge pesticide application information.

CROP	PRODUCT	RATE/ACRE	PRICE	COST	GROSS MARGIN
Soybeans	Fusilade	20 oz	$67.00/gal	$64.00/gal	$3.00/gal
Wheat	Harmony	.75 oz	$12.50/oz	$10.80/oz	$1.70/oz
Alfalfa	Ambush	10 oz	$101.30/gal	$91.35/gal	$9.95/gal

■■■ WORKING CAPITAL

Logan flipped through his notes to make sure he had accounted for all costs and revenues. Just as he was finishing, one of his employees came in to his office and asked Logan if it was okay to bill a load of feed on credit to a customer who had been a bit slow lately in paying. Logan gave his reply and turned back to his notes. A thought suddenly hit him, triggered by the employee's question—he hadn't included anything to account for the increase in working capital that would be required to support the additional sales and service volume. To handle this, Logan decided to assume that all the custom application revenue and the additional sales volume would be put on customers' accounts. BFS's days sales in receivables (DSR) ratio typically ran about 45 days. But, to make things a bit easier for purposes of his budget, Logan assumed a DSR of 60 days (two months). He wasn't sure exactly how to include this increase in working capital in his budget, so he decided to give it a rest and think about it for a while.

■■■ THE PROBLEM

After assembling the data presented above, Logan sharpened a couple of pencils, dusted off his calculator, and pulled out another legal pad. He knew he would need some additional information for his analysis. First, BFS's marginal tax bracket was 34 percent. Second, Logan typically used 20 percent as his after-tax cost of capital number. In addition, he knew he could borrow money to finance the Spra-Coupe at the prime rate plus 2 percent—if he came up with a 20 percent down payment. Checking the *Wall Street Journal,* he found the prime rate was 6 percent. Finally, he had read recently that inflation was forecast to run about 3 percent per year for the foreseeable future. Combining this information with that provided above, decide if the Spra-Coupe sprayer would be a wise use of limited capital.

■■■ *QUESTIONS*

1. What is the payback period for this project?
2. What is the real (as opposed to nominal) after-tax cost of capital Logan is using in his analysis? Which cash flows will be discounted using the nominal after-tax cost of capital and which will be discounted using the real after-tax cost of capital?
3. At a 20 percent cost of capital, is the net present value of this project positive?
4. What assumptions are the most critical in this analysis? How would you evaluate the importance of these assumptions?

Attachment A

■ A SPECIAL REPORT FROM MELROE

The 220 semi-high clearance Spra-Coupe, manufactured by the Melroe Company of Bismarck, North Dakota, is a self-propelled ground sprayer with capacity and power to handle small grain or row crop spraying applications.

One in a family of Spra-Coupe models offered by Melroe, the 220 is a one-man, all-season machine built high enough from ground to mainframe to help the applicator complete his spraying needs. It is loaded with features which give the applicator spraying versatility when he needs it.

Smooth Ride, Steady Boom

Ask a Spra-Coupe operator which feature he likes best and he's most apt to say the smooth ride and steady boom structure. The 220's automotive-type suspension and shock absorbers on the boom structure combine to give the operator a steady ride and smooth boom.

A heavy-duty coil spring with shock absorbers supports a rugged front fork assembly connected to the A-frame, cushioning the ride considerably. The wheels, instead of the boom, absorb the initial shock from riding over center pivot tracks, water furrows, dead furrows, irrigation pipe, and natural low spots.

Coupled with the machine suspension is a rear suspension system which holds tension on the boom, absorbing shock and keeping the boom steady and horizontal to the crop. The driver rides comfortably while the booms direct the chemical where it will do the most good . . . on the crop.

Total Spray System Control

An adjustable boom, spanning 60 feet, gives the operator a wide spray swath and the ability to spray more acres in a day. Electric actuators, controlled from inside the cab, allow the boom to be folded, unfolded, raised or lowered as needed. The boom tip lift will raise the outer edge of the boom up to 48 inches to clear fence posts and other obstacles.

The 220's booms are adjustable to allow spraying at heights from 24½ inches to 64½ inches, ensuring the best possible tip-to-tip coverage.

Melroe has designed a boom structure with two hinge points to allow break-away if an object is struck. A hinge at the outer end of the boom permits the boom to swing back about 90 degrees at an upward angle. Once clear of the obstacle, the boom returns and automatically locks back into its original position.

Another hinge point near the base of the inner boom allows the boom to break-away at a lesser angle, returning to its normal position once the object is cleared.

Rounding out the features of the Spra-Coupe's total spray system is a 210 gallon polyethylene tank with an offset jet agitator inside. The tank supplies enough liquid for maximum coverage in minimum time. Spray pressure is provided by a Hypro centrifugal pump with electromagnetic clutch.

Standard flat-tip nozzles are spaced at 20 inch intervals to obtain the correct 30 percent overlap and most consistent top of the nozzle to the top of the crop coverage. The 31 nozzle assemblies can be fitted with nylon, brass, or stainless tips.

The 220 is light . . . 6,440 pounds loaded . . . and its three-wheel design minimizes soil compaction since only one wheel passes through a row on a single pass. An optional wide front assembly can be mounted to conform to tread widths from 80 to 108 inches.

Ideal for small grains and specialty row crops, the 220's adjustable tread spacings are suitable for most farming practices. The 220's rear axle is adjustable from 78 to 101 inches, and an optional extension axle extends rear tread spacings from 101 to 120 inches.

Power and Transport

The 20 Spra-Coupe is powered by a 75-horsepower, 1.8 liter Volkswagen water-cooled engine. A four-speed transaxle transmission supplies spraying speeds up to 21 miles per hour.

Melroe has designed the 220 and other Spra-Coupe models so they can be readily towed from field to field. According to instructions provided by Melroe in the Spra-Coupe operator's manual, the operator disconnects the rear axles, empties the spray tank, checks all tire pressures, and attaches the transport hitch. (The towing vehicle should be of adequate capacity to handle the weight of the Spra-Coupe it is towing.)

MODEL 220 SPRA-COUPE
SPECIFICATIONS
(Specifications and design subject to change without notice)

General Specifications

Shipping Weight (220-78") lbs. (kg.) (Does not consider optional equipment.
Weight will be more if equipped with options) .... Approx. 4550 (2066)
Shipping Weight (220-72") (Does not consider optional equipment. Weight
will be more if equipped with options) .... Approx. 4675 (2122)
Operating Weight (220-78") lbs. (kg.) (With spray tank full) (Weight will be
more if equipped with options) .... Approx. 6305 (2861)
Operating Weight (220-72") lbs. (kg.) (With spray tank full) (Weight will be
more if equipped with options) .... Approx. 6428 (2918)
Speed Ranges—mph & (km/h) (With Standard Rear 7.50 × 16 "General"
Mud Grip Tires) 5.0 (8.0), 9.2 (14.8), 14.6 (23.5), 21.5 (34.6)
Tires (Standard) .... 11L × 15 Imp. Rib. (Front) Inflate to 26-30 psi (179-207 kPa)
7.50 × 16 "General" Mud Grip (Rear) Inflate to 60 psi (413 kPa)
Tires (Optional) .... 29 × 12.50 - 15 Bar Lug (Rear) Inflate to 30 psi (207 kPa)
29 × 12.50 - 15 Xtra-Traction Flotation (Rear) Inflate to 25-30 psi (172-207 kPa)
31 × 13.50 - 15 Lt Rib (Rear) Inflate to 30 psi (207 kPa)
Rear Suspension .... Swing Type-Coil Springs and Shock Absorber
Front Suspension .... Wheel Fork-Coil Spring and Shock Absorber
Tread Spacing (rear) 220-72" - in. (cm) .... 72 (182.9) to 87.25 (221.6) w/rims reversed
Tread Spacing (rear) 200-78" - in. (cm) .... 78 (198.1) to 101.25 (257.2) w/rims reversed
Tread Spacing (wide front 220 = 72") in. (cm.) .... 72 (182.9) to 96 (243.8)
Tread Spacing (wide front 220 = 78") in. (cm.) .... 80 (203.2) to 108 (274.8)

Engine

Make .... 75 H.P. 1.8 Liter Volkswagen-Industrial, Water Cooled
Type .... 026.2, 4 Cylinder, 1781 cc Displacement - 108.6 cu. in.
Governed Operating RPM .... 3800 No-Load - 800 Low Idle
Fuel .... Regular Gasoline, not lower than 87 Oct.
Fuel Tank Capacity—gallons (litres) 22 (83.27)
Engine Oil Capacity—quarts (litres) 3.2 (3.03)
Engine Oil .... SAE 15W-40 SF/CD or equivalent to Mil-L-2104D.
(Ambient Temp. range from 0°F (–18°C) to 92°F (33°C). See page 30 for other recommendations.

Transmission

Type .... Heavy Duty, Synchromesh Transaxle, 4 Speeds Forward and 1 Reverse
Transmission Oil Capacity - pints (litres) 5.3 (2.507)
Final Drive .... 1:3.5 No. 60 Chain, Chain Sprockets and Roller Chain Running in Oil, Left and Right Hand
Final Drive Oil Capacity - pints (litres) 9 (4.26)

Spraying System

Spray Control .... Electric "Left - Center - Right" Boom On/Off Spray Control Valves
Flow Control .... Electric Control Pressure Adjust Valve
Agitation .... Offset Jet Agitator Inside Tank
Liquid Tank—gallons (litres) 210 (796.1)
Sprayer Pump .... Centrifugal 130 Max. psi With H.D. Electric Clutch
Filtration .... Pump Outlet Strainer w/40 Mesh Screen
Sprayer Manifolds and Feed Lines .... 36 Nozzle Jet Assemblies with 80" 8002 Brass Tip
.... w/50 Mesh Screen Standard

Booms

Boom Controls .... Hydraulic "Top Lift"   "Fold/Unfold"—"Raising/Lowering"
Boom Height - in. (cm) .... Approx. 222 (55.9) to 64 (162.6)
Boom Width - ft (m) 60 (18.3)
Nozzle Spacing - in. (cm) .... 20 (50.8 Standard)

CASE

11

Lil's Place

Lil's Place is a small restaurant in a downtown area of a small midwestern city called Midtown. The owner, Lil, features live entertainment nightly and a full dance band on weekends. She opened the place on the July 4th weekend with a big-name entertainer (a friend of Lil's). For Midtown this was quite an event. With interest in Lil's Place running high, the stage was set for rapid growth.

Lil started out with $20,000 she had managed to save from her rather brief career as an exotic dancer in a Chicago nightclub. The land and building—a not-so-prime downtown location—cost her $19,000 (land $10,000, building $9,000). The equipment—tables, chairs, bar, kitchen facilities—ran an additional $7,500. Redecorating the building to a Gay Nineties theme cost $3,000. Lil decided that she must have $5,000 cash at the outset to cover other costs of operation for the first few months.

To finance her initial business venture she convinced a local banker of the future potential for such an establishment. He eventually agreed to loan her the needed amount—one-half due by July 1 next year and the remainder over a five-year period with payments starting in January.

During the first few months, Lil's business boomed. She managed to pay off $4,250 of her bank note ahead of schedule and meet all her current expenses. But then disaster struck Lil's Place. The local WCTU, which had never quite approved of the idea of a "nightclub" in Midtown, succeeded in getting Lil's Place closed down on the unofficial grounds that it contributed to the moral decay of the community. (The police acted on rumors that Lil's had been the scene of various illegal activities.)

The solution to all this, as Lil saw it, was to dissolve the business and move to a larger city. Lil figures the concept would be even more profitable there. (Besides, here the mayor's wife was the chairperson of the local WCTU.) Lil has hired you to draw up a balance sheet for her business as of July 4th—the day she opened—and June 15th—the day she closed.

This case was prepared by W. David Downey, Professor of Agricultural Economics, Purdue University, as a basis for classroom discussion rather than to illustrate either correct or incorrect handling of an administrative situation.

121

You find that Lil has $8,500 in her business checking account and owes $1,000 for wages and other unpaid bills. Depreciation is estimated at 10 percent on the building, 20 percent on the equipment, and depreciation of $500 on the improvements for the period she was in business. There is $200 of prepaid insurance on the establishment. She has beer bottles left in the back room on which she has paid deposits of $300.

■■ QUESTIONS

1. Draw up the requested balance sheets.
2. How much profit or loss did Lil realize?

SECTION

III

MANAGEMENT STRATEGY

CASES

Scenic Hills Cooperative

Ed Over, general manager of Scenic Hills Cooperative (SHC), sat at his desk, contemplating his options for the future. He had only been manager for two years, yet it seemed like an eternity. Nothing was going right—sales were dropping, large losses were being experienced, cash flow was extremely tight, employees had not had any pay raises in three years, member dividends had just been suspended, and needed capital expenditures were not being made because of the shortage of funds. With the current $289,000 deficit, SHC had the ignoble distinction of having lost more than $1 million in four years. Sales had dropped 25 percent during the same period and stood at about $6.5 million.

SHC was a supply cooperative serving dairy farmers with four product lines: (1) feed services (60 percent of sales), including grinding, mixing, grain sales, and supplements; (2) fertilizers (14 percent); (3) agricultural chemicals (7 percent); and (4) general farm merchandise (19 percent), running from small tools to tractors. SHC was well known for having high-quality products and sold dry, blended fertilizers under its own brand name. Because SHC was a cooperative, its customers were also its owners and were called members. Each member bought one share of stock, which represented the right to vote on cooperative business, primarily the election of members to the board of directors who set policy for SHC. Members were served from five mill sites (referred to internally as branches). All branches offered the same mix of products and services, handling everything except major equipment sales. In addition to the mill branches, a farm-and-home center specializing in lawn-care products, hardware items, and major equipment sales and service was in Centerton. (See the map in Exhibit 1 for all branch locations.) The administrative offices for the general manager and accounting staff were also at Centerton.

This case was prepared by H. Christopher Peterson, Department of Agricultural Economics, Michigan State University, as the basis for classroom discussion rather than to illustrate either effective or ineffective handling of an administrative situation.

◼◼◼ THE EXTERNAL ENVIRONMENT

The farming environment in each part of Scenic County was being affected by different forces. In the Eastburg area, suburban sprawl from a growing city in a neighboring county was fast reducing the number of farms. Already only a few large dairy farms were left in the area. Many small "recreational" farms, often with horses, still remained. New subdivisions were springing up everywhere, filled with new homes with new lawns needing annual doses of fertilizer and other turf-care products. As a result, the Eastburg branch was grinding and mixing more horse feed and selling increasing amounts of lawn care items.

In the Oldville and Shortville areas, many farms were being bought by members of a conservative religious sect who preferred dealing with their own people. Often their feed needs were being met by a portable mill operated by a sect member coming from 50 miles away. The sect was known for its very efficient farmers who were highly conscious of saving money wherever possible. The "right" deal or a sales rep with the "right" background might have made inroads with the sect members, but SHC had done little to attempt either approach.

The area west of Centerton was known for its profitable, progressive dairy farms. The area was not threatened by suburban sprawl, and the future was considered good for the continued strength of these farms.

SHC faced tough competition throughout its area. A large regional supply cooperative had branches in every community served by SHC, except Shortville. In Westown and Eastburg, there were also several proprietary mills. Two competing mills had just closed in the Eastburg area for lack of business volume.

The other growing concern was the pressure from the state's environmental resources department to improve control over the chemicals and fertilizers on all of SHC's branch sites. New regulations were going to create

EXHIBIT 1   Cooperative locations in Scenic County.

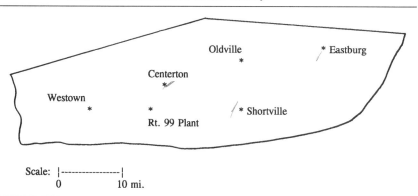

the need for some substantial and costly renovations to several of the firm's operations. At the same time, members were beginning to request that the cooperative develop ways to help them manage chemicals and fertilizers more efficiently on their farms. On the one hand, the members wanted to use less of both these inputs, and that would hurt SHC's sales even further. On the other hand, the new services needed to support changing farm methods could be a source of new revenue.

■ THE INTERNAL ENVIRONMENT

Exhibit 2 provides some selected financial data on each of the branch operations and the cooperative in total for the two most recent years. Exhibit 3 presents some further information for the five major operating branches. Exhibit 4 gives some comparative industry data.

Within the bounds of board policy, each branch manager was responsible for sales, credit, pricing, and other day-to-day operating decisions within his district. The general manager played the lone coordinating role in attempting to reconcile any conflicts that arose among the branch operations. Ed Over's time and energy always seemed overly consumed by fighting fires here and there among the branches rather than being focused on the broader, long-term interests of the whole organization.

EXHIBIT 2   Selected financial data ($ in thousands).[a]

	PRIOR YEAR		CURRENT YEAR	
BRANCH	Sales	Margins	Sales	Margins
Farm & Home	$ 562	$ (17)	$ 502	$ (34)
Westown	2,350	100	2,389	75
Route 99 Plant	1,660	(31)	1,395	(120)
Oldville	1,072	(29)	954	26
Shortville	767	2	645	(11)
Eastburg	745	(8)	710	15
Main Office Expense		(239)		(240)
Total	$7,156	$(222)	$6,595	$(289)

TOTAL COOPERATIVE	PRIOR YEAR	CURRENT YEAR
Current Assets	$2,213	$1,934
Total Assets	$3,651	$3,277
Total Liabilities	$1,367	$1,373
Total Equity	$2,284	$1,904

[a]Numbers in parentheses represent losses. Margins is another name for profits (the difference between sales and related expenses). Main office expense produces no direct sales revenue but is necessary to the operation of SHC.

The Route 99 plant was a large, modern facility less than 10 years old. It was highly automated and capable of great efficiency in the production of large feed batches. Unfortunately, the proximity of the Westown, Oldville, and Shortville branches to Route 99 meant that it was very much underutilized. In fact, it could handle three times its current level of sales. This underutilization resulted in higher maintenance costs than would be expected in order to keep infrequently used parts of the plant in working order. The other mills were all more than 30 years old. Shortville equipment was in particularly poor condition, while Eastburg sales floor facilities were not well suited to attract the new suburban trade potentially available to it.

Complicating matters at Route 99 was the internal competition with Westown. The Westown manager, George Guber, believed he was carrying the rest of the cooperative by his good performance. He refused to attend management meetings and went out of his way not to cooperate with any efforts made by the general manager to bring about change or central coordination. George would even underbid the Route 99 manager to take away new business. Most recently, George had refused sales help offered to the cooperative by a major manufacturer and supplier of feed supplements. George had been overheard saying, "If those lousy salespeople come into my territory and mess with my customers, I'll tell my customers to shift to the competition." SHC only had two sales reps working the whole county, and the added sales help would have been a considerable benefit. The general manager seemed powerless to do anything about the situation since the board members from that area (5 out of 19 board members) staunchly

EXHIBIT 3   Additional information on mill operations (three-year average).

BRANCH	COST OF SALES	SALARIES AND WAGES[a]	OTHER EXPENSES[a]	RECEIVABLES OUTSTANDING[b]
Westown	82.4%	7.1%	5.2%	108 days
Rt. 99 Plant	73.0%	9.3%	15.8%	111 days
Oldville	86.4%	8.0%	7.5%	74 days
Shortville	84.7%	8.3%	7.3%	45 days
Eastburg	78.1%	13.0%	8.8%	18 days

[a]As a percent of sales.
[b]The average number of days it takes for a member to pay a bill for goods purchased from the mill. Members were supposed to pay their bills within 30 days.

EXHIBIT 4   Selected industry averages.

Profits/Sales	1.9%
Sales/Total Assets	2.8x
Receivables Outstanding	27 days
Cost of Sales/Sales	74%

Source: Robert Morris Associates.

defended the Westown manager at every turn. Ed was convinced that Westown should actually be performing better than it was, given the rich farming area it served.

The central office staff seemed able to handle little more than the basic accounting functions and billing. There was little computer use. Financial statements were only made available quarterly, and even then many numbers were estimates. No true volume data was kept, only dollar sales. No form of budgeting was used by the management of SHC.

The farm-and-home center was on a back street in Centerton. It had adequate parking facilities, but was not well suited for attracting any customers other than the farm trade. The farm equipment business was becoming a particular burden since new sales were falling each year and yet skilled mechanics had to be retained to handle repair work.

■■■ ED'S PREDICAMENT

Ed wondered how to proceed. The board was demanding a plan of action for reversing SHC's decline. What strategic direction should be taken? There appeared to be several broad alternatives.

First, branches could be closed down and consolidated. Operating efficiency would become the focus of all managerial attention. This could result in some layoffs and save some other operating costs. But which branches should go? Which services could and should be consolidated? Would members accept these changes when they often equated service with the nearness of their own local branch? Could Ed sell the assets of closed branches, or would that bring even more competition from the new owner or owners? The portable mill operator had expressed some interest in buying the Shortville facilities, and a producer of hog and chicken feeds had made some initial inquiries about purchasing the Route 99 plant.

Second, new marketing efforts could be mounted. Centerton and Eastburg could be dedicated to serving nontraditional suburban customers at a profit. But how would traditional customers perceive this change in strategy? Did SHC have the facilities and know-how to serve these customers? New promotional efforts could also be developed for use with farmers in the central and western parts of the county. New sales reps could be hired. No matter which approach might be taken, a key question remained: What would be the source of funds for change?

Third, some board members were beginning to ask if SHC should simply sell out to its competitors. This seemed like an option of last resort to Ed. Would other competitors treat the members as well as SHC did? Was there even a buyer who would want SHC's assets and business?

Ed was not sure what to do next. What should he recommend as a plan? Should he emphasize new marketing efforts or cost cutting? In either case, what were the specific actions needed to bring about change? Or should he recommend that the board explore exiting the business altogether? The new operating year was already at hand, and Ed knew he needed a plan as soon as possible. The very survival of SHC was at stake.

■■■ QUESTIONS

1. State the problems facing SHC. (Use available financial information to support your assessments of the problems.)
2. Explain the causes for SHC's problems. (Consider both the external and internal environments.)
3. How does George Guber's behavior contribute to the cause of SHC's problems? How would you handle the situation with George? Be specific.
4. What plan would you recommend to the board if you were Ed Over? (Be prepared to justify your plan. What are the threats and opportunities in the external environment? What are the strengths and weaknesses in the internal environment? What strategic options make sense given your analysis? You may wish to expand upon the three options suggested by Ed.)
5. What are the key steps needed to implement your plan? What are the risks of your plan and how will you manage them?

Arizona Beef Company

Bud Darling started through the file on the beef processing industry again. He hoped the answers to his questions would reveal themselves.

Bud was born into the cattle business in Arizona. His family's Rocking D brand is still carried by several thousand head of cattle in southeastern Arizona, an area that was still the Wild West when his grandfather settled there in the late 1800s. Soon after graduating from college, Bud had become the managing partner in a feedlot operation and over the years built it up to be one of the largest in the southwest. Now he represented a group of investors interested in buying Arizona Beef Company.

Arizona Beef Company (ABC) owns and operates a beef packing plant located on 240 acres of land about 15 miles southwest of downtown Phoenix. The company generates annual sales of about $500 million in a high-volume, low-margin meat packing business with 200 employees. ABC kills, dresses, and processes 1,000 head of cattle each day. The facility was constructed by a major meat packing firm in 1966, and at that time the plant was considered one of the most modern in the United States. ABC bought the packing plant five years ago when high labor costs made the plant uncompetitive and the large meat packer shut it down. The new owners of Arizona Beef reopened the plant using nonunion labor and were able to operate at a profit because of an $800 per hour reduction in overall wage costs.

Arizona Beef had been very open in giving Bud information. Exhibit 1 shows that although ABC's net income as a percentage of sales is lower than the industry average, profitability seems to be higher than the industry average.

Why do they want to sell? That question went through Bud Darling's mind over and over again as he thumbed through the file.

Articles in the file described the fundamental changes that had occurred in the beef industry. The starting point for the industry was and still is the cow/calf operation. Grass is the basic raw material and cow/calf

This case was prepared by Michael W. Woolverton, Continental Grain Professor of Agribusiness, Department of World Business, American Graduate School of International Management, as a basis for classroom discussion rather than to illustrate either effective or ineffective handling of a business situation.

operations are located where grass is available. When calves are large enough, they are placed in feedlots to gain weight rapidly. Although they are sometimes called fat cattle, the weight gain is mostly muscle tissue. Feedlot operators try not to put too much fat on the animals, as they respond to price signals indicating consumer desires for leaner beef.

A change has occurred in the location of cattle feeding. Feedlots were mostly small and were located on farms in the Midwest. Farmers could increase the value of their grain and utilize unused labor in the winter months. In the late 1950s, some farmers started to increase the size of their feedlots. They had learned to become very efficient and profitable at cattle feeding. The location of cattle feeding slowly shifted southwest out of the Corn Belt. There were several reasons for this:

1. Moving feedlots closer to the location of cow/calf operations reduced the high cost of transporting live animals.
2. The development of irrigated grain sorghum production in the High Plains and the Southwest meant that surplus grain was available. At the same time, export markets for corn and soybeans opened up, and many Midwestern farmers found it just as profitable with less work and risk to sell their grain rather than feed it to livestock.
3. Feeding efficiency was greater in the Southwestern states because the winter weather was better than in the Corn Belt states.

Some farm economists are now predicting that cattle feeding may shift back to the western Corn Belt because grain exports are down and farmers would like to increase the returns to their grain production. Also, rising irrigation costs in the High Plains and Southwest are making it more expensive to produce in those regions.

Bud ran across a curious report about feeder calf production and cattle feeding in Arizona. Of the 350,000 or so feeder cattle that are produced in the state each year, about 300,000 head are transported to feedlots in the High Plains areas of Texas, Oklahoma, Kansas, and Colorado. The remaining 50,000 go into Arizona feedlots along with about 50,000 head of dairy animals. Joining the Arizona cattle in feedlots are Gulf Coast-produced feeder calves, about 600,000 head of them per year. Of the cattle finished in Arizona feedlots each year, about 400,000 are slaughtered in-state and about

EXHIBIT 1 ABC's net income.

| | NET INCOME AS A PERCENTAGE OF | | |
	Sales	Total Assets	Net Worth
Industry	0.8	5.5	9.0
Arizona Beef Company	0.3	6.0	16.0

300,000 are shipped out. Many go to packing plants in California, but a higher and higher percentage are being shipped east, to the large packing plants in the High Plains.

When cattle feeding was concentrated in the Corn Belt states, the beef packing industry extended from Chicago to Kansas City. The major meat packers built large processing facilities in the terminal market cities. The stockyards in these cities became famous for their steak and infamous for their stink.

When the location of cattle feeding shifted, packers followed. They built modern plants near the large feedlots in the High Plains and the Southwest. Even though investment costs were high, the cost of processing beef dropped. Procurement costs dropped because the packers could buy large numbers of cattle from a few sellers. Also, there was little shrinkage because cattle did not have to travel long distances to reach the processing plants. The processors, at first, were able to escape the high-priced, unionized labor found in the large Midwestern cities. Some of the plants were subsequently unionized.

In 1961, a small company was organized in Dennison, Iowa, using a Small Business Administration loan for financing. The company, Iowa Beef Processors (IBP), grew quickly and threw the large, established meat packers into a panic with its revolutionary approach to processing and distribution. Before IBP's innovations, beef was shipped in sides and quarters either hanging from overhead racks or stacked like wood. Expensive hand labor was required to load and unload the meat. At the destination, the sides and quarters would be broken into salable cuts of meat. Meat purveyors and grocery chains paid union wages to highly skilled butchers to perform this additional processing step.

IBP's approach was to perform nearly all cutting operations in its plants, where it could be done more efficiently and at lower costs. (IBP took care to locate plants in rural areas and to treat employees well. Its plants have not been unionized, and IBP's labor rates are relatively low.) The cutting and trimming reduces the weight of the carcass by about 200 pounds of by-products that can easily be collected, processed, and sold, adding to processing revenues. The beef carcass is reduced to primal and subprimal cuts that can be cut into consumer cuts in retail stores by semiskilled, nonunion meat cutters.

IBP also introduced boxed beef. To improve shelf life of the primal and subprimal cuts, they are put into vacuum-sealed bags. The bags are placed into boxes to a total weight of about 80 pounds. The boxes are stacked on pallets and moved with forklifts. Refrigerated trucks can be loaded to maximum weights with boxed beef. With hanging sides and quarters, volume limitations were often reached before weight limitations.

IBP was recently acquired by Occidental Petroleum Company. IBP's closest competition is Excel, which was the old MBPXL Company, now owned by Cargill, Inc. Together, IBP and Excel have about a 30 percent market share. Cargill's meat packing company was quick to adopt the boxed beef concept. IBP and Excel have about 60 percent of the boxed beef market. Also, both companies have been able to use their cash resources to build very large processing plants. Studies have shown substantial economies of size in beef processing. These companies have been able to capture many of the economies by building processing plants that have capacities exceeding 1 million head per year. Exhibit 2 shows estimated kill costs associated with beef processing plants of various size.

Bud reached for the sheet of paper showing the estimated costs to upgrade Arizona Beef's plant so that it could produce boxed beef. The estimates are as follows:

Reconditioning the plant to increase the speed of the processing line by 50%	$5,000,000
Construction of boxing line and equipment	2,500,000
Additional refrigerated storage	1,600,000
Other	350,000

One thing that bothers Bud and many of his fellow cattlemen is the current trend in beef consumption in the United States. U.S. per capita beef consumption hit a peak in 1976 of 129.4 pounds. Consumption is now below 100 pounds per capita. Some are saying that the downturn is due to poor economic conditions, and consumption will increase again as the economy improves and consumers feel better off. There is no doubt that some of the reduction in beef consumption is due to substitution of relatively lower-cost poultry and pork. Maybe people have grown to like these meats and won't

EXHIBIT 2   Kill cost per head versus yearly capacity.

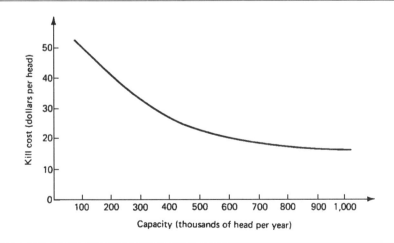

return to beef even when beef prices return to more competitive levels. Nutritionists are saying that the decrease in beef consumption is permanent because of changes in eating habits.

Arizona cattlemen are encouraged by the fact that Arizonans are beef eaters. They eat 5 to 6 percent more beef per capita than the national average.

Also, the 2 million plus population of the Phoenix metropolitan area is predicted to grow at a high rate. Bud reasons that Arizona Beef is in a good location to serve this market.

But ABC's location might be a problem. Bud has heard rumors that the management of Arizona Beef was under increasing pressure to solve its pollution problem. The plant uses more than 800,000 gallons of water each day. When the water leaves the plant, it carries a high load of waste materials. ABC pays about $8,000 a month to the local community for processing the sewage. The agreement with the community stipulates an upper limit on waste in the sewage water. ABC is almost always at the upper limit and has exceeded it on several occasions.

Local residents have also been complaining about the odor. Normally, odor can be controlled but when breakdowns occur, waste materials accumulate in the hot Arizona sun.

Land developers have been buying property surrounding ABC's plant. Parcels of land have been purchased for $15,000 to $60,000 per acre depending upon size and location. The developers would like to start building on the properties but hesitate because they are afraid potential buyers might be offended by the odor. Rumor has it that the developers may bring legal action to have the plant declared a nuisance, in which case the court might require expensive pollution control equipment or shut the plant down.

Bud Darling has a meeting tomorrow morning with the group of investors. They are going to ask for his recommendation: Should they pursue the purchase of Arizona Beef Company or drop it? Bud decides to sleep on it.

Whirlwind Egg Company

■■ BACKGROUND

The Whirlwind Egg Company processes and markets about 10,000 cases of eggs each week. About 25 percent of the volume arises from contract production, 25 percent from its own production facilities, and the remaining 50 percent is purchased from independent producers. In addition to shell egg processing, this firm owns an egg-breaking plant and sells liquid and frozen eggs.

The egg-processing equipment consists of two Penbreaker in-line, egg-handling systems. Each system has a capacity of 70 cases per hour and has mechanical packers. Each handling system is operated two shifts. Egg production facilities for all flocks are modern cage layer systems.

The firm considers itself to be progressive. It has an excellent retirement program for its employees and a profit-sharing plan.

Bill Pearson, general manager, has been with the company since the corporation was founded in 1960, and has been general manager for the past 10 years. The firm has grown considerably under his management. Bill is 46 years old, married, and has two teenage children. He is hard working and eager to make the business as efficient as possible.

The corporation employs 48 people. Bill realizes that he cannot run the business by himself and must depend on his assistant managers and key supervisory personnel. Several of the newer employees have been with the firm for only a few months. Bill identified five key persons exclusive of the sales manager upon whom he relies to run the business. When asked about these individuals, Bill describes them and their responsibilities as follows:

1. *Jim Mellon.* Jim is in charge of egg processing. He has three supervisors reporting to him. They are the day and night supervisors for the shell egg processing operation and the supervisor of the breaking plant.

This case was prepared by A. Kermit Birth, Professor Emeritus of Agricultural Economics, Department of Agricultural Economics and Rural Sociology, Pennsylvania State University, as a basis for classroom discussion rather than to illustrate either effective or ineffective handling of a business situation.

Jim is 40 years old and has had considerable experience in running the egg-processing facilities. He seems to get the job done, even though he sometimes fails to spell out detailed instructions on how things are to be done. His processing costs for shell eggs are among the lowest in the state. However, the costs for the egg-breaking operation have been excessive since this operation was undertaken.

Jim is well known in the state industry and is often sought out to participate in industry training programs because of his success at Whirlwind's modern plant. He has had offers to manage other plants but has elected to stay with Whirlwind. Jim is married and has one child. He has held his present position for 15 years.

2. *Joe Short.* Joe is assigned supervisory responsibility for the day shift for shell egg plant operations, including receiving, candling, cartoning, packaging, and storing eggs. He also has responsibility for making up orders for delivery.

Joe is directly responsible to Jim Mellon and is normally responsible for 10 to 12 employees. Joe keeps a close eye on the processing plant crew to assure himself that they concentrate on their jobs. He also makes periodic inspections to see that eggs packed in cartons meet the requirements of the firm and frequently consults with state inspectors on this matter.

Joe is 27 years old and unmarried. He is a competent bowler and is in two leagues.

3. *Dick Hits.* Dick's responsibilities entail supervising the egg-breaking operation. He schedules work since the breaking operation is not operated continuously. When not supervising the breaking operation, he assists elsewhere in the plant.

Dick is 57 years old, and a man everyone likes. He feels that the people who work for him know their jobs and he doesn't have to bother them. He is married and has been with the company since it was founded.

4. *John Grouse.* John is the maintenance foreman and normally has a part-time assistant. His responsibilities include preventive maintenance for trucks owned by the company.

John is 25 years old and has been with the Whirlwind Egg Company since graduating from high school. He was an honor student in the auto mechanics program. He does a good job, and there are seldom any serious maintenance problems. He works well with others. He is married and has four small children. His chief hobby is hunting.

5. *Fred Coon.* Fred is manager of the egg production department. Whirlwind depends on him to run their egg production operation. His responsibilities include supervising the contract and independent producers. He is also responsible for managing the flock supervisors.

One of his responsibilities is to see that the layers are arranged to give a fairly uniform production of eggs throughout the year. This is necessary to keep costs of processing eggs at a minimum.

Fred sees that the production operations are run smoothly. Everyone in the egg production department is supervised by Fred. He is 55 years old and began work for the corporation 22 years ago. His children are all married and live away from home.

He was production foreman for another firm before coming to work for Whirlwind. He knows the egg production business well and quickly recognizes jobs that need to be done. He is the kind of supervisor that keeps people jumping when he is around. If someone is not busy, Fred will see that he has a job, and quick! Some of the new employees don't seem to get along well with Fred, but he sees that they do what they are told.

Bill also identified two other persons who are not management personnel but are essential to smooth operation of the egg-processing plant.

1. *Susan Jones.* Susan is chief candler on the day shift. She is responsible for training new candlers. Susan takes considerable pride in her work and considers herself a good worker. She has two children who are married and live nearby. Susan's husband operates a business in town. Her chief reason for working is to have a supplemental income to spend for such things as that "special" vacation.

2. *Dick Pheasant.* Dick is responsible for supplying 30 dozen empty cases and wire baskets to the egg-packing stations. He is also responsible for transporting eggs from the packing area to the cooler and stacking outgoing eggs to facilitate loading out of eggs.

Dick is single and the newest employee in the firm. He just graduated from high school. He is an excellent bowler. He won the trophy for the highest season average in the high school league last spring. Dick is looking forward to becoming a member of the "Bad Egg" bowling team sponsored by the Whirlwind Egg Company.

■■ THE SITUATION

Whirlwind has experienced two years of low profits while industry profits had been adequate to good. Bill Pearson decided something had to be done. He asked Mr. Porter, a recently retired chief executive from a similar West Coast firm, to take a thorough look at Whirlwind. Bill asked him to spend as much time as he needed observing what was going on, looking over facilities and equipment, studying records, and told him he should feel free to talk to any of the employees.

Mr. Porter said that he would be glad to do that, especially in light of the fee being paid, but that he would probably be much better at identifying problems than in suggesting solutions. Bill said, "That's fine! If we know what they are, we can solve them ourselves. We think we have good facilities, markets, and people, yet profit-wise we are not doing well, and we don't know where to start."

Mr. Porter spent two weeks poring over records, looking at facilities, and observing operations. He concluded early in his investigation that Whirlwind's problems resulted from incurring slightly higher unit costs than those of competitors. On the other hand, marketing seemed to be doing very well by industry standards. After observing operations a few days, he concluded that the facilities and equipment were modern, well organized, and extremely well maintained. However, even with good facilities and equipment, the egg processing and egg production operations were not achieving the output per dollar of cost that one would expect.

Upon talking to employees, he found that those working in sales and for John Grouse seemed to be enthusiastic and happy with their jobs. However, he had a feeling that those working for Fred Coon and Jim Mellon were not quite as satisfied. They had treated Mr. Porter with suspicion for the first few days until they knew more about him and what he was up to; then they started to open up. Mr. Porter thought that for the most part they were all competent employees and had the ability to make the operations as sound as any in the industry.

Mr. Porter's report to Bill Pearson stated:

1. Productivity/dollar of input is low by industry standards in egg processing and in the company-owned egg-producing operations.
2. Equipment and facilities are as good as any and hence do not appear to be a constraint on productivity.
3. Morale of employees, however, seemed to be low in processing and production. (Mr. Porter thought that perhaps this could be the source of much of the problem. "After all," he said to Bill, "in a low-margin business like egg production and marketing, a few cents here and there can really change your profit picture.")

Bill inquired, "What would you do?" Porter replied, "I told you that I thought I could more likely find the problem than solve it, and I'm afraid I really don't know!"

■ QUESTIONS

1. Based on what you know, define the problem(s) for your own use as if you were general manager.
2. What would you do to counteract the problem(s)? Explain the goals you wish to achieve and develop plans and actions to accomplish them. Will you have to make changes in the way you operate?

Francis Farms

■■ SETTING

John Francis flicked through the 44 channels he was able to receive via his satellite dish with growing frustration. Midweek TV was worse than he had imagined possible. He'd seen all the soap operas that he could stomach. He had never thought that a period of enforced rest would be so difficult.

Two weeks ago John had been awakened at 3 AM by the sound of the warning alarm from one of his weaning sheds. Cussing himself for not switching off the alarm in the shed that was empty for cleaning, he guessed that it had probably gotten too cold in there. Still, there was no way to be certain without checking out the sheds, and it was not worth the risk of resetting the alarm without taking a look. A sudden drop in temperature in one of the full houses could cause substantial death losses.

Hastily pulling on coveralls and a pair of boots, he had hurried outside, still fastening the buttons. In his rush he forgot about the patch of ice on the back stairs. His fall carried him to the bottom of the stairs, where he landed on his hip. The resulting fracture had put him in the hospital for two days and in plaster for four to six weeks, depending on the healing process. The doctor had been emphatic that the more rest he got and the less movement, the faster the healing would be.

John had taken these instructions seriously. His father, Jerry, was able to give up retirement for a month or so to help out with the daily chores and keep a close eye on things, while Dan, his swine manager, effectively took on full responsibility for the first time.

They kept him informed each day, and so far there had been no problems that they had been unable to handle. John slowly started to grow confident that the day-to-day operations would be tended to. The realization that the operations of the business could be handled without him led John to think that he needed to reevaluate his management priorities.

This case was prepared by Dave Hitchens and Steve Sonka, Food and Agribusiness Program, University of Illinois at Urbana-Champaign, as a basis for classroom discussion rather than to illustrate either correct or incorrect handling of a business situation.

Perhaps he was spending too much time on the day-to-day operations and not enough on managing the direction of the business. After all, he had a swine manager who appeared to be able to run things as he would, and the cropping program was in winter recess. This period of enforced confinement could give him an opportunity to really focus on the management of the business. With that thought firmly in mind, John switched off the third replay of Saturday's ball game and asked his wife to help him move down to the farm office. He was sure that several tasks could benefit from his attention.

■■■ MANAGING INFORMATION

The following day John was back in the farm office. For as far back as he could remember, this was the first time he'd had two uninterrupted days in the office. John usually did most of the paperwork at night and spent only odd hours of the day in the office to make phone calls and the like. After two days of his attention, the routine paperwork was all done, and his desk was almost clear.

The one last stack of papers was an assortment of advertising flyers and brochures that John had put to one side to read when he had time. With the wastebasket close at hand, he pulled the stack toward him and began to glance through it with something less than enthusiasm. The wastebasket was almost full by the time a booklet from Knowledgeworks, Inc., caught John's attention. The brochure was an example of a strategic herd analysis for a swine operation that used farm records to assess the various components of herd performance. Attachment A contains selected portions of this brochure.

John returned the brochure to his desk for later reference and began to think through the situation at Francis Farms. What would be required if he was to prepare such a detailed analysis of his swine operations? How would he get this information from his existing records? Was it available?

John also thought about a number of magazine articles that he had read recently. He remembered being surprised at how many articles in the pork productions magazines had focused on the need for producing better quality pork. Some university people were even saying that producers should grow different kinds of pork for different types of consumers. But John knew that until the packer routinely provided detailed cut-out data to the producer, he couldn't produce a better hog.

John had also seen articles in the *Wall Street Journal* and other business periodicals about suppliers and manufacturers working together to produce higher quality products at lower cost. Sometimes the articles called this Total Quality Management. Some articles stressed that collecting and sharing detailed, timely information was a key requirement of the supplier in such a system.

Francis Farms produced a top-quality product. John knew it, or at least he sure thought so. The idea of producing a premium product appealed to John. But as John thought about his production and financial information, he began to wonder if Francis Farms might miss out on such opportunities if it couldn't provide the needed data. Maybe John's thinking about improvements to the information systems on Francis Farms should include developing the capacity to interact with the packer and the processor. But what would that cost? How much more data would they have to collect out in the production facilities?

This was confusing. John and his wife had been thinking about some new living room furniture. John thought this would be a great time to go look at what the new discount furniture store in Davenport had to offer.

■■■ BACKGROUND

Francis Farms consisted of 1,500 acres of medium to heavy soil in the undulating country of eastern Iowa with a 750 sow-intensive stop-swine farrow-to-finish hog operation. The farm had been established by John's grandfather, who had managed to raise a grub stake for some cheap depression-priced land and held out until the end of World War II, when John's father returned from military service. In the postwar years, the farm size increased from 300 to about 1,000 acres. The increase in land area had been in moderate-sized steps of 150, 220, and 330 acres. At times the debt level had been uncomfortably high to accomplish these increases, but safety margin in the plans had always been sufficient to enable them to get by. The remaining 500 acres was an inheritance from John's mother's family in 1967.

The first swine on Francis Farms came about as an indirect result of the inheritance. On that farm, a 20-acre area had been set aside to finish feeder pigs when favorable opportunities arose. Self-feeders, feeding troughs, and wind-break shelters were set up in the corner of the field. John's father had no plans to use the area for hogs, but had allowed John to keep a small number of animals during his high school years to earn a little money.

John made enough in his first year that he decided to finish a slightly larger herd the following year. The enterprise required relatively little work, and John could do most of what was needed while home from college on the weekends. Each year the number of animals he finished was increased a little. In his senior year at Iowa State University, John finished just under 600 animals.

After completing his BS in agribusiness, John (who's now 41) came home to work full time on the family farm. Gradually he increased his responsibilities until three years ago when his father, Jerry, retired. Then he took full control of the operations and general management. His father remained the major equity partner and is actively involved in major financial decisions.

At the time John returned from college, Francis Farms was entirely dedicated to growing corn and beans, with appropriate acreage set aside for participation in government programs. Apart from John's feeder pigs, there were no other livestock. There were a number of swine operations in the county, some of them fairly large, but many area farms were grain-only operations.

■■■ SWINE OPERATIONS

Shortly before finishing college and returning to the farm, John persuaded his father to invest in swine-operating facilities rather than purchase additional land as a way to expand. John had used two main arguments in making his case to his father. First, they could use grain that was produced on their own farm and convert it to a high-value product—hogs. Second, they had reached the physical limits of the amount of cropped area that they could plant and harvest with their available equipment and labor. Any significant increase in crop area would require a great deal more equipment or the use of contract planters and harvesters.

John's father had agreed with the two arguments, but felt uncomfortable about going into a livestock operation that he would know very little about. However, the thought of feeding his own corn to grow hogs was appealing. Before Jerry would consent to making an investment of this sort, he felt that someone had to be familiar with swine management practices. It would be too expensive to learn on the job when there was no one with any experience.

John was adamant that he could learn by doing, but his father would not change his position, and John agreed that Murphy's Golden Rule[1] could not be broken. John then took a job as a general hand in a 150 sow-farrow to finish operation 65 miles from home to learn the job of herdsman and daily management. To gain a technical knowledge of swine management, he also took a one-month intensive course in swine management run by the agricultural extension group of the local university.

With a great deal more urging from John, Francis Farms began construction for an intensive sow handling and farrowing facility sufficient to maintain a breeding herd of 200 sows in 1975. A weaning shed followed immediately, but it was three more years before the addition of intensive finishing sheds. At the time of the additions, farrowing space for another 100 sows was constructed. The finishing sheds were large enough to finish all animals farrowed on the property.

By this stage, Francis Farms's swine operations had two full-time employees in addition to John and the occasional help from his father. At

---

[1]Murphy's Golden Rule: He who has the gold makes the rules!

planting and harvest time, an extra part-time hand was brought in to help out in the swine operation, while John moved across to the grain operations at periods of peak workload. John's father operated the rest of the farm with the assistance of one full-time farm hand.

The expansion to 300 sows had resulted in a less than optimal layout of the facilities. The original farrowing shed had not been situated with sufficient thought for future expansion. The positions of the sheds meant that animals had to be moved from one end of the facility to the other and back again during their growing cycle. This did not result in very large inefficiencies, but John was frustrated that he had not planned the layout with sufficient room for growth.

The source of his frustration was also a source of pride. The swine operation had surpassed both his father's and his own expectations. It had made good profits in all but the first year, and the level of production efficiency had been pleasing. The consulting veterinarian that visited Francis Farms at least four times per year had told John in 1980 that his operation was in the top 25 percent of farms in Iowa for production efficiency.

Confident that he could manage a larger scale operation effectively, John then set about developing a set of physical plans for Francis Farms's swine enterprise to grow to a size of 1,050 sows. These plans were developed with the assistance of a consulting design engineer and would ensure that expansion was logical. The expansion could be modular, allowing capacity to be added in units of 150 breeding sows.

John had used these plans to expand in 1981 and again in 1987. At the time of the last expansion, two modules were constructed, bringing the total size of the operation to 750 sows. By the time the last expansion was operating at capacity, Francis Farms was marketing almost 15,000 hogs per year at approximately 240 pounds liveweight.

Each of the expansion stages had worked well in John's opinion. Daily operations had not been disrupted excessively by construction, and each phase had allowed the testing of new equipment and stall designs that could be incorporated into the facilities if they proved effective.

By this time, John employed seven full-time employees. The most senior employee at Francis Farms, Dan Jenkins, had been employed in 1982 as the breeding herd manager. He holds a degree in animal science from the University of Minnesota and, before joining Francis Farms, worked for five years as a herdsman for a large integrator. When John assumed full responsibility for the management of Francis Farms in 1988, Dan's responsibilities increased to include overall responsibility for the day-to-day operations.

John spent roughly half his time overseeing the physical operation of the swine enterprise and continued to handle the hiring of staff and all worker problems. He also took on his share of weekend chores, feeding and checking the farrowing pens. Weekend work was kept to a minimum, and, with eight people, each person was required to work only one weekend per month.

■ RECORDKEEPING

Prior to the 1970s, the farm records for Francis Farms had been stored in a cardboard box, and an annual trip was made to deliver the contents to the local accountant and financial adviser. The farming operations had been a relatively simple business, and John's father had not felt the need for more information than to know the bank balance at the end of each month and a cash budget at the beginning of each year.

In 1971 a state extension specialist had given a seminar to introduce a farm recordkeeping system that would be supported by the university. John's father decided to adopt the system after discussing the benefits with his accountant. The accountant assured him that it would reduce the time needed to prepare his annual tax returns and financial statements, and that he could save some of the annual subscription fee by reduced accounting charges.

In the first years of using this system, a separate, manual record of all checks and receipts was kept and mailed into the university at the end of the year. The recordkeeping service processed the forms sent in by Francis Farms along with those of all other subscribers to the service. The service then calculated the average performance of producers of commodities who were of a similar size. Each subscriber received a listing of his or her own farm's performance compared with that of the average of similar subscribers.

The comparison included average yields, costs of production per acre and per bushel, and prices received for approximately 25 similar producers in the region. The comparison was made for each enterprise (at the time, corn and beans only) and for the whole farm. The system was unable to look at different physical parts of the farm.

One disappointment with the service was that the record summaries were not available soon enough to suit the farm's accountant. Thus, the accountant was not able to take the information directly from the reporting service printouts. Also, occasional small errors required the accountant to go back and reconcile the bank accounts. These corrections took as long as if he had prepared the books himself from scratch. The end result was no time or cost saving in the tax accounting for Francis Farms.

About the time that John returned to the farm, an additional feature was added to the university reporting service. By mailing in all canceled checks to the reporting service, Francis Farms could receive a monthly report on business expenditures. The checks were specially printed to give extra space for additional information on each check. When each check was written, a four-digit code was included to identify what was being paid. The total amount of each check could be divided into three separate items to ensure accuracy. The farm receipts were recorded manually the same as before, except that now they were sent in each month. The monthly reports were usually received from the university by the end of the following month.

The monthly reports did not provide a comparison with other farms using the service, but did compare monthly expenditure with a cash-flow budget that was prepared at the beginning of the year. At year end, the farm's performance was compared with other users of the monthly and annual service.

The monthly service provided a profit and loss statement for each month and a full list of all payments and receipts by category. A profit and loss statement could also be prepared for the tax year and provided to the accountant. In general, the accountant was happy with the information provided by the reporting service, but it was not in the exact format needed for him to prepare tax accounts. He transcribed the figures into his own format manually. However, he felt that the information he needed was more readily available than it had been before and that the categorization of expenditure was convenient to sort through.

One problem in preparing the tax accounts from these reports was that some of the allocations made at the time of writing the checks did not conform with the requirements of the IRS for allowable business deductions. This problem arose primarily at the time of coding the checks because the writer of the check was not always fully conversant with the relevant tax law.

The monthly reports for Francis Farms were not always examined closely by John's father, but Jerry felt that the information kept him more up to date with their financial position than he had been without them. He rarely referred to any report other than the most current. Sometimes historical figures were used at the time of preparing the next year's budget, and these reports helped identify when payments had been made and income received.

■■ THE FIRST COMPUTER

In 1984, Francis Farms bought a personal computer to operate its financial recordkeeping system. A software package especially designed for farming businesses, Financial Manager, from the company FMS, was bought to run on the computer. Financial Manager had been developed in the late 1970s and early 1980s.

Getting used to a computer had taken John a while. Although he attended a two-day training course when the machine was bought and another three-day course from the software company, it was more than a year before John felt that he was sure of what he was doing.

Using Financial Manager was fairly simple. As checks were written, the amount and the purpose were recorded; receipts were recorded similarly when they came in. These amounts were entered into the program once or twice per month. As bank statements were received, the canceled check numbers were entered into the program along with any bank fees and interest amounts. This system allowed John to track outstanding checks and provided him with much more current information than the mail-in reporting system. Francis Farms, however, continued to use the annual comparison service offered by the university by sending in a Financial Manager printout.

One of the more frustrating aspects of using Financial Manager was the frequent revisions to the software. Every year there seemed to be a new version that was just a little bit different. John agreed that each new version was usually better than the last, but each time he had to convert all his files to the new format, and once he completely lost two years of historical information. He still had the old printouts of course, but he could not use the data to compare current years without reentering it manually.

■ GROWING INFORMATION NEEDS

Adding swine operations to Francis Farms greatly increased the amount of information that was required to run the day-to-day operations. The most intense aspect of this was managing the sow breeding herd. Decisions had to be made on which sows to mate, how many to mate, how long to keep a sow in the breeding herd, and so on.

John had not really experienced this demand for information before. Managing a cash grain operation required relatively little continuous information, and at the end of each season the effects of the previous year's decisions were assessed by looking at yields and overall farm profit. Knowledge of soil types and which farming practices had worked best on each were memorized and not systematically recorded anywhere. This worked well enough because the cropping program was often modified in the field to adjust for the prevailing conditions. Formal recordkeeping systems were not flexible enough to accommodate all the different types of information and, anyway, were not easily available at the time they were needed.

As the swine enterprise had grown, John had given little thought to the information he would require to operate this business. He had not dealt with this in his one-year experience with the farrow to finish operation 65 miles away. Decisions had been made by the owner, and John had focused on learning the tasks of animal husbandry. He had kept basic records on each aspect of the enterprise, such as sow mating, farrowing, and weaning figures, but he had never been required to use these records in his job.

John decided that he would use a system similar to that used at the place he had worked. This decision was made primarily because he was not aware of any other information needs. His system consisted of a set of index cards, one for each sow, on which was recorded each sow's performance.

Cards were updated from sheets kept in the farrowing sheds that recorded the sow's identification number, date of farrowing, number of piglets born alive, number of piglets weaned alive, and the date of weaning. These sheets were removed from the shed at the end of each weaning cycle, or roughly once per month.

The card system was simple to use but did not provide a great deal of information for making decisions such as sow culling. Obtaining overall information for the enterprise was laborious and not done more than once a year. Thus, selection decisions were made one at a time, without being related to previous decisions or the current status of the enterprise.

Shortly after Dan Jenkins arrived to work at Francis Farms, he suggested using the PigCHAMP Breeding Herd Monitor from the University of Minnesota. The PigCHAMP service was a mail-in system that used information similar to that already being recorded at Francis Farms. At the end of each month, a record of each sow that had been mated, culled, or weaned or had farrowed was sent to the university. The data were entered into a computer program that used a number of selection index criteria developed by the university's College of Veterinary Medicine. The sow's breeding performance was rated on the number of piglets born alive, number weaned, parity, and days to return to service. The index value ranked sows according to their breeding performance and was useful in deciding which sows to cull and when.

A drawback of the system was that the information often did not get back to Francis Farms until it was too late, and sometimes errors in filling out the cards caused further delays. These errors were found by the university staff, who would write back to Francis Farms requesting correction. Making corrections was difficult and sometimes impossible. Cards misplaced or incorrectly completed were the main source of the problem. By the time the error was noted, a great deal of searching was required to find the right information.

The main benefit of the mail-in service was the year-end comparison with all other PigCHAMP subscribers. John could compare the performance of the breeding herd at Francis Farms with other producers. From this comparison he was able to identify areas in which performance was below or above average. Discussing the result with the veterinarian had resulted in improving some areas of the operation. It was hard to identify the dollar value of these improvements, but the averages were definitely getting better. Attachment B shows only a sample of the many production performance reports available.

■ AN UPGRADE

Early in 1990 the floppy disk drives on the original computer at Francis Farms began to fail. The computer repairman had laughed when John asked if the computer could be fixed. Of course it could, but the cost would be half that of a new machine, and any new computer would be at least 10 times as powerful as the old one. It seemed that the decision to upgrade was made for him. Francis Farms purchased a new computer with 40 megabytes of hard disk storage capacity. This was a great improvement from the earlier computer, which had no hard disk. The new machine actually cost slightly less than the previous computer.

The arrival of the new computer meant that Francis Farms now had a system capable of running its own version of PigCHAMP. The software was sold and supported by the University of Minnesota. At the end of each year, John could send in his floppy disk with the year's records, and the university would prepare the same sort of herd performance comparison as before.

Having PigCHAMP on site made quite a difference. Sow information was entered into the program by John's wife once a week, and the sow breeding herd index was printed out for use that same week. More up-to-date information was available on each sow at the time decisions were being made about culling and mating. Errors that occurred in recording information were more easily resolved because John could attend to them immediately, before the information got lost or buried.

Shortly after beginning to use PigCHAMP on site, John found that the sow index card system was unnecessary. All the previous information, plus much more, was now available to him on PigCHAMP. In fact, so much more detail was kept on each animal that it was sometimes a bit confusing to try to take it all in.

At the time of upgrading, John added an automatic check writer to Financial Manager. With the check writer, John now entered information directly into the computer from the invoice, and a special printer printed the payroll sheets and the checks. This did not create much of a time saving as far as John could tell, but it was a good discipline for him to ensure that his records were always up to date.

■■■ FUTURE INFORMATION NEEDS

John leaned back in his chair and stretched. According to the X's on his desk calendar, this was the 34th day since his accident. His hip was better, and some first signs of spring were appearing. John felt good because the swine operations had continued to function smoothly. He wasn't as pleased with his progress on the farm's record systems. It was becoming obvious to him that while he had a great deal of data from the records at Francis Farms, he did not really have as much information as he would like.

Dan and John had several good discussions about Dan's perspective from the production management side of the business. Overall, Dan felt pretty good about the data they had, particularly the quality. Dan worked hard with new employees to stress accuracy. Dan believed, however, that they should be able to determine the profitability of each part of the swine operation. He was pretty sure that their software would let them do more in this area, but he was concerned about the potential extra time and trouble for the employees. Also, both Dan and John were curious about some of the performance claims that the feed supplier was making about a new ration formulation. To use this new ration formulation they would need to be able to track the costs and output of each part and they did not have that sort of information—at least not with the level of accuracy that would be needed.

John had also begun to think about using some of this sort of information to report to the employees on their performance, and maybe even have some sort of incentive system that was monitored on a profitability basis for the area that the individual was responsible, or perhaps an overall profit-sharing scheme that all employees shared.

To do all this John must decide what the right level of profit reporting was and if it could be achieved. But he did not want the addition of a great deal of work, if there was no tangible benefit. Should he try to report on the functional parts of the swine operation, such as breeding, weaning, growing, selling and so on? Or should he treat each module of Francis Farms as a separate profit center and measure the bottom line? Could he do both?

To do both, the system would need to track all inputs such as labor, feed, and drugs at the relevant level of detail (either whole farm, module, or function). All outputs (animals, weights, prices) would need to be monitored at the same level of detail. In addition, John would need to develop some sort of efficiency measure or performance criteria if any of it was going to be meaningful. He realized that he already had more data than he could deal with, so any new system must convey meaning and interpretation rather than a mass of numbers on a page.

John's local lender had been an interesting source of information. Francis Farms had a long and solid relationship with the local banker, Tom Davis. Tom was comfortable with the amount and quality of information that Francis Farms provided. But when John shifted the discussion to that of a potential major capital expansion at Francis Farms, Tom got nervous and uncomfortable. Tom immediately said it was a bad idea. Later in the conversation, it became apparent that Tom's bank couldn't handle the financial needs that a substantially larger Francis Farms would require.

John then talked to a couple of other large producers and a financial consultant they used. He was interested in their reports of some alternative sources of financing. Often these included a combination of more aggressive banks, Farm Credit, and, in some cases, outside equity. The financial reporting needs in such situations grew as well. Projected 12-month budgets needed more justification and the ability to look at fluctuations of revenues and costs from the projected levels. Monthly comparisons of budgets with actual performance were essential. Documenting the relative profitability of the components of the business seemed important to some outside equity investors. John really doubted if his existing financial information would support these needs.

■■ SPRING ARRIVES

"Boy, thinking about all this stuff makes your head swim," John mused to himself. Although still confused, John thought he was starting to get a handle on the problem. Maybe the thing to do would be to call a couple of software vendors that he'd read about. They seemed to have some powerful new programs. Some were even supposed to be able to integrate financial and production data. That must be a good feature.

John had talked to Sharon McColl over at Mirage Farms in Illinois. Mirage Farms had an operation similar in size to Francis Farms and seemed happy with the farm's computerized information systems. They had hired someone to write programs. Maybe that's the way to go. Then you could be assured of getting the information the way you want it. Maybe it would be worth a visit to Mirage Farms.

Hmmm, what to do next? Just then the phone rang. It was Dan at the south farrowing unit. John's dad, Jerry, had left early because he seemed to be coming down with that lousy flu that was going around. This didn't cause a big problem, but a number of sows were farrowing, and it was getting pretty hectic. Dan said the litter sizes seemed really good, but he could use a bit of help right now. He wondered if John's hip was well enough for him to come down.

John thought about the question for a second and then said, "Yep, that sounds like a good idea. Give me 10 minutes to dress and drive down there."

As he grabbed his cane to leave the office, John thought, "Getting out of the office will clear my head about all this recordkeeping stuff. Anyway, I can get back to it tomorrow, or some other day if dad's still sick tomorrow."

Attachment A

Breeding herd performance, hog farm, 1 April 1988–31 May 1990.

	APR 88 JUN 88	MAY 88 JUL 88	JUN 88 AUG 88	JUL 88 SEP 88	AUG 88 OCT 88	SEP 88 NOV 88	OCT 88 DEC 88
Total number of services	521	551	534	550	584	586	554
Number of sows farrowed	422	431	409	444	473	483	464
Total pigs weaned	3,619	3,700	3,661	3,780	4,070	4,132	4,098
Average female inventory	762	780.4	804	823.9	832.8	834.3	836.6
Ending boar inventory	73	76	77	73	74	69	66
Average gilt pool inventory	1	1	1	1	1	1	1
Entry to first service interval	0	0	0	0	0	0	0
Replacement rate	61.1	54.9	54.3	45.3	44.3	48.1	57.4
Culling rate	33.7	11.2	14.8	20.2	34.8	41.8	46.5
Breeding herd mortality	7.4	7.1	7.9	4.8	6.7	4.8	5.2
Average parities/sow lifetime	3.6	4.0	4.0	5.2	5.5	5.1	4.0
Average non-productive sow days	59.7	61.2	61	62.5	59.4	54.8	49.8
Farrowing rate	80.7	82.6	85.6	89	88.2	86.6	84.8
Average pigs born alive/litter	9.4	9.4	9.4	9.7	9.6	9.9	9.8
Pre-weaning mortality	10.8	8.4	8.7	9.2	10.7	10.3	10.7
Age at weaning	22.2	22.1	22.6	22	21	20.9	21.9
Average weaning weight	0.0	13.7	13.5	12.8	12.3	12.5	12.9
Adjusted 21 day litter weight	0.0	122.0	120.0	120.0	119.0	118.0	117.0
Daily gain in lactation	0.000	0.620	0.597	0.582	0.586	0.598	0.589
Litters/mated female/year	2.17	2.22	2.15	2.34	2.45	2.46	2.27
Pigs weaned/mated female/year	18.4	18.8	18.9	19.9	21.4	21.6	20.6
Pigs sold/sow/year	16.8	15	12.4	12.4	11	12.8	14.6
No. farrowing crates	164	164	164	164	164	164	164
No. females/farrowing crate	4.6	4.8	4.9	5.0	5.1	5.1	5.1
Pigs weaned/crate/year	88.3	90.2	89.3	92.2	99.3	100.8	100.0
Feed delivered (tons)	280	255	255	276	289	313	313
Tons feed/sow, boar, gilt	1.3	1.1	1.1	1.2	1.3	1.4	1.4
Breeding herd feed cost	40,817	40,344	43,327	81,350	83,028	86,044	51,034
Feed cost/ton	146	158	170	295	287	275	163
Feed cost/pigs weaned	11.28	10.9	11.83	21.52	20.4	2022	12.45

Source: © 1990, Knowledgeworks, Inc.

Breeding herd performance, continued.

	NOV 88 JAN 89	DEC 88 FEB 89	JAN 89 MAR 89	FEB 89 APR 89	MAR 89 MAY 89	APR 89 JUN 89	MAY 89 JUL 89
Total number of services	547	541	532	563	561	565	539
Number of sows farrowed	469	484	495	484	478	486	468
Total pigs weaned	4,157	4,456	4,199	4,220	4,140	4,626	4,437
Average female inventory	843.6	848.1	840.5	832.7	823.9	824.1	821.7
Ending boar inventory	66	66	65	61	60	58	60
Average gilt pool inventory	1	1	0.9	0.6	0.3	0	0
Entry to first service interval	0	0	0	0	0	0	0
Replacement rate	64.4	67.9	70.4	77.3	73.7	65.7	63.7
Culling rate	48	68.4	80.1	78.8	69.8	61.3	57.5
Breeding herd mortality	3.8	4.3	4.3	6.9	7.2	7.3	4.8
Average parities/sow lifetime	3.5	3.5	3.4	3.1	3.1	3.5	3.5
Average non-productive sow days	49.5	53.2	54.9	53.2	47.8	47.3	48.5
Farrowing rate	85	85.7	87.6	87.4	86.6	87.7	88
Average pigs born alive/litter	10	9.9	10	10	9.9	10	10
Pre-weaning mortality	9.4	10.1	9.9	10.1	9.3	7.9	7.9
Age at weaning	21.6	20.4	19	20.2	21.1	21.1	21
Average weaning weight	12.8	13.3	13.6	14.0	13.5	12.7	12.5
Adjusted 21 day litter weight	120.0	129.0	138.0	136.0	129.0	123.0	120.0
Daily gain in lactation	0.593	0.652	0.716	0.693	0.640	0.602	0.595
Litters/mated female/year	2.25	2.36	2.41	2.37	2.25	2.3	2.22
Pigs weaned/mated female/year	20.3	21.8	20.5	20.8	19.6	21.9	20.8
Pigs sold/sow/year	15.6	15.6	14.3	16.2	16	18.8	16
No. farrowing crates	164	164	164	164	164	164	164
No. females/farrowing crate	5.1	5.2	5.1	5.1	5.0	5.0	5.0
Pigs weaned/crate/year	101.4	108.7	102.4	102.9	101.0	112.8	108.2
Feed delivered (tons)	322	317	334	327	309	294	295
Tons feed/sow, boar, gilt	1.4	1.4	1.5	1.5	1.4	1.4	1.3
Breeding herd feed cost	52,339	51,954	54,986	55,040	52,484	49,851	49,396
Feed cost/ton	163	164	165	168	170	170	167
Feed cost/pigs weaned	12.59	11.66	13.1	13.04	12.68	10.78	11.13

Breeding herd performance, continued.

JUN 89 AUG 89	JUL 89 SEP 89	AUG 89 OCT 89	SEP 89 NOV 89	OCT 89 DEC 89	NOV 89 JAN 90	DEC 89 FEB 90	JAN 90 MAR 90	FEB 90 APR 90	MAR 90 MAY 90
530	563	560	595	578	563	541	530	536	524
505	472	480	440	432	459	470	499	479	488
4,615	4,405	4,323	4,253	4,003	4,267	4,130	4,848	4,659	4,910
824.1	826.9	832.1	838.4	842.8	844.3	842.7	838	832.9	830.8
60	62	59	62	61	61	61	61	58	60
0	0	0	0	0	0	0	0	0	0
0	0	0	0	0	0	0	0	0	0
55.4	68.1	62	78.5	67.3	65.3	53.4	49.8	54.7	53
53.4	50.9	60.6	61.7	58.4	52.6	49.1	52.8	53.7	54.4
4.8	4.3	4.3	4.3	4.7	6.6	6.7	5.8	3.9	4.3
4.4	3.3	3.7	2.7	3.1	3.4	4.3	4.8	4.3	4.3
54.7	59.7	65	64.3	61.1	54.9	53.1	50.5	47	38.7
88.8	86.8	85	83.2	80.9	81.8	82.9	85.7	87.1	86.5
10.2	10.1	10.1	9.8	9.8	9.8	10.2	10.6	10.6	10.5
7	8.2	7.3	8.2	6.6	6.6	5.9	5.7	6.6	6.4
20.1	21.4	21.3	22.6	21.8	21.9	21.5	20.4	20.2	20.8
11.7	11.8	11.9	12.9	13.1	13.5	13.0	12.2	11.6	11.9
118.0	112.0	114.0	116.0	122.0	124.0	125.0	126.0	123.0	122.0
0.582	0.551	0.559	0.571	0.601	0.616	0.605	0.598	0.574	0.572
2.41	2.27	2.31	2.15	2.08	2.2	2.29	2.41	2.33	2.29
21.9	21.1	20.8	20.7	19.3	20.6	20.2	23.6	22.7	23.1
17.6	16.1	20.1	19	18.8	17.2	18.1	20	19.8	18.4
164	164	164	164	164	164	164	164	164	164
5.0	5.0	5.1	5.1	5.1	5.1	5.1	5.1	5.1	5.1
112.6	107.4	105.4	103.7	97.6	104.1	100.7	118.2	113.6	119.8
313	299	320	317	305	284	290	326	339	355
1.4	1.3	1.4	1.4	1.3	1.3	1.3	1.5	1.5	1.6
51,003	48,221	50,161	49,359	47,460	44,160	45,336	49,781	51,686	51,674
163	161	157	156	156	155	156	153	152	146
11.05	10.95	11.6	11.61	11.86	10.35	10.98	10.27	11.09	10.52

Breeding herd performance, continued.

TRENDS		QUARTERLY AVERAGE
Total number of services	Down, cyclic	—
Number of sows farrowed	Up	—
Total pigs weaned	Up	—
Average female inventory	Slight drop	836
Ending boar inventory	—	60
Average gilt pool inventory	Not recorded	—
Entry to first service interval	Not recorded	0.0
Replacement rate	Down, now steady	52.7
Cutting rate	Down, now steady	52.5
Breeding herd mortality	Down, cyclic	5.2
Average parities/sow lifetime	Up	4.4
Average non-productive sow days	Down	47.3
Farrowing rate	Up	85.5
Average pigs born alive/litter	Up	10.5
Pre-weaning mortality	Down, now steady	6.1
Age at weaning	Steady	20.7
Average weaning weight	Down	12.2
Adjusted 21 day litter weight	Up, now steady	124.0
Daily gain in lactation	Up, now down	0.587
Litters/mated female/year	Up	2.3
Pigs weaned/mated female/year	Up	22.4
Pigs sold/sow/year	Steady	19.1
No. farrowing crates	—	164.0
No. females/farrowing crate	Steady	5.1
Pigs weaned/crate/year	Up	113.1
Feed delivered (tons)	Up	328
Tons feed/sow, boar, gilt	Up	1.5
Breeding herd feed cost	Up	49,619
Feed cost/ton	Down	152
Feed cost/pigs weaned	Steady	10.71

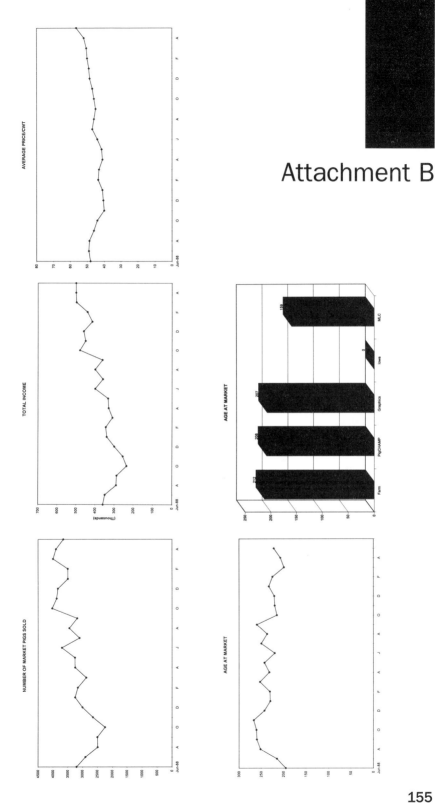

Attachment B

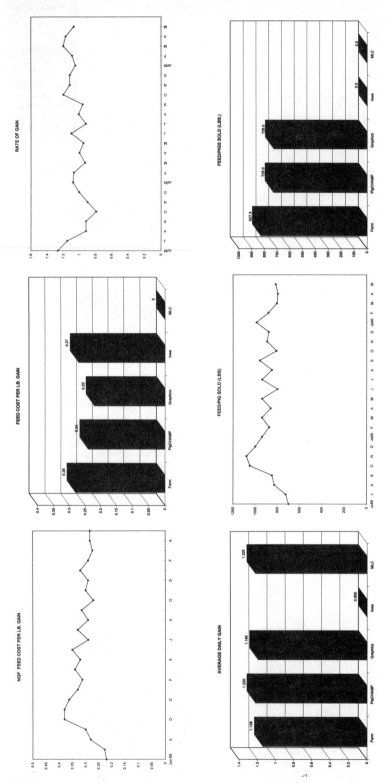

156

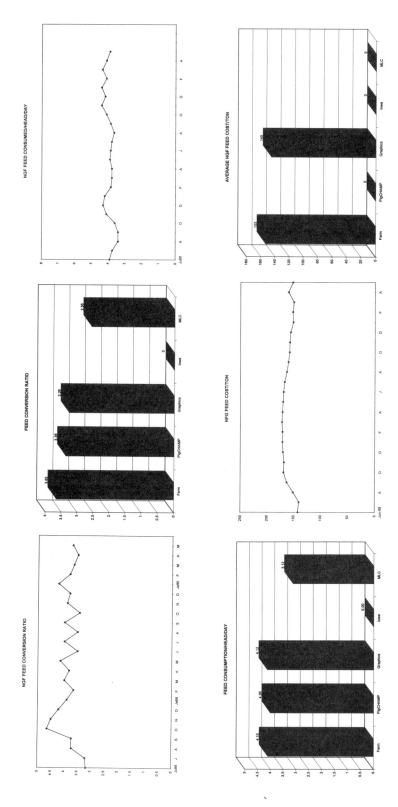

Congrain

Congrain, Inc., is a privately owned, widely diversified, multinational trading firm. The grain trade is the largest contributor to sales and, in most years, to profit. The company's trading activities are not restricted to grain, however; the firm's managers see themselves as agribusiness commodity merchants. As such, they buy and sell all types of agriculturally related commodities, performing necessary functions such as processing, warehousing, transporting, and financing. Every merchant's goal is to conduct operation to make a profit. Congrain's policy is to continuously evaluate opportunities to expand business. Top management establishes guidelines by which opportunities are evaluated. The guidelines are loosely applied in some cases, but each manager and merchant knows them well.

1. The opportunity must be in agribusiness. Congrain had its origins in agriculture. Most of its employees come from agricultural backgrounds or studied agribusiness. Nearly all the company has branched into other businesses. For example, the company has a Plastics and Resins Department within the Chemical Division, but it evolved within the Processing Division as an effort to develop methods to further process soybean oil.

2. The opportunity should fit Congrain's existing business as nearly as possible. The same physical facilities, transportation facilities, methods of financing, and geographical areas should be involved.

3. The new business should initially require little extra management input from Congrain. The company operates with a thin management hierarchy. Each person is given as much responsibility as he or she can handle and is rewarded according to performance. The company is not

This case was prepared by Michael W. Woolverton, Continental Grain Professor of Agribusiness at the American Graduate School of International Management in Glendale, AZ; and George J. Seperich, Associate Professor in the School of Agribusiness and Environmental Resources at Arizona State University in Tempe, AZ, as a basis for classroom discussion rather than to illustrate either correct or incorrect handling of a business situation.

interested in new business that requires extensive training of personnel or hiring many additional people.

4. The potential should exist for Congrain to become a dominant factor in the relevant market. The company has a track record of entering a new business and within a few years becoming one of the top five firms in terms of market share.

5. The initial investment in a new business opportunity must pay back in five years. Although the company has the financial resources to make very large investments, top management insists on the five-year pay-back.

Dave Sheets, manager of business development, had been invited to a meeting in mid-July by Douglas Johnson, vice president of the Input Supply Division. At the meeting was Wally Wilson, manager of the Fertilizer Department. The two had asked Dave to examine the pesticide industry in general and Congrain's future involvement in the industry in specific.

The memoranda in Attachment A represent the correspondence among the three during July and August. Several phone calls and informal conversations also occurred, but they were either not relevant or were to clarify material presented in the memos.

Dave Sheets is preparing for the meeting scheduled for September 2, the Friday before Labor Day. At that meeting he is to make final recommendations to Doug and Wally.

Attachment A

CONGRAIN INTERNAL MEMORANDUM

Date: July 21, 1994

To: Doug Johnson/Input Supply
           Wally Wilson/Fertilizer

From: Dave Sheets/Business Development

Subject: Pesticide Meeting Follow-Up

To summarize our meeting on July 18:

1. Pesticides are vitally important to crop and livestock
   production.
2. Congrain is already in the pesticide business through
   the activities of various departments, although the
   Fertilizer Department does not now handle pesticides.
3. Since fertilizer and pesticides are normally sold by
   the same people, the Fertilizer Department may have an
   opportunity to enter the business.

At the conclusion of the meeting, I agreed to prepare
a report on pesticide production and distribution. In the
report, I am to recommend the approach that should be
taken by the Input Supply Division and the Fertilizer
Department of Pesticide Distribution. I will have the
report on your desks within two weeks.

You agreed to fund the project through the Fertilizer
Department. I will ask the Accounting Department to bill
you at our usual hourly rate using an interdepartmental
voucher.

CONGRAIN INTERNAL MEMORANDUM

Date: August 4, 1994

To: Doug Johnson/Input Supply
           Wally Wilson/Fertilizer

From: Dave Sheets/Business Development

Subject: Pesticide Production and Distribution

BACKGROUND
   Pesticides is an all inclusive term. It includes
insecticides, herbicides, fungicides, mitacides, rodenti-
cides, and so on. A pesticide is a compound, usually a
chemical or a mixture of chemicals, used to control any
plant or animal organism considered a pest.
   In the U.S., 10,000 species of insects, 600 species of
weeds, 1,500 plant diseases, and 1,500 species of nema-
todes destroy an estimated $15-20 billion dollars worth
of crops, livestock, and forest each year. Fortunately,
most of the damage is caused by just a few pests, and we
can cut down on the damage by concentrating on them.
   Before 1940, pesticides were unsophisticated and consisted of natural compounds such as pyrethrum, arsenics,
sulphur, copper sulfate, and others. During World War II,
the insecticidal properties of DDT were discovered, and
DDT was used widely to save lives by destroying disease-
carrying pests. The herbicide, 2,4-D, was also discovered
during the war but was classified top secret because of
its potential use as a weapon. It might have been used to
destroy enemy food supplies. After the war, both of these
products became widely used in agriculture.
   From the late 1950s through the 1970s, many new products were discovered and came on the market. These products tended to be more specific, more effective, and
safer. Few new products reached the marketing stage in
the 1980s because of high development costs.
Manufacturers concentrated on improving the effectiveness
of existing products.
   Total world sales of pesticides is now approximately
$22 billion. U.S. sales are about $8.9 billion, or about
40 percent of the total. Western Europe and Japan are

the other major use areas. The real potential for growth
in the use of pesticides, however, is in the developing
countries. Sales are expected to grow at least 10 percent per year in the developing nations. In 1993, U.S.
export sales grew 0.9 percent, with sales of herbicides
and insecticides accounting for $1.86 billion of the
$2.08 billion total. This understates the involvement of
U.S. pesticide manufacturers, however, since most have
aggressively moved into the emerging markets by building
production facilities overseas.

INDUSTRY STRUCTURE

BASIC PRODUCERS: The major producers of agricultural
chemicals include large chemical, petroleum, and drug
companies. In the U.S. this list includes 23 companies.
The six largest firms, with sales exceeding $6 billion,
have about 70 percent of the total U.S. agricultural
chemical sales. Basic producers are facing serious problems. R&D costs are rising, primarily due to the stringent regulation of the industry by the Environmental
Protection Agency (EPA). Discovering a new product is
becoming more difficult because hundreds of thousands of
compounds have already been screened. Developing a new
pesticide from screening process to final regulatory
clearance can now take as long as 10 years at a cost of
as much as $20 million. The short period of time (total
patent life is 17 years) to recoup R&D costs and pay
for a plant is causing many companies to cut back on
new R&D. Competition in the marketplace is increasing:
Old patents expire, new or improved products are introduced, and foreign manufacturers are moving into the
U.S. market.

FORMULATORS: As patents expire, formulators move into
manufacture of product. When this happens or when a basic
producer wants to increase market penetration, the basic
producer sells technical product to formulators. A relatively low level of technical expertise and low investment
are required to become a formulator.

WHOLESALE DISTRIBUTORS: Basic producers and formulators market products primarily through wholesale distributors. The functions of a wholesale distributor include
warehousing product, distributing to retailers just
before use season, providing training and technical
assistance to retailers, and providing the necessary

credit. For providing these services, wholesale distributors generally receive about 10 percent margin.

RETAILERS: A retailer sells and services farmers. A retailer performs the following marketing functions: warehousing, delivery when product is needed, exchange for unused product, technical expertise, custom application, and credit. A retailer generally makes 10-15 percent profit but can almost double margin by providing custom application of pesticides.

CURRENT SITUATION

Basic producers are weeding out some of the weaker wholesalers and are redefining relationships with end-use customers. At the same time, they are strengthening relationships with strong wholesalers to build tight-knit, integrated distribution systems. Profit margins have improved slightly in the industry as the better firms stress service rather than low price. Most basic producers still offer early-take and early-pay discounts. Wholesalers and retailers are trying hard to stick to recommended prices with about a 10 percent average markup at the retail level. Most wholesalers are still warehousing, although this is becoming less important. Some wholesalers, however, resist taking delivery on the product until just before the use season, and in some cases, product is moving directly from basic producers to full-service retailers. Retailers who are service-oriented are doing well. The services themselves, such as custom application, can be quite profitable.

Demand for pesticides is strong. Domestic sales grew by 7.2 percent in 1993. Herbicides continue to lead all pesticides with about 52 percent of sales. Insecticides make up about 16 percent of pesticide sales, and fungicides 6 percent. Five major crops (corn, cotton, soybeans, small grains, and vegetables) account for about 58 percent of agricultural pesticides sales in the U.S. Corn accounts for 34 percent of the herbicides consumed in the U.S. and for 17 percent of the insecticides. Soybeans are the second largest market for agricultural chemicals. In 1993, soybeans accounted for 30 percent of total herbicides and for 18 percent of total pesticides. Cotton is the next largest market even though the acreage for cotton is a lot less than that for corn. Cotton takes about 6.5 percent of all herbicides and about 33 percent of all insecticides, which amounts to about 11 percent of the total pesticide usage. Herbicide use on small grains, such as wheat and oats, amounts to about 5 percent of total consumption. Fungicides are used on citrus and other fruit, as well as on vegetable crops. Although total volume is low, the market for fungicides has been growing and increased in sales by 4.3 percent in 1993.

The National Agricultural Chemical Association included biologicals under the category Agricultural Chemicals for the first time in 1993. Biologicals include biologically based, natural compounds with pesticidal properties and living organisms such as predator insects that attack damage-causing pests. Biologicals constitute a growing market that has the potential for becoming very large. Although currently undergoing definition and measurement, this portion of the industry may generate close to $2 billion in yearly sales in the near future.

The U.S. export market for pesticides has grown rapidly in the last few years and now exceeds $2.08 billion per year. The market growth potential for pesticides in developing countries is far greater than in the more developed countries such as the U.S., Western Europe, and Japan. Insecticides and fungicides are more important in some parts of the world than they are in the U.S. because the climates of many countries tend to support high levels of fungal and bacterial as well as insect infestations. Farmers growing labor-intensive crops, however, tend to rely on tillage instead of herbicides. Most basic producers of pesticides are manufacturing or are at least formulating outside the U.S. They find that shipping technical product and then formulating it outside the U.S. is more economical than shipping manufactured product. Some pesticide manufacturers, for one reason or another, have not developed international markets for their products and may be looking for help. One large manufacturer is interested in our Canadian distribution system. Another, a producer of an excellent rice insecticide, has had problems getting its production and distribution system operating and may welcome help in Asian countries.

SIGNIFICANT FUTURE DEVELOPMENTS

During the last decade, technology has been developed to alter plant genetic structure. For example, some

genetically altered plants have the capacity to grow in
high-salt soils (halophytes), or in low-water regions
(xerophytes), or to fix nitrogen, which eliminates the
need for nitrogen fertilizer. Congrain has followed these
developments with interest because of the potential to
increase grain yields in regions of the world not noted
for grain production. This new technology will also
impact the pesticide industry. For example, scientists
are placing the genes of insect-killing bacteria into the
genetic structure of crop plants. These transgenetic
plants then have the ability to resist specific insects,
and insecticide does not have to be applied. This development is very close to the marketing stage, and the
impact on pesticide use in certain crops (cotton, for
example) may be substantial.

Anticipating this development, pesticide manufacturers
have become involved in the seed business and in genetic-
engineering research. Several firms are working to alter
the genetics of soybeans and other plants to give the
crops the ability to resist specific low-cost herbicides.
If a major weed infestation occurs, herbicide is broadcast
over the entire field. The weeds are destroyed while the
crop grows to maturity. The result is fewer herbicide
applications and lower production costs for the farmer.
Some herbicide-tolerant crops are already being marketed
jointly by agricultural chemical firms and seed companies.

CONGRAIN'S APPROACH

The first step in Congrain's approach to the pesticide
industry should be to coordinate and/or consolidate present
activities. The following departments are already involved
in pesticide marketing or could become involved: Fertilizer,
Seed, Feed, and Country Elevator. The Fertilizer Department,
with its warehouses and distribution system, would be in a
position to act as a wholesaler to Country Elevator retail
operations. The Fertilizer Department could fill Seed's
internal requirements and also might rely on Seed salespeople in the field to generate sales at the farm level. The
Fertilizer Department might act as a wholesaler of animal
pharmaceuticals and for chemical feed additives to be sold
to and through the Feed Department. Outside the Input
Supply Division, the Chemical Division might be useful in
helping to formulate new products, for example, the encap-
sulation of insecticides.

Congrain's approach to the pesticide industry outside the company should be as a wholesaler/formulator. The following are important to basic pesticide producers in sizing up wholesalers: strong financial backing, good distribution in major crop areas, warehouse space availability, and field sales force that can sell and service products. Most basic producers are not adding new wholesalers unless they can foresee excellent future expansion of sales. All pesticide producers contacted did want to talk to Congrain as a potential wholesaler. The following seemed to interest basic producers most: Congrain's capital, internal demand that would immediately expand sales volume, warehouse space and broad distribution, and import/export capability.

The basic production of pesticides and strictly retail operations do not look attractive for the following reasons. Basic production of pesticides presents many problems such as rapidly increasing R&D costs, stringent regulation by both state and federal governments, patent expirations, severe price competition on commodity-like products, and competition from international suppliers. The retailing of pesticides is becoming service oriented rather than product oriented, and managerial control is one of the biggest problems. Basic production of pesticides is a highly seasonal business, and unless this business can be complemented by another business such as a grain elevator, spreading overhead is difficult. Farmer cooperatives present strong competition in most areas and tend to keep margins on products and service depressed at the retail level.

CONGRAIN INTERNAL MEMORANDUM

Date: August 8, 1994

To: Dave Sheets/Business Development
          Wally Wilson/Fertilizer

From: Douglas Johnson/Input Supply

Subject: Pesticide Regulations

I found your report interesting. We may want to consider some of the alternatives you discuss. It is apparent that the industry is in transformation.

I have some concerns about the regulatory situations. Which federal and state agencies are involved? How much control would they have over our operations? Could we get caught with pesticides we could not sell? Could our entry into this business be jeopardized by the new biotechnology products?

CONGRAIN INTERNAL MEMORANDUM

Date: August 12, 1994

To: Doug Johnson/Input Supply
          Wally Wilson/Fertilizer

From: Dave Sheets/Business Development

Subject: Pesticide Regulatory Situation

The Environmental Protection Agency (EPA) now has
full authority over pesticide regulation. The Food and
Drug Administration (FDA) is still responsible for the
surveillance of residue tolerances, and the U.S.
Department of Agriculture (USDA) continues to be the
principal research agency for pest control. Combining all
pesticide regulation under the EPA has helped clear up
confusion and eliminate delays in dealing with various
government agencies and their overlapping jurisdictions.
Individual states, however, still retain the authority to
enact and enforce stricter programs as long as they do
not require changes in packaging and labeling. Most
states follow the lead of the EPA, but in some cases
lack of uniformity in state regulations causes problems
in interstate marketing.

The EPA receives its power from Congress to implement
the laws regulating pesticides. The following are important points of the laws:

- Classification of pesticides into two usage groups:
  General Use: materials that can be applied by end
  users within the label restrictions.
  Restricted Use: Highly toxic chemicals that only
  licensed applicators can apply.
- The EPA can suspend registration and halt sales of any
  pesticide that it deems an imminent hazard. It can
  also deny registration of a product that could
  adversely affect human health or the environment.
- EPA has the power to seize pesticides found to be
  illegal, seek court injunctions, and ask for civil and
  criminal penalties against violators.
- Pesticide manufacturers are required to register production facilities as well as products with the EPA.

The EPA can inspect plants, take product samples, and examine books and records.

- The government must make indemnity payments to manufacturers and users holding stocks of pesticides ordered off the market after the EPA granted clearance.
- The EPA can control end uses of a pesticide.

The EPA's approach has been to reduce the labeled uses of a potentially hazardous pesticide slowly without sacrificing essential uses. DDT was an exception, and then Aldrin and Dieldrin were suddenly banned from all uses. Ordinarily, the EPA gives the industry several years notice of impending registration cancellation and gives manufacturers involved the opportunity to present evidence supporting the continued use of the pesticides. Before cancellation, the EPA compares the benefits of use with the potential hazard to the environment and gives considerable weight to the availability of economical alternatives that the user can substitute for the pesticide in question.

The impacts of genetically altered crops may be spread out over time because of the regulatory process. For example, it is not hard to imagine the difficulty facing the company trying to get a genetically altered wheat through the regulatory process. If Calgene, Inc.'s FLAVR SVR™ tomato or Monsanto's BST (Bovine Somatotropin) hormone are any indication of the regulatory impediments, companies involved in the development of these products must be prepared for the frustration and expense of a long review and approval process. Of course, the lengthy approval process reflects public fear of genetically altered food products. Perhaps with time and acceptance of early biotechnology products, the public attitude will change.

CONGRAIN INTERNAL MEMORANDUM

Date: August 4, 1994

To: Dave Sheets/Business Development
          Doug Johnson/Input Supply

From: Wally Wilson/Fertilizer

Subject: The Pesticide Business

As I see it, Congrain has a lot to offer the pesticide industry: its prestige as a trading company, a large internal demand for pesticides, capital, strategically located facilities, and widespread coverage of major crop-growing areas with good people. With our broad market coverage, we could become a strong force in the pesticide business.

Developing an Ag Chemical marketing system within the Fertilizer Department would give us the ability to offer a complete range of products and services to our customers. Our fertilizer warehouses can be used to warehouse ag chemicals. Out of the warehouses, we'll supply our own country elevators and sell products to other retailers. With our ability to operate with few people, our costs should be lower than competitors, giving us an advantage.

The Fertilizer Department is ready to go with this. Doug, with your permission, I'd like to ask Dave to transfer into Fertilizer to head up our pesticide business. Dave, how soon can you come on board?

CONGRAIN INTERNAL MEMORANDUM

Date: August 17, 1994

To: Doug Johnson/Input Supply
          Wally Wilson/Fertilizer

From: Dave Sheets/Business Development

Subject: Agricultural Chemicals

   I agree with your assessment of Congrain's strong
points as a potential marketer of agricultural chemicals.
I would like to comment from the viewpoint of a pesticide
basic producer. To your list of Congrain's name, money,
facilities, services, internal requirements, and sales
coverage, I would add export capability. Our human
resources and facilities worldwide, in general, are in
areas of major agricultural production. They constitute a
natural world sales distribution network for agricultural
chemicals. We would be in an excellent position to perform valuable marketing functions for basic producers who
want to avoid the time and expense of developing export
capabilities. You state that Congrain's human resources,
facilities, and services could be combined to form an
efficient agricultural chemical marketing system. I
agree, especially if we organize to emphasize the farm-
center concept. We would be in position to meet the complete input needs of growers as well as to perform their
output marketing functions. This, plus the wide geographic area we cover, would give us the marketing flexibility
that basic pesticide producers look for in wholesale distributors. We could distribute complete lines of pesticide products in many end-use markets. We should also
possess the internal flexibility to deal with the large
grower who wants to buy product at a low price without
service directly from basic producer or wholesaler. More
and more growers are falling into this classification.
They tend to disrupt normal channels of distribution. I
believe our integrated marketing system could offer basic
pesticide producers a way to sell to these individuals
without causing hard feelings and a breakdown in their
normal three-step distribution system.

One note of caution: A function that is very important for a wholesaler of agricultural chemicals is the selling and servicing of products in the field. This is becoming less important as retailers and large growers become more familiar with pesticides and their use characteristics, but it is a capability that basic producers will be looking for in a wholesaler. This is one function that could be performed by the cross-application of present sales personnel from other lines of interest which, as you state, would give Congrain immediate broad market penetration. In order for these people to perform this and other sales functions related to agricultural chemicals, they must be educated and motivated. Education presents no problem. It would just be a matter of time and training. In fact, basic producers would help train our sales personnel. Motivation, however, can come only with the full cooperation of the other Congrain departments involved. The various departments will have to be convinced that adding agricultural chemicals to their lines of products and services will not detract from but will add to the effectiveness of their present sales forces. As a general rule, in selling to growers the company most likely to be successful is the one that can come closest to completely meeting one grower's needs.

In addition, biotechnology-based products will be commonplace in the 21st century. Today, the industry needs time to develop, demonstrate its promise, and gain public acceptance. Once this industry-public loop is closed, the potential for new agricultural products, production processes, and even new crops is staggering. I mention this because our decision for Congrain today has important implications for the future.

Wally, your offer to have me develop the pesticide business for the Fertilizer Department comes as a surprise. Although I think there may be a good opportunity for Congrain in pesticides, I'm not sure it is a business to which I want to make a personal commitment. I'd like to have a little time to think about it.

CONGRAIN INTERNAL MEMORANDUM

Date: August 22, 1994

To: Wally Wilson/Fertilizer
            Dave Sheets/Business Development

From: Douglas Johnson/Input Supply

Subject: Crop Protection Chemicals

First of all, I would like to suggest we no longer use the term *pesticides*. *Crop protection chemicals* may be more acceptable to those who don't want anything to do with pesticides.

Wally, I agree with your assessment of the potential for Congrain in the crop protection chemical business. I do think that if we decide to enter the business we should do it on a pilot project basis. I don't want to jump in with both feet only to find the water is over our heads.

Dave, I know you've been looking for a good opportunity to move from your staff position to a line management job. This looks to me as if it might be a good opportunity for you. Your hesitancy concerns me. If, after the good research you've done on this project, you personally don't want to enter the business, maybe Congrain shouldn't either.

Let's get together to talk about the crop protection chemical business before we make any decisions. Unless either of you have a conflict, let's meet in the conference room next to my office at 9AM Friday, September 2.

Carnation Dairy

■ INTRODUCTION

The sun was finally appearing over the Superstition Mountains as Charles Bogar, general manager of Carnation Company's Phoenix facility, stole a few moments from his desk work to gaze out the window behind his desk. Next to watching the sun rise over the carefully placed trees and manicured greens of a golf course, he liked this view from his office. This was the view he saw most often. It afforded a momentary distraction from daily activities to think about the future.

And the future was very much in his mind. When Nestle/USA, Inc., purchased Carnation in 1985, he expected to learn to work within the framework of a new corporate culture; however, that did not happen. Carnation, Phoenix was often left to make its own decisions and set its own course. Charles liked that. And now, as of May 1992, Main Street & Main had bought out the Nestle interest in Carnation, Phoenix. Once again Charles had to wonder about the future autonomy of Carnation, Phoenix. For the present, though, a big decision lay before him—NAFTA.

The North American Free Trade Agreement was on everyone's lips in 1992. For Arizona, a border state, the ramifications of it loomed large. Debate was rampant within the state. U.S. delegations, both official and unofficial, regularly visited sister states across the border. Similarly constituted Mexican delegations visited Phoenix, Tucson, and Yuma. People saw potential opportunities or problems arising across the border in the sister state of Sonora.

Charles knew that the name Carnation was almost synonymous with the terms *dairy* and *dairy products*. The footfalls of opportunity could almost be heard approaching the dairy plant's door. Yet there was doubt. He had his share of visitors from both sides of the border who were "heavy on promise, light on delivery."

This case was prepared by Daniel L. Vertz, graduate student; and George J. Seperich, Associate Professor in the School of Agribusiness and Environmental Resources at Arizona State University as a basis for classroom discussion rather than to illustrate either correct or incorrect handling of a business situation.

As he pondered the full visibility of the sun through his window, single words floated before him. Words such as *opportunity, problems,* and *trust.* Nevertheless, a decision would have to be made and soon.

▬ THE ENTERPRISE FOR THE AMERICAS INITIATIVE (EAI)

President George Bush on June 27, 1990, announced the Enterprise for the Americas Initiative (EAI). The initiative offered market access, financial and technical resources, and debt reduction opportunities to countries that liberalized their trade and investment regimes, maintained sound economic policies conducive to investment and competition, and responsibly managed their international debt obligations.

Mexican acceptance of the Brady plan, discussed below, was instrumental in bringing Mexico, Canada, and the U.S. together on NAFTA.

▬ THE BRADY PLAN

In March 1989, U.S. Secretary of the Treasury Nicholas F. Brady announced the Brady debt plan, and in April discussions began between Mexico and its creditors. In February 1990, the fifth renegotiation was signed, with 49 percent of Mexican banks choosing to exchange $22 billion of debt for lower-interest fixed-rate bonds of the same face value. Another 41 percent chose to exchange $20 billion of debt for floating-rate bonds at 35 percent discount to face value. Ten percent chose a third option: to buy new money. In June of that year, Mexico returned to the international capital markets. See Exhibit 1 for an economic profile of Mexico.

Mexican debt statistics for 1992 vary depending on sources. One estimate put the total at $114.96 billion under the Salinas administration (1988–92).

Servicing this debt cost the nation more than $20 billion in 1991. The Mexican government has managed to bring down the ratio of debt to gross domestic product (GDP). In 1982 it rose sharply to 50.6 percent, climbing even higher to 78 percent by 1986. By 1991, the figure had fallen to 36.8 percent. For a comparison of Mexico's GDP with that of the U.S. and the European Community, see Exhibit 2.

Mexico's capacity to repay strengthened the debt-to-export ratio. The cost of debt servicing in 1987 increased to $16.505 billion, according to Finance Secretariat (SHCP) sources, with exports reaching $20.494 billion, representing 80.5 percent of the GDP.

Data for 1991 show the percentage going down to 74 percent, with exports expanding to $27.12 billion and debt repayments amounting to

EXHIBIT 1   An economic profile of Mexico.

	1989	1990	1991
Population (millions)	84.5	86.0	90.0
GDP (billions of $)	279.5	291.8	302.3
Unemployment	2.9%	2.9%	2.6%
Inflation	19.7%	29.9%	16.6%
Average exchange rate	2,462.0	2,812.0	3,018.0
Minimum wage	$0.52	$0.54	$0.55
U.S. Exports (billions of $)	24.9	28.4	33.0
U.S. Imports (billions of $)	27.2	30.8	31.5
Interest rates	45.0%	34.8%	19.3%
Budget deficit (billions of $)	10.0	9.1	5.0

Source: International Monetary Fund; International Labor.

EXHIBIT 2   Comparison of gross domestic products of EC, US, and Mexico.

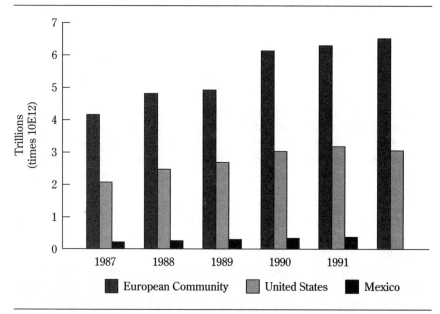

$20.137 billion (Exhibit 3). Improvements in debt-to-export and debt-to-GDP ratios still leave analysts skeptical of Brady's statement that Mexico's debt crisis is dead and buried (Exhibit 4). The peso changed greatly in value during the peak debt crisis period (1986–88), which may have sustained the skepticism (Exhibit 5).

In July 1992, Brazil became the last major Latin American country to accept Brady plan guidelines. Brady said that the Brazil deal repre-

EXHIBIT 3   Rate, servicing, and burden of Mexico's foreign debt.

YEAR	TOTAL EXTERNAL DEBT ($ MILLIONS) [1]	COST OF SERVICING DEBT ($ MILLIONS) [2]	GDP IN PESOS (MILLIONS) [3]	PESO-DOLLAR EXCHANGE RATE [4]
1970	$6,091	$1,300	444,271	12.50
1980	$57,378	$9,739	4,470,077	22.95
1981	$78,215	$13,250	6,127,632	24.51
1982	$86,230	$21,151	9,797,791	57.44
1983	$93,062	$17,407	17,878,720	120.17
1984	$95,317	$17,040	29,471,575	167.77
1985	$96,617	$15,123	47,391,702	256.96
1986	$101,065	$13,731	79,191,347	611.35
1987	$107,541	$16,505	192,801,935	1,366.72
1988	$100,969	$15,222	389,258,523	2,250.28
1989	$95,157	$20,326	503,677,765	2,453.17
1990	$98,210	$21,040	678,923,486	2,807.30
1991	$103,687	$20,137	852,783,201	3,006.79

YEAR	GDP IN DOLLARS (MILLIONS) 5 = [3/4]	EXPORTS [6]	DEBT-GDP RATIO % [1/5]	DEBT-EXPORTS RATIO % [1/6]
1970	35,541.7	3,254.0	17.1%	187.2%
1980	194,774.6	22,406.0	29.5%	256.1%
1981	250,005.4	28,014.0	31.3%	279.2%
1982	170,574.4	28,003.0	50.6%	307.9%
1983	148,778.6	28,944.0	62.6%	321.5%
1984	175,666.5	32,902.0	54.3%	289.7%
1985	184,432.2	31,572.1	52.4%	306.0%
1986	129,535.2	25,198.9	78.0%	401.1%
1987	141,069.1	31,437.2	76.2%	342.1%
1988	172,982.3	33,887.4	58.4%	298.0%
1989	205,317.1	38,090.6	46.3%	249.8%
1990	241,842.2	45,066.9	40.6%	217.9%
1991	283,619.1	45,797.8	36.6%	226.4%

*Includes capital and interest.
Source: Hacienda, Banxico, and World Debt Tables.

sented "a milestone in finally putting the Latin American debt crisis behind us."

One clause of NAFTA was specifically designed to further President Bush's Enterprise for the Americas Initiative. According to that clause, nations other than the three original signatories might join the agreement in the future. Chile is, apparently, next in line. Economic reform in Latin America and the Caribbean put the region on the map as a major export market. The region's economy turned around from the debt crisis of the 1980s to growth in the 1990s. The attraction of the Latin American and Caribbean market has always been its considerable size, its large resource base, and its proximity to the U.S. In 1991, the total population in the region was estimated at 451 million, 8.4 percent of the world total.

The GDP of Latin America and the Caribbean was about $943 billion in 1990, or nearly four times that of Mexico for that year. It is also more than three times that of Eastern and Central Europe and is larger than the entire Southeast Asia market. More than 50 percent of the region's trade is with the U.S.

It is estimated that each $1 billion in U.S. exports creates about 20,000 U.S. jobs. Total U.S. merchandise exports reached a record $394 billion in 1990, up from $277 billion in 1986, an increase of nearly 73 percent. The $63.5 billion in U.S. exports to Latin America and the Caribbean in 1991 supported more than a million American jobs. More than one-half of those jobs were created since 1986, as a result of U.S. export growth to the region.

A 10 percent surge in the value of U.S. agribusiness exports to Latin America and the Caribbean brought two-way agribusiness trade to $15.2 billion in 1992 and lowered the U.S. trade deficit in agricultural products to its lowest level since 1984. U.S. investment in Latin America and Caribbean agribusiness, measured in terms of the total U.S. direct foreign investment, jumped nearly 20 percent between 1987 and 1990, reaching $3.1 billion.

More than half of U.S. capital in Latin America and Caribbean agribusiness is invested in Mexico (where U.S. investment more than doubled between 1989 and 1990) and Brazil, with lesser amounts invested in Argentina, Venezuela, and Colombia. In the Caribbean Basin, where 99.6 percent of all agricultural exports to the U.S. receive duty-free treatment through the Caribbean Basin Initiative (CBI), U.S. investment expanded 17 percent per year during 1987–90.

U.S. agribusiness exports in 1991 increased 10 percent over those of 1990 to $5.7 billion. Exports of animal products and live animals have grown rapidly, with growth averaging 8 percent per year between 1983 and 1990 before surging 60 percent in 1991 to $1.1 billion. Prepared foods exports also increased sharply, expanding to just under $2 billion in 1991.

During the period of 1989–90, Mexico received U.S. exports of butter and milk fat (nearly 10,000 metric tons), condensed milk (nearly 3,000 metric tons), dry whole milk (more than 28,000 metric tons), and nonfat dry milk (more than 100,000 metric tons). Other Latin American countries generally received nonfat dry milk only. Guatemala, Bolivia, and Chile together received nearly 7,000 metric tons of nonfat dry milk in that same period.

U.S. agribusiness imports from Latin America and the Caribbean were relatively unchanged at $9.5 billion in 1991. Milk prices in Latin America

EXHIBIT 4   Mexican foreign debt against exports.

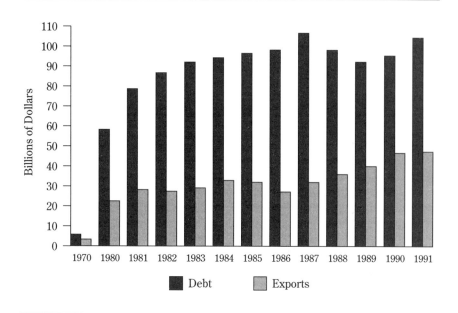

EXHIBIT 5   Peso–dollar exchange rate.

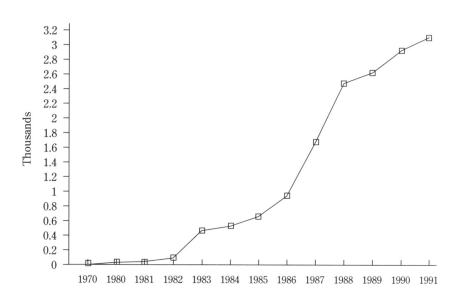

are nearly the same as in the U.S., that is, between $12 and $13 per hundredweight. Farm wages are comparable to those in Mexico. A large portion of the area's milk goes into cheese, and there currently is a deficit for fluid milk.

■■ NAFTA

The U.S., Mexico, and Canada began negotiations on NAFTA in June 1991 to remove barriers in goods, services, and investment and to provide protection for intellectual property rights. A successful agreement would link the U.S., its largest trading partner, Canada, and its third-largest trading partner, Mexico, in a single continental free-trade zone.

Export is the fastest growing sector of the U.S. economy today, and Mexico is the fastest growing market in the world for U.S. exports. U.S. merchandise exports have increased 22 percent per year for each of the past five years. The states exporting the most to Mexico are California (more than $5.5 billion in goods and services in 1991), Texas, Arizona, Michigan, Illinois, Ohio, New York, and Pennsylvania.

From 1986 to 1991, as Mexico reduced its import barriers, U.S. merchandise exports to Mexico grew twice as fast as exports to the rest of the world, from $12.4 billion to $33.3 billion. U.S. agricultural exports rose 173 percent to $3 billion. Consumer goods exports tripled to $3.4 billion. Capital goods increased from $5 billion to $11.3 billion. Under a successfully negotiated NAFTA, the U.S. anticipated even greater export growth since Mexico still has higher trade barriers than the U.S. Mexico's average duty is 10 percent; the U.S. duty is 4 percent.

In 1992, the Office of the U.S. Trade Representative presented these economic statistics about the potential of expanded U.S.–Mexico trade:

- For each $1.00 Mexico spends on imports, $.70 is spent on U.S. goods.
- For each $1.00 growth in Mexico's GNP, $.15 is spent on U.S. goods.
- More than 600,000 U.S. jobs were related to U.S. exports to Mexico in 1991.
- A net increase in jobs relating to U.S. exports to Mexico over the next several years is projected to be 130,000.
- In 1990 prices, a gain in U.S. GDP of $35 billion is projected by 2002.

■■ DAIRY AND DAIRY PRODUCT EXPORTS

Historically, Mexico has been the most important international market for U.S. dairy products. Since 1985, Mexico has imported slightly more than $102 million in U.S. dairy products annually, or 23 percent of total annual

U.S. exports. Mexican imports have fluctuated, and they peaked in 1989 at almost half of total U.S. exports. Exhibits 6 and 7 show the Mexico–U.S. trade balance for 1981–91. Exhibit 8 shows the value of each group of agricultural products for 1990. Many of these imports have been government-to-government exchanges because the Mexican government controls trade by requiring import licenses and is the largest importer of dairy products. Exhibit 9 shows U.S. exports of dairy products to Mexico from 1988 to 1990.

Freer trade policies would stimulate import demand and Mexico's domestic production, but dairy product demand would increase much faster than Mexico's domestic industry could expand to meet it. Although Mexico's milk production would expand, the U.S. would benefit from the technology and other inputs needed for this expansion, since they likely would be imported from the U.S. Although fluid milk prices were allowed to increase 17 percent in October 1991 in Mexico City, producers reported that they could not break even, much less expand and invest in additional cattle. Mexico City was the largest fluid milk consumer center in Mexico. Raw milk prices were estimated to be undervalued by 20 percent in April 1992. Should the government of Mexico liberalize the producer price of milk, real economic expansion would likely occur throughout the country's dairy industry.

Mexico has a large, young and growing population that underconsumes dairy products, especially fluid milk. From 1990 to 1992, per capita fluid milk consumption increased from 107 pounds to 120 pounds, compared with 237 pounds in the U.S. (Exhibit 10).

EXHIBIT 6   Value of U.S.–Mexican agricultural trade 1981–1991 (billions of dollars).

YEAR	U.S. EXPORTS TO MEXICO	MEXICAN EXPORTS TO U.S.	U.S. TRADE BALANCE
1981	$2.43	$1.10	$1.33
1982	$1.16	$1.16	$0.00
1983	$1.94	$1.28	$0.66
1984	$1.99	$1.28	$0.71
1985	$1.29	$1.56	($0.27)
1986	$1.93	$1.12	$0.82
1987	$1.90	$1.12	$0.79
1988	$1.90	$1.73	$0.18
1989	$2.09	$2.77	($0.67)
1990	$2.57	$2.66	($0.09)
1991	$2.52	$2.87	($0.35)
Total	$21.73	$18.64	$3.10

Source: Government Accounting Office from USDA (1981–84), U.S. Embassy, Agricultural Affairs Office Briefing Paper, January 10, 1992 (1985–91).

EXHIBIT 7   Value of U. S.–Mexican agricultural trade, 1981–1991.

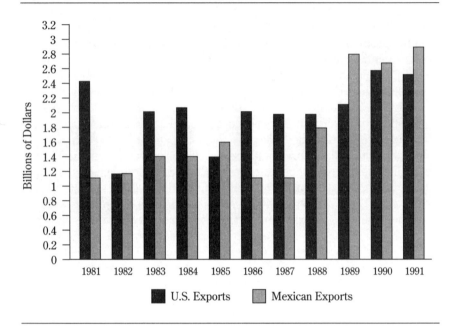

EXHIBIT 8   Value of U. S. agricultural exports to Mexico, 1990.

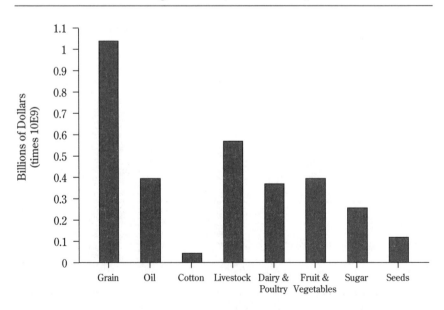

EXHIBIT 9   U. S. exports of dairy products to Mexico.

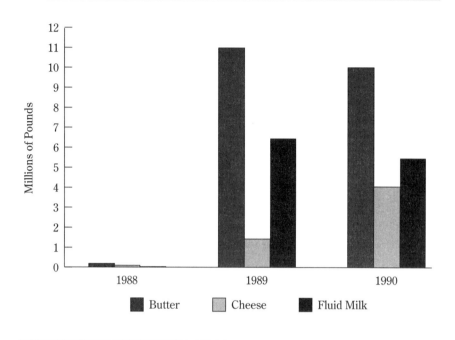

■ Butter   ☐ Cheese   ■ Fluid Milk

■■ MEXICO'S FLUID MILK PRICE CAP

Mexico's fluid milk imports into the "free zone," cities within 25 miles of the U.S. border, have sharply increased in the past few years, especially from U.S. border states. In June 1992, more than 80,000 gallons of fluid Grade A milk was imported into the free zone from Arizona's dairy industry every week (Carnation's share was 25,000). The retail price of Mexico's milk was controlled by the Mexican government's retail price cap (Exhibit 11). U. S. milk prices for the same period are in Exhibit 12. A lack of refrigerated transport, higher freight costs, and a policy of controlled retail cap prices on imported fluid milk have prevented expansion of fluid milk imports. The Secretariat of Commerce (SECOFI) for the state of Sonora asks fluid milk importers and distributors to sell imported fluid milk at prices similar to or lower than the controlled fluid milk price. If importers/distributors do not do so, they can be fined or subjected to other punitive actions. This situation persists even though imported fluid milk has higher fat and protein content and a longer shelf life when compared with domestic product. The gap in quality between U.S. and Mexican fluid milk is narrowing, however. The Mexican government approved new health and quality standards for domestic fluid milk in July 1992. These standards

EXHIBIT 10   Mexico's supply and domestic consumption of dairy products (1992 data is forecasted).

MILLIONS OF POUNDS	1990	1991	1992
Milk production	20,526.0	22,440.0	23,540.0
Fluid milk	9,178.0	9,915.0	10,351.0
Fluid factory use	12,188.0	13,409.0	14,102.0
Cheese	871.0	913.0	935.0
Butter	77.0	81.0	84.0
Nonfat dry milk	431.0	301.0	361.0
Whole dry milk	22.0	33.0	55.0
Total Domestic Consumption	22,768.0	24,653.0	25,887.0
Consumption minus production	2,242.0	2,213.0	2,347.0

MILLIONS OF GALLONS	1990	1991	1992
Milk production	2,387.0	2,609.0	2,737.0
Fluid milk	1,067.0	1,153.0	1,204.0
Fluid factory use	1,417.0	1,559.0	1,640.0
Cheese	101.0	106.0	109.0
Butter	9.0	9.5	9.7
Nonfat dry milk	50.0	35.0	42.0
Whole dry milk	2.6	3.8	6.4
Total Domestic Consumption	2,647.0	2,867.0	3,010.0
Consumption minus production	260.7	257.3	273.0

POUNDS PER CAPITA ANNUALLY	1990	1991	1992
Milk production	238.7	260.9	273.7
Fluid milk	106.7	115.3	120.4
Fluid factory use	141.7	155.9	164.0
Cheese	10.1	10.6	10.9
Butter	0.9	0.9	1.0
Nonfat dry milk	5.0	3.5	4.2
Whole dry milk	0.3	0.4	0.6
Total Domestic Consumption	264.7	286.7	301.0
Consumption minus production	26.1	25.7	27.3

EXHIBIT 11   Producer and consumer fluid milk prices in Mexico.

STATES, CITIES & REGIONS	AVERAGE PRODUCER PRICE/CWT	AVERAGE PRODUCER PRICE/GAL.	CONSUMER PRICE PER GALLON[a]
Aquascalientes	$12.30	$1.06	$1.82
Baja California	$12.71	$1.09	$1.88
Baja California Sur	$11.48	$0.99	$1.70
Campeche	$11.48	$0.99	$1.70
Coahuila	$12.71	$1.09	$1.88
Cuenca Lagunera			$1.82
Border Cities			"free"
Carbonifera			$2.01
Chiapas	$10.66	$0.92	$1.58
Chihuahua	$13.12	$1.13	$1.94
Colima	$13.56	$1.17	$2.01
Distrito Federal (Mexico City)	$13.53	$1.16	$2.01
Durango	$12.30	$1.06	$1.82
Estado de Mexico	$12.71	$1.09	$1.88
Guanajuato	$12.30	$1.06	$1.82
Guerrero	$13.53	$1.16	$2.01
Hidalgo	$12.30	$1.06	$1.82
Jalisco	$13.53	$1.16	$2.01
Michoacan	$10.26	$0.88	$1.52
Morelos	$13.12	$1.13	$1.94
Nayarit	$9.85	$0.85	$1.46
Nuevo Leon	$13.12	$1.13	$1.94
Oaxaca	$10.66	$0.92	$1.58
Puebla	$13.12	$1.13	$1.94
Queretaro	$12.30	$1.06	$1.82
Quintana Roo	$12.30	$1.06	$1.82
San Luis Potosi	$12.30	$1.06	$1.82
Sinaloa	$13.53	$1.16	$2.01
Sonora	$13.94	$1.20	$2.07
Sonora[b]	$15.54	$1.34	$2.31
Tabasco	$11.89	$1.02	$1.76
Tamaulipas	$13.53	$1.16	$2.01
Tlaxcala	$13.53	$1.16	$2.01
Veracruz	$12.15	$1.05	$1.94
Yucatan	$11.48	$0.99	$1.70
Zacatecas	$12.71	$1.09	$1.88

[a]Retail price for pasteurized fluid milk.
[b]Market survey revealed government cap on milk with more stringent sanitary standards was labeled *preferente especial* and changed to 1,900 pesos per liter.
Source: National Livestock Confederation (CNG).

EXHIBIT 12   International Association of Milk Control Agencies supermarket whole milk price survey summary June 8–12, 1992.

MARKET	PRICE	MARKET	PRICE
Arizona		Nevada	
Phoenix	$2.45	Las Vegas	$2.42
		Reno	$2.37
California		New York	
Los Angeles	$2.74	Buffalo	$2.16
San Francisco	$2.34	New York City	$2.30

include a mesophile count (equivalent to the U.S. standard plate count) of 30,000 bacteria per milliliter, a coliform count of less than 20 (the U.S. standard is 10), as well as solids, protein, and fat standards and provisions for the prevention of adulteration of milk with water, starch, oils, antibiotics, and pesticides. Producers whose milk has a bacteria count below 230,000 per milliliter and a butterfat content of 3.3 percent or greater receive a premium of 230 pesos ($0.07) per liter for their milk. (Grade A raw milk in the U.S. must have a plate count of less than 100,000 per milliliter.) All milk is monitored by Mexican government inspectors who take random samples to the state laboratory in Sonora. Milk meeting the new standards is labeled *preferente especial* and can be sold for the new retail cap price of 1,900 pesos per liter.

Because profit potential is limited by the retail cap, several buyers and supermarket chains are importing increasing amounts of canned, powdered, or sweetened condensed milk products with flexible prices that are not subject to the strict governmental price controls of fluid milk.

Supermarket chains are also purchasing increased amounts of other imported dairy products. U.S. yogurt, ice cream, and butter are attractive items among Mexico's middle and upper classes. La Corona Foods, Arizona's only yogurt plant, ships more than 47 percent (900,000 pounds per month) of its yogurt to Mexico, despite higher costs to the consumer than the Mexican domestic product. Exhibit 13 shows the prices of assorted dairy products in selected markets in Sonora, Mexico.

▬ NAFTA OPPOSITION

Environmental Problems

Those who opposed a free trade agreement with Mexico cited the environmental problems along the Mexico–U.S. border. In 1991 the two nations

EXHIBIT 13   Market survey of dairy products for 1992 in Sonora, Mexico.

PRODUCT	MEASURE	NOGALES	HERMOSILLO	OBREGON
Water	gallon	$0.82		$0.84[a]
Whole milk	gallon	$2.07	$1.77	$2.10[b]
Whole milk	half gallon		$0.90	
Whole milk	liter[c]	$0.52	$0.43	$0.58
Chocolate milk 1.5%	gallon	$2.62		$2.38
Half & half	250 ml.	$0.49		
Cream 30%	900 ml.	$2.56	$2.26	
Cream 30%	16 ounce	$1.14	$1.08	$1.00
Cream 30%	8 ounce	$0.58		
Whipped cream	500 grams	$1.93		
Sour cream	32 ounce	$2.13		
Cottage cheese	16 ounce		$2.95	$3.19
Ice cream	half gallon	$3.96		
Ice cream	16 ounce	$1.14		
Ice cream	4.5 liters		$9.59	$9.89
Ice cream	liter		$2.65	$3.64
Orange juice	64 ounce	$2.29		$3.26
Drinks	64 ounce	$1.03		
Drinks	gallon		$1.80	$1.98
Yogurt	32 ounce	$2.24	$2.36	
Yogurt	8 ounce	$0.55	$0.64	$0.88
Yogurt drink	8 ounce	$0.63	$0.64	$0.88
Whey yogurt drink	80 ml.	$1.52		

Table 13 converted using 3,280 pesos per dollar.
[a]Town House water out of Oakland is $0.87 for one gallon.
[b]Ranges from $1.77 for Oro Pura to $2.19 for Yaqui brands.
[c]Retail cap price for *preferente especial* is $0.58 per liter.

attempted to thwart an environmental controversy with a plan to boost pollution enforcement, build sewage treatment plants, and exert control over hazardous chemicals.

Mexico put $460 million into cleaning up industrial pollution along the border in 1991. The EPA had asked Congress for $240 million in 1993 to fund the U.S. contribution; however, this is far from the estimated $5.5 billion that is needed for an effective cleanup by the Border Trade Alliance, a business group that supports NAFTA.

Mexico began a crackdown on *maquiladoras,* or border manufacturing plants, in 1991. The 80 temporary closings have been Mexico's best weapon against pollution. "Environmental consciousness has risen dramatically over the last 18 months," says Javier Guerra, president of Quimica Omega, a hazardous waste treatment plant near Mexico City. After one of its border plants was temporarily shut down in 1991, General Motors announced plans to spend $20 million on waste-water treatment facilities at 31 of its *maquiladoras.*

Loss of U. S. Jobs

Another argument posed by opponents of NAFTA was that many U.S. jobs will be lost. Many economists think these fears are exaggerated. Edward E. Leamer, an economist at the University of California at Los Angeles, predicted that over several years the commitment of Mexico and the U.S. to free trade will reduce real annual wages for low-skilled workers in the U.S. by about $1,000 and that annual earnings for high-skilled workers could rise as much as $6,000. "Everyone need not benefit from increased international commerce," he concludes. Gary Hufbauer and Jeffrey Schott at the Institute for International Economics calculate that the increased trade flowing from the tariff-reducing pact will create about 325,000 new jobs in the U.S. by 1995 and will eliminate about 150,000 unskilled factory jobs, some of which will be lost to Mexican competition. One of the ironies of the trade pact is that just as Americans fear that their jobs will move to Mexico, where wages are markedly lower, Mexicans fear that jobs in their less efficient economic sectors, particularly in the dairy sector, will move to the U.S., where production standards are higher.

Labor remains a sticky issue in NAFTA. To obtain hard data, the American Chamber of Commerce of Mexico studied the labor practices of U.S. companies operating in Mexico. The survey questioned companies on unionization, wages, benefits, and the likely effects of NAFTA. Voluntary responses from 125 chamber members revealed that Mexican workers at U.S. firms were well-protected and that NAFTA will create jobs for the Mexican and the U.S. economies.

The average daily wage paid by U.S. companies to Mexican blue-collar workers was more than twice the national minimum wage, according to survey results. The national minimum wage was $.55 (1,700 pesos) per hour. Participants reported that the mean daily gross wage of Mexican blue-collar workers was $10.36 (32,300 pesos) per day, or $1.30 (4,048 pesos) per hour. (In March of 1992 one U.S. dollar in Mexico was worth 3,114 pesos.)

Large U.S. companies pay the highest wages, averaging $11.14 (34,700 pesos) per day, followed by small companies at $9.71 (30,200 pesos) per day. The lowest salaries or wages were paid by medium-sized companies, who offered the average employee $8.94 (27,800 pesos) per day, or $1.12 (3,480 pesos) per hour. For comparison, Arizona's dairy product manufacturers paid blue-collar workers an average wage of $11.00 per hour or $88.00 per day, more than eight times its Mexican counterpart.

Under Mexican law, labor relationships are presumed permanent. As a result, the law requires an array of employee benefits. For example, employers must pay employees who are dismissed without cause a lump sum equal to three months' pay plus 20 days' pay for each year of service. Employers must pay 1 percent of the payroll, to a maximum of 10 times the minimum wage in the federal district (13,330 pesos, or $4.28 per day), for child day care programs. The mandatory Christmas bonus is equivalent to 15 days' pay.

Surveyed companies reported that they provide additional compensation to workers through contributions to Social Security and other programs. These include the items listed in Exhibit 14.

Trade liberalization has already increased U.S. exports to Mexico. Since the liberalization of the Mexican economy in 1986, 63 percent of the surveyed participants reported an increase in U.S. imports. On the average, U.S. imports to these companies increased 57 percent.

■■■ NAFTA AGREEMENT

The U.S., Canada, and Mexico reached an agreement on NAFTA on August 12, 1992. Among the provisions of NAFTA that would affect the dairy industry are market access, rules of origin, and sanitary standards.

Market Access

All U.S. and Mexican tariffs on dairy products would be phased out over a 10-year period. All Mexican import licensing requirements for dairy products would be eliminated immediately and converted to 20 percent tariffs to be phased out over 10 years. All Section 22 dairy import quotas would be converted to tariff-rate quotas vis-à-vis Mexico, but retained for all other countries. The tariff quota levels for these products for Mexico would be approximately 5 percent of current Section 22 quantities for individual product categories, and these quotas would increase by 3 percent per year. For over-quota cheese exported from the U.S. into Mexico, the tariff was 40 percent for fresh cheese and 20 percent for all others. The over-quota tariffs,

---

EXHIBIT 14   Extra work benefits (respondent percentages) of surveyed U.S. companies operating in Mexico.

Paid vacations	92%	Transportation allowance	59%
Health insurance	87%	Health care on premises	53%
Profit sharing	83%	Maternity care	42%
Subsidized groceries	70%	Subsidized medication	34%
Disability insurance	64%		

which initially range between 70 and 96 percent, would also be phased out over 10 years. Nonfat dry milk was the only dairy product with a Mexican tariff-rate quota. Mexico will give the U.S. a 40,000 metric ton (88.2 million pounds) duty-free quota for nonfat dry milk, which will increase at 3 percent per year. Mexico's over-quota tariff for nonfat dry milk would begin at 139 percent and be phased out over 15 years. The tariff was 10 percent for fluid milk exported to Mexico, 92–94 percent for fluid milk imported from Mexico, 20 percent for most manufactured dairy products exported to Mexico, and 87–96 percent for the same imported from Mexico.

Each initial tariff level would be reduced by 10 percent per year until elimination after 10 years, except the tariff applied to U.S. nonfat dry milk exported into Mexico in quantities above the duty-free quota level. This tariff would be reduced from its initial level of 139 percent by 4 percent per year for the first six years of NAFTA and by 11.5 percent per year thereafter until elimination after 15 years.

Under NAFTA rules of origin, all dairy products must originate 100 percent in NAFTA countries to be considered of NAFTA origin.

■■■ OPTIONS

The following several options are available to processors or investors who are interested in expanding into the Sonora, Mexico, markets.

Option I

Carnation might continue delivering milk to the Mexican border to be purchased and distributed by a Mexican importer. Carnation is currently selling milk to Mexican importers at the border for a price that returns a profit of from six to eight cents per gallon, or roughly half that from the local Arizona markets. The bulk of this milk is sold in the free zone border cities. The remainder finds its way into nontraditional market channels to other areas of Sonora, Mexico, and other states or is purchased at the border by individuals and distributed from family to family throughout Mexico.

The potential market is about 4 million consumers in Sonora, Sinaloa, and Nayarit. The per capita milk and milk products intake exhibits a steady growth trend. With the new cap price of 1,900 pesos per liter for *preferente especial* milk, a processor could negotiate a higher price for its milk at the border.

Option II

Carnation and La Corona Foods have had a good business relationship for many years. La Corona provides yogurt to the Mexican states of Sonora,

Nuevo León, Baja California, Jalisco, and Chihuahua and to Mexico City (an area with more than 20 million customers). If these areas are opened to manufactured milk products, Carnation could enter into a joint agreement with La Corona to supply many of those products using La Corona's vast distribution network.

Option III

There are about 25 producers in the Obregon, Sonora, region with a total herd size of 3,200 cows, producing from 20,000 liters (46,000 pounds), or more than 5,000 gallons per day, to 60,000 liters (138,000 pounds), or nearly 16,000 gallons a day.

These producers are dissatisfied with the processors purchasing their milk and wish to enter into a joint venture to start their own processing plant. They would like an investor with processing and marketing expertise. A dairy plant in the Obregon area could potentially supply the entire Pacific region of Mexico, which has a population of more than five million. The regions south and east of Obregon are devoid of dairy operations. The large deficit in fluid milk and manufactured dairy products could be supplemented with milk from Arizona's dairy producers as part of the venture agreement. Exhibits 15, 16, and 17 compare the costs of processing milk in the U.S. with the costs of doing so in Sonora, Mexico.

Additionally, the seaport of Guaymas is less than 60 miles west of the Obregon region. With a foothold in the Pacific region, a processor could eventually enter the South American markets by taking advantage of the existing trade agreements that Mexico has with many of these countries.

Option IV

The *ejido* (common public land) association in Caborca, Sonora, has already received government permission and aid (25 percent) to enter into a joint venture to purchase 1,600 head of milking cows and to construct a production and processing facility. It has set aside another 25 percent for the venture. Carnation could expand into Sonora, Mexico, by investing in this venture.

Ejidos originated after the Mexican Revolution of 1920, during which peasants seized their ancestral lands from wealthy landowners. Under the revolutionary constitution, private farms were limited in size to 200 hectares (each hectare equals 2.47 acres) for crops and to 600 hectares for livestock. Approximately two thirds of the agricultural land was eventually granted to landless peasants organized in *ejidos*. Since the revolution, more than 90 million hectares have been redistributed to peasant farmers. Under the con-

EXHIBIT 15   Fluid milk manufacturing: Sales and administrative costs per gallon (producer summer rate) United States and Mexico (in pesos).

MANUFACTURING COSTS	U.S.	CARNATION	SONORA
Labor	$16.68	$39.86	$4.31
Fringe benefits	$2.78	$14.73	$10.75
Supplies	$13.90	$24.26	$18.00
Repairs	$5.56	$27.73	$24.00
Taxes	$2.78	$8.67	$0.00
Insurance	$0.00	$1.73	$0.00
Depreciation	$11.12	$19.06	$16.50
Rentals	$0.00	$1.73	$0.00
Services purchased	$8.34	$0.00	$0.00
General expense	$0.00	$26.00	$22.50
Subtotal expense	$61.16	$163.78	$96.07
Handling cost	$269.65	$251.31	$217.52
Total	$314.00	$394.00	$326.09

SALES AND ADMINISTRATIVE COSTS	U.S.	CARNATION	SONORA
Delivery and selling	$255.76	$188.05	$162.77
Administrative general	$63.94	$43.33	$37.50
Total	$303.00	$220.00	$200.27
Total costs	$617.00	$614.00	$526.36
Producer paid ($/cwt)	$14.50	$14.50	$15.70
Producer paid (pesos/liter)	$1,080.51	$1,080.51	$1,170.00
Tariffs & expenses	$170.00	$170.00	$0.00
New total	$1,868	$1,865	$1,696
Retail market gets	170	170	170
Retail price	$1,900	$1,900	$1,900
Profit	($138)	($135)	$34

Data on Sonora from market survey, Sept. 25, 1992. Exchange rate: 3,280 pesos per dollar.

stitution, *ejido* land belonged to the nation. Although *ejido* farmers could cultivate the land and will the right to use it to their children, they could not sell, rent, or mortgage the land. Corporations, whether domestic or foreign, could not own land for agricultural production and could not associate with *ejido* farmers.

EXHIBIT 16   Fluid milk manufacturing: Sales and administrative costs per gallon (producer summer rate) United States and Mexico (in U. S. dollars).

MANUFACTURING COSTS (U. S. $)	U. S.	CARNATION	SONORA
Labor	$0.019	$0.046	$0.005
Fringe benefits	$0.003	$0.017	$0.012
Supplies	$0.016	$0.028	$0.021
Repairs	$0.006	$0.032	$0.028
Taxes	$0.003	$0.010	$0.000
Insurance	$0.000	$0.002	$0.000
Depreciation	$0.013	$0.022	$0.019
Rentals	$0.000	$0.002	$0.000
Services purchased	$0.010	$0.000	$0.000
General expense	$0.000	$0.030	$0.026
Subtotal expense	$0.071	$0.189	$0.111
Handling cost	$0.311	$0.290	$0.251
Total	$0.382	$0.479	$0.362

SALES AND ADMINISTRATIVE COSTS	U. S.	CARNATION	SONORA
Delivery and selling	$0.295	$0.217	$0.188
Administrative general	$0.074	$0.050	$0.043
Total	$0.369	$0.267	$0.231
Total costs	$0.75	$0.75	$0.59
Producer paid ($/cwt)	$14.50	$14.50	$12.50
Producer paid ($/gal)	$1.25	$1.25	$1.08
Tariffs & expenses	$0.196	$0.196	$0.000
New total	$2.194	$2.189	$1.668
Retail market gets	$0.196	$0.196	$0.196
Retail price	$2.193	$2.193	$2.193
Profit	($0.197)	($0.193)	$0.328

Data on Sonora from market survey, Sept. 25, 1992. Exchange rate: 3,280 pesos per dollar.

EXHIBIT 17   Fluid milk manufacturing: Sales and administrative costs per gallon (producer fall rate) United States and Mexico (in U. S. dollars).

MANUFACTURING COSTS (U.S. $)	U.S.	CARNATION	SONORA
Labor	$0.019	$0.046	$0.005
Fringe benefits	$0.003	$0.017	$0.012
Supplies	$0.016	$0.028	$0.021
Repairs	$0.006	$0.032	$0.028
Taxes	$0.003	$0.010	$0.000
Insurance	$0.000	$0.002	$0.000
Depreciation	$0.013	$0.022	$0.019
Rentals	$0.000	$0.002	$0.000
Services purchased	$0.010	$0.000	$0.000
General expense	$0.000	$0.030	$0.026
Subtotal expense	$0.071	$0.189	$0.111
Handling cost	$0.311	$0.290	$0.251
Total	$0.382	$0.479	$0.362

SALES AND ADMINISTRATIVE COSTS	U.S.	CARNATION	SONORA
Delivery and selling	$0.295	$0.217	$0.188
Administrative general	$0.074	$0.050	$0.043
Total	$0.369	$0.267	$0.231
Total costs	$0.75	$0.75	$0.59
Producer paid ($/cwt)	$11.50	$11.50	$12.50
Producer paid ($/gal)	$0.99	$0.99	$1.08
Tariffs & expenses	$0.196	$0.196	$0.000
New total	$1.936	$1.931	$1.668
Retail market gets	$0.196	$0.196	$0.196
Retail price	$2.193	$2.193	$2.193
Profit	$0.061	$0.065	$0.328

Data on Sonora from market survey, Sept. 25, 1992. Exchange rate: 3,280 pesos per dollar.

This is changing. The *ejido* association in Caborca has been given government support in entering into a joint venture with a U. S. corporation that wants to invest in the project mentioned above.

The *ejido* landowners in Caborca, Sonora, did not receive their land from the government, but purchased it and chose to organize as an *ejido* system because of the advantages of government support and assistance.

Another possibility would be for Carnation to invest in the producer venture in Caborca, but process that milk in Arizona and then market and distribute the fluid milk and manufactured dairy products in Mexico. A part of that venture agreement could be to supplement Mexico's dairy product deficit with milk from Arizona's producers.

Option V

There are three major dairy processors in Sonora, Mexico: Oro Pura in Hermosillo, Yaqui in Obregon, and La Pearla in Caborca. These plants do not process enough milk to meet the increasing demands of the Mexican markets. It may be feasible for Carnation to enter into a venture with any one of these plants to supply deficit milk and expand its processing facilities. As part of a venture agreement, the milk deficit in Mexico's markets could be supplied by Arizona producers.

■■■ SUMMARY

Because of its proximity to Arizona, the state of Sonora, Mexico, could become an important market for Arizona milk and dairy products. The most promising pathway into that market is through direct investment in and joint ventures with Mexico's dairy industry.

At present, fluid milk profits are low because of the Mexican government's retail price cap. In 1992, this cap jumped from 1,700 pesos per liter to 1,900 pesos per liter for *preferente especial* milk. After NAFTA is passed by Congress, this cap will likely be raised again. At present, yogurt and yogurt products, cottage cheese, and ice cream are overpriced in the Mexican markets. Charles Bogar understood this situation, and knew it was time to act. But which alternative should he choose?

Ontario Flower Growers' Cooperative (2)

On November 14, 1984, Harry Stueben was elected president of the board of directors of the Ontario Flower Growers' Cooperative (OFGC) of Mississauga, Ontario, at its annual meeting. He would hold the position for one year, and he felt that much could be done to build on the organization's strengths. Stueben's own major interest was in making the cooperative more attractive as a source of floricultural products. He saw his immediate task as deciding what his agenda would be for the board's next meeting on December 12, 1984.

■ THE COOPERATIVE

The OFGC was established in 1972 by a group of plant and flower growers with the assistance of the Ontario provincial government to help Ontario growers sell their floricultural products. All were interested in providing a single location where growers could get together with buyers. Initially, this was accomplished through an auction held in a rented industrial building in Georgetown, Ontario, but in 1974, the OFGC moved 30 kilometers to its current location in a rented building of 65,000 square feet in Mississauga on the outskirts of Toronto. Two other methods or programs for selling these products had been added recently: presales and direct sales.

The OFGC had distinctive features because, as a co-op, it was viewed as an extension of the growers' or farmers' enterprises. Each grower who wished to use the co-op to sell products had to become a member. Growers became members by providing part of the capital needed to operate the co-op, and as members they had equal voting rights with all other members no matter how much they used the co-op. The profits generated by the co-op

This case was prepared by Kenneth F. Harling and Alan DeRoo, Department of Agricultural Business and Economics, University of Guelph, Guelph, Ontario, Canada, under a grant from the Small Business Secretariat of the Department of Regional Industrial Expansion, Ottawa, as a basis for classroom discussion rather than to illustrate either correct or incorrect handling of an administrative situation.

were considered to be savings for the members who used it and were passed back to them each year as patronage dividends. These were not taxed at the level of the co-op but were part of the individual farmers' taxable income.

Memberships

To qualify for membership a grower had to be situated in Ontario. The co-op's bylaws also required that members only sell through the OFGC product that had been in the greenhouse for 60 days or more. In recent years the board of directors had felt that more growers wanted to sell through the OFGC than there were buyers, so it had required that prospective members go through a trial year in which they had to ship good-quality product regularly to the OFGC. After one year of acceptable performance, they were made full members. The sales of individual members through the OFGC ranged from nothing to over $500,000 (Exhibit 1). This variation was due to differences in both grower size and the proportion of business growers sent through the cooperative. In recent years, the larger growers had accounted for an increasing proportion of the volume.

Organization

The OFGC's organizational structure, presented in Exhibit 2, shows the two groups that affect the OFGC's activities: the board of directors and management. The board's seven directors oversaw the management of the OFGC. Each director was elected by the members to serve a two-year term but could be re-elected an unlimited number of times. The directors did not always agree on what needed to be done. Personalities sometimes expanded these differences to the point where there was personal and emotional conflict among members. Further details on individual directors appear in Exhibit 3.

The executive positions on the board were allocated by the board in a private discussion following the election of the new directors. The board had several committees, with each committee being served by directors who had an interest in the subject matter of the committee. The building and marketing committees were very active during 1984. The building committee was looking for land for a new building and arranging for an architect to draw up plans for it. The marketing committee was looking for ways to expand sales and had a particular interest in direct sales. The finance committee had done little because it had been waiting for the previous president, Bert Roosevelt, to come to an agreement with the finance committee's chairman, Pat Haefling, about how the new building would be financed. Roosevelt had wanted the OFGC to finance the building, while Haefling had wanted it to borrow the money from the members.

EXHIBIT 1 Grower members' sales through the cooperative.

DOLLAR RANGE OF INDIVIDUAL MEMBERS' SALES	1982		1983		1984	
	Number of Members	Total Dollars	Number of Members	Total Dollars	Number of Members	Total Dollars
None	28	—	27	—	27	—
1–250	5	657	2	179	2	104
251–10,000	33	123,611	28	99,827	25	110,998
10,001–50,000	44	1,139,632	44	1,062,598	39	1,040,963
50,001–100,000	28	1,995,703	25	1,735,130	29	2,189,611
100,001–250,000	16	2,848,727	24	3,373,315	24	3,578,526
250,001–500,000	3	1,429,087	4	1,230,318	6	1,877,853
Over 500,000	1	509,185	3	1,831,149	3	1,992,910
Total	158	8,046,602	157	9,332,516	155	10,790,965

Source: Annual Reports of the Ontario Flower Growers' Cooperative.

EXHIBIT 2   Organization of the Ontario Flower Growers' Cooperative.

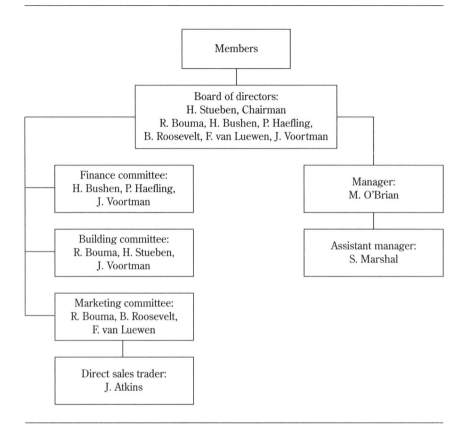

The directors were all active members who ran their own floricultural businesses. This meant that they were very interested in the daily operations of the OFGC and devoted much attention to how they could be improved. The directors often called on their own experiences and instincts when addressing problems arising in this area. Conflicts of opinion about what should be done were not uncommon at the monthly board meetings, as each director promoted what he thought was best for OFGC.

The OFGC functioned with a small staff of three management people: the manager, the assistant manager, and the direct sales trader. The manager, Mildred O'Brian, was responsible for the operation of the auction and reported to the board. Except for 1980 and 1981, she had been the manager of the OFGC since it had started. She relied on the board to "tell her what it wanted." The assistant manager reported to the manager and was responsible for the presales program and providing support for the manager. The current assistant manager had been hired six months earlier and

EXHIBIT 3   Members of the board of directors.

Name	Ron Bouma	Henry Bushen	Pat Haefling	Bert Roosevelt
Age	55	34	57	55
Role on board	Member and serves on the marketing committee and building committee	Treasurer and serves on the finance committee	Member and serves on the finance committee	Vice president (past president) and serves on the marketing committee
Years on board	4	2	5	5
Business interests	Cut flowers $150,000 sales/year	Potted plants $120,000 sales/year Sells two-thirds to wholesalers	Imported tropical plants $1,500,000 sales/year Sells one-half wholesale and from his greenhouse	Potted and tropical plants $2,000,000 sales/year Sells wholesale to all types of retailers
Use of OFGC	Sells all his product through the auction	Sells one-third through the auction	Sells one-half through the auction Heavy user of the buyback mechanism	Sends one-fifth to the auction Buys at auction occasionally to meet wholesaling needs
Expressed interests	None	None	Would like to see volume on the auction increased and dumping prevented Wants the auction to build its own building	Has been pushing hard for direct sales

EXHIBIT 3   Continued.

Name	Harry Stueben	Frank van Luewen	John Voortman
Age	59	54	50
Role on board	President and serves on the building committee	Secretary and serves on the marketing committee	Member and serves on the finance committee and the building committee
Years on board	1	5	2
Business interests	Garden center and traditional florist $500,000 sales/year	Potted chrysanthemums $700,000 sales/year Sells two-thirds to retailers on a contractual basis	Sells cut roses $150,000 sales/year
Use of OFGC	Bought $500 at auction in the previous year Has sold nothing at co-op in recent years	Sends one-third to the auction	Sends one-half to the auction
Expressed interests	Wants to help the OFGC attract more buyers	Wants direct sales expanded	Wants the problem with the auction solved

his previous experience had been in operating a theater. The direct sales trader was responsible for the direct sales program and reported to the three-member marketing committee of the board. He had been in his job since the fall of 1983 and before that had been a grower and a salesman.

Activities

The OFGC participated in the floricultural industry, which is described in Attachment A. It provided markets where growers and buyers could work together and played an active yet impartial role in helping transact sales. This was different from other marketing alternatives which required either the grower or the buyer to seek out the other and then to carry out the sales negotiations. The co-op carried out its role through three programs: auction, presale, and direct sale. Each program was viewed as a separate business because it attracted different sellers and buyers. The original and still the most important program was the auction—it was the only one in Ontario.

The Auction

The auction was really a series of frequent auctions carrying the full range of floricultural products. An auction was held every Tuesday, Thursday, Friday, and on other days during peak sales periods. It started at 6 or 7 in the morning and was usually over by 11. Growers would deliver their product prior to the auction in boxes and pails on carts waiting to be taken into the auction. Buyers could identify who grew the product by looking at invoices attached to the carts on which the containers stood.

The auction was conducted in a tiered gallery with seats for 200 buyers. They sat at tables and looked down on the auction floor and a Dutch clock mounted on the wall behind it. Product was rolled in front of them on carts. Each box on the cart was considered a lot and was auctioned off separately, although buyers could ask for more boxes when they had a winning bid. The Dutch clock behind the floor indicated the price of the product being auctioned. The clock started at the grower's asking price and, as the clock rotated, the price dropped until a buyer pressed the button on the table at which he sat to indicate that he would buy the product at the price indicated on the clock. At the back of the gallery were buttons that enabled growers to remove their product from the auction by "buying it back." Growers did so when they thought the auction price had dropped too low. Buybacks were treated as sales, however, and the grower had to pay the OFGC its sales commission. The commission was about 10 percent of the value of the product sold.

A buyer could participate in the auction personally by renting a seat in the gallery either for the day, if one was available, by paying $35, or for the year by winning a competitive bid for it. If he did not want to participate personally, he could deal through a commission agent who sat at the back of the gallery and charged a 10 percent fee on the value of product bought. Most buyers had to pay cash for their purchases before they left the building. Before growers left the auction, they were given a check for the product they had sold that day.

The auction had attracted a variety of buyers. The estimated purchases by customer type in millions of dollars were wholesalers, 2.5; plant and flower shops 2.5; greengrocers, 2.0; garden centers, 1.5; and florists, 1.0. Approximately 60 percent of the dollar volume was from sales of potted flowering and foliage plants, 25 percent cut flowers, and 15 percent bedding plants. No separate record of volume under the presales program was kept, as it was minimal.

From the buyers' perspective, the auction had several positive and negative features. On the positive side: (1) a wide range of products were traded, (2) prices were observed by all present, (3) available quantities could be purchased by anyone willing to pay the necessary price, and (4) prices on average were lower than those of terminal wholesalers. On the negative side: (1) prices and quantities could vary considerably from day to day, (2) the auction seemed to attract a disproportionate amount of poor-quality product during peak buying periods, (3) any buyers buying a large amount quickly raised the auction price, and (4) the buyer had to be a good judge of quality.

From the grower's perspective, the auction also had several positive and negative features. On the positive side: (1) growers were able to bring all varieties and qualities they had to sell, (2) growers were paid their cash immediately following the auction, (3) it was a fast way of selling product, and (4) prices were better than those of terminal wholesalers. On the negative side: (1) many buyers seemed reluctant to pay premium prices, and (2) bringing a large quantity of product to the auction depressed auction prices.

Presales

The presales program was introduced as a way of guaranteeing that buyers who definitely wanted a particular item would be able to get it when they wanted it. Under the program, a buyer was able to use the services of the OFGC to get a grower to supply him with a particular item of a certain quality. The buyer paid the OFGC nothing for this service, while the grower paid a 5 percent commission. The grower was given a check when the product was sold. Growers charged higher prices on these sales because they knew the buyer wanted the product.

Direct Sales

The direct sales program was a new program similar to an earlier export sales program, which had lost $73,000 over 1980 and 1981. The previous program had so angered some members that a motion had been passed at the 1981 annual meeting banning export sales. Nevertheless, members had agreed recently to the direct sales program as a way of pursuing buyers who were not using the auction or presales program. It was also argued that this program would reduce the supply of product at the auction and thus improve prices there.

This program was run by a person employed by the OFGC, the direct sales trader. He would contact both growers and buyers to see what was available and what was wanted. When he had a match he would arrange a sale, with the identity of buyers and sellers kept confidential. Thus sellers and buyers would have to continue to rely on the trader to set up further transactions and sales would continue to be made through the OFGC. The program was different from regular wholesale operations in several ways. First, the trader acted as an honest broker between the buyers and sellers by helping each get a "fair" deal rather than to maximize the margin he made on the transaction. Second, by being continually in the market for both growers and buyers, he acted as a clearinghouse for sales, usually being able to provide a buyer or seller in the market for the product.

Shipments of product to direct sales program customers were all sent from the OFGC's building, where products from several growers were consolidated and repackaged if necessary. This approach had proven useful because it permitted medium-sized growers to sell to large customers. The trader was also able to see the quality of product that the growers were shipping—an important factor to many buyers under this program. In this way the trader was able to judge whether a certain grower was providing the quality desired by the customer. The buyer used his impressions of quality when deciding on which growers to include in future deals.

The cost for using this program was 5 percent commission paid by the grower. Growers were paid when product was received at the OFGC's warehouse and buyers paid the OFGC within 60 days of receiving the product. By mid-1984 sales through the program had been largely top-quality potted plants going to retail chains in the United States. These sales had been especially lucrative for the OFGC because growers had been paid in Canadian dollars at the time of the sale and the OFGC had received payment in more valuable U.S. dollars later as the Canadian dollar continued to decline in value.

Buyers liked the program because they could negotiate the price, quality, and timing of a sale. Medium-sized and large growers liked the program for the same reason.

Finance

The permanent capital needs of the OFGC were not great. (The balance sheet information for the years 1982 through 1984 is provided in Exhibits 4 and 5.) The last large purchase by the OFGC had been $150,000 in 1983 for a new computer for use in the auction. No major assets were purchased in 1984, but in 1985 the OFGC planned to take delivery of a new electronic Dutch clock that would cost $130,000.

The building committee of the board was also negotiating the purchase of land as a building site for a building that would replace the leased one that was now used. The decision to build its own building had been prompted by

EXHIBIT 4   Balance sheet 1982–1984 (September 30, 1984).

	1984	1983	1982
Assets			
Current			
Cash	$162,264	$120,809	$141,926
Term deposits	122,850	122,850	—
Accounts receivable: auction	36,570	41,197	36,054
Accounts receivable:			
direct sales	88,019	26,852	—
Carton and label inventory	82,542	41,279	42,901
Deposits and prepaid expenses	19,896	15,966	42,041
Total current assets	$512,141	$368,953	$262,922
Fixed			
At cost	$473,173	$438,808	$290,308
Accumulated depreciation	303,159	243,031	186,774
Net fixed assets	$170,014	$195,777	$103,534
Other	3,787	3,787	3,787
Total assets	$685,942	$568,517	$370,243
Liabilities and Equities			
Current liabilities			
Accounts payable: auction	$ 37,330	$ 13,479	$ 33,831
Accounts payable: direct sales	9,068	4,097	—
Due on redeemed shares	—	—	2,800
Deposits on shares	21,000	15,000	—
Shareholder loan	144,831	144,831	—
Total current liabilities	$212,229	$177,407	$ 36,631
Equities			
Common shares	$152,500	$141,500	$145,000
Retained earnings	301,213	249,610	188,612
Total equities	$453,713	$391,110	$333,612
Total liabilities and equities	$665,942	$568,517	$370,243

Source: Annual Reports of the Ontario Flower Growers' Cooperative.

the landlord asking for a new lease for the building in Mississauga starting in September 1985 of $250,000 a year for three years. After that he proposed that the rate increase at 6 percent per year—the estimated rate of inflation. Many members felt that having their own building would be a good investment: Why should some one else be getting rich owning a building they were paying for? The building committee of the board anticipated it would need a new building of 80,000 square feet. The cost of land and construction of the building would be $2.5 million, and moving to the new building would cost an additional $100,000.

Until recently, equity had been sufficient to finance the limited capital needs of the OFGC. There were two components of equity in the OFGC: common stock and retained earnings. Ten common shares were sold to each member when he or she joined the OFGC. Early members had paid $500 for these shares, while recent members had paid $3,000. Growers tended to view this purchase of stock as an entry fee, as they were never required to make further contributions to equity. Retained earnings had never accumulated because each year the preceding year's earnings were distributed as a patronage dividend to avoid paying income tax at a rate of 46 percent per year.

Anticipating the decision to build a new building, the finance committee had asked the members in 1983 for financial contributions so that it could make a down payment on the land needed. Members had been unwilling to provide further equity investment in the OFGC, so it had taken loans from shareholders. Initially, each member had been asked for $2,000, on which the OFGC promised to pay market rates of interest. Some members contributed, but the poor response led the board to reduce the contribution to $400 for those who felt $2,000 was too much. Those who did not contribute were barred from selling through the OFGC for a year. In the end, the OFGC was able to raise about $145,000.

The manager had discussed the OFGC's financing needs with its banker and had been told that if the OFGC were to use a mortgage to build, it would have to raise $600,000 of equity for a $2 million mortgage at the long-term market rate of 13.5 percent. The mortgage would require an annual payment of $293,000, of which $263,000 would be interest on average for the first five years.

EXHIBIT 5 Statement of retained earnings 1982–1984 (September 30, 1984).

	1984	1983	1982
Retained earnings, beginning of year	$249,610	$188,612	$204,318
Net income for period	301,903	239,172	176,294
Total	$551,513	$427,784	$380,612
Less patronage dividend	249,300	178,174	192,000
Retained earnings, end of year	$302,213	$249,610	$188,612

Source: Annual Reports of the Ontario Flower Growers' Cooperative.

Performance

The OFGC was profitable and had demonstrated continuing financial success for the year just ended (Exhibit 6). The total value of product marketed through it had increased considerably over time, from nearly $5 million in 1976 to over $10 million in 1984 (Exhibit 7). In 1984, total sales volume was greater than planned, although auction sales, the principal component, were below plans. The actual volume of the auction was unknown because buyback sales were incorporated with regular sales through the auction. Moreover, although direct sales had failed to cover direct costs by $18,000 in 1983, these sales contributed $25,000 after direct costs in 1984.

Measures of performance other than sales volume that were also used

EXHIBIT 6   Income statement 1982–1984 (September 30, 1984).

	1984	1983	1982
Total sales	$10,790,965	$9,332,516	$8,046,602
Auction sales[a]	9,870,007	9,282,319	8,046,487
Direct sales	920,602	49,697	—
Revenues			
Auction			
Commissions	$ 915,169	$ 847,953	$ 775,604
Seat rental	59,093	51,394	36,579
Total	$ 974,262	$ 899,347	$ 812,183
Direct sales			
Commissions	$ 46,073	$ 3,696	—
Markup and foreign exchange	166,367	6,670	—
Total	$ 212,440	$ 10,366	—
Other	27,214	17,702	35,478
Total revenues	$1,213,916	$ 927,415	$ 847,661
Expenses			
Auction	$ 383,371	$ 346,034	526,913
Direct sales	183,351	27,824	—
Unallocated			
Building rental	144,883	144,883	144,883
Other	200,408	105,333	—
Total expenses	$ 912,013	$ 684,074	$ 671,796
Net income before taxes	$ 301,903	$ 239,172	$ 176,294
Provision for taxes	—	—	—
Net income for the year	$ 301,903	$ 239,172	$ 176,294

[a]Auction sales include buybacks.
Source: Annual Reports of the Ontario Flower Grower's Cooperative.

EXHIBIT 7   Performance and goals (thousands of dollars).

Year	SALES			COMMISSIONS	PATRONAGE DIVIDEND	COST OF MARKETING THROUGH OFGC
	Auctions and Presales[a]	Direct Sales	Total Sales			
Actual						
1976	$ 4,704	—	$ 4,704	$421	$ 36	8.2%
1977	5,683	—	5,683	513	105	7.2%
1978	5,409	—	5,409	496	61	8.0%
1979	6,002	—	6,002	547	109	7.3%
1980	6,492	$ 398	6,890	634	36	8.7%
1981	7,303	66	7,369	706	192	7.0%
1982	8,047	—	8,047	776	178	7.4%
1983	9,283	50	9,333	855	249	6.5%
1984[b]	9,870	921	10,791	961	302	6.1%
Planned						
1984	$10,175	$ 500	$10,675			
1985	11,193	1,000	12,192			
1986	12,312	2,000	14,312			
1987	13,543	3,000	16,543			
1988	14,897	3,600	18,497			
1989	16,387	4,320	20,707			
1990	18,257	4,968	22,994			

[a] Includes buybacks by members.
[b] Cost of marketing through the OFGC assumes that all savings are paid to members as dividends.
Source: Actual from Annual Reports of the Ontario Flower Growers' Cooperative; *planned* was a finance committee document.

by the board were commissions charged, patronage dividends, and the cost of marketing. Commissions were important because they provided about 90 percent of the co-op's total revenues. Commission revenues were supplemented by seat rentals and interest on the OFGC's bank account. Patronage dividends had also been used to measure the performance of the OFGC. The cost of marketing through the OFGC was a calculation that some growers made on their own and represented commission paid less patronage dividend for the year. It reached its lowest point in 1984 when it only cost 6.1 cents for a grower to market a dollar of product through the OFGC.

■ THE ISSUES

Most members felt that there were not enough buyers. Although the OFGC had a list of 500 buyers, only 75 to 100 usually attended an auction. Members felt that more buyers would have to be found so that they could sell more volume through the OFGC. Members disagreed, however, over how these buyers should be sought. Some felt that the auction program should be promoted and efforts made to make it a more attractive marketing alternative for buyers. Others felt that the direct sales program should be used to pursue the U.S. market.

Members interested in the auction saw various ways of improving it. One problem they saw was that some members were inconsistent users of the auction. They only brought product when they were unable to sell it elsewhere, and sometimes the amounts they brought were large. Moreover, these growers did not worry about prices they received at the auction because they had already made their profits from other sales. They would sell product for whatever they could get. The members referred to this practice as "dumping." The result was that prices on the auction for that day were seriously depressed. The manager was talking to these growers and asking them to "treat the auction like a customer," in other words, bring amounts to the auction in line with their customer demands outside the auction. Several board members thought that the quantity of product delivered by members should be much more tightly controlled.

Another problem related to the quality of products marketed at the auction. Some members complained about the poor-quality product that members would bring to it. One cause was that members would sell their poor-quality product through the auction at low cost with minimum effort. The manager had used her "treat the auction like a customer" presentation on these growers as a way of minimizing this problem. Roosevelt, a member of the board and a grower of tropical plants, felt that another cause was that importers of tropical products were not holding the plants in their greenhouses for the 60 days required by the OFGC. He argued that the OFGC needed to enforce the 60-day requirement and seemed to have the support of several board members for such action.

Buyers at the auction also expressed concern about the quality of product. Some buyers, mostly occasional buyers, found it difficult to judge and compare product. They wanted grading so that they knew what they were buying. Van Luewen, a member of the board, argued that quality was a subjective thing that should not be graded. He was very critical of a previous attempt by the OFGC to grade product on a rigorous set of standards. This attempt had ended with the OFGC leaving it up to each grower to grade his own product. Now buyers were complaining about the uneven quality in individual product lots, as some growers would put several poor-quality pieces in with good quality. The result was that the buyer wound up buying poor-quality product that he could not sell. Some members proposed that lots be graded to ensure that the quality of a lot was consistent.

Whether a direct sales program should be used at all was subject to debate, although one was operating. Growers relying on the auction complained that the availability of top-quality product at the auction had been made worse with the introduction of the direct sales program. They said that direct sales was taking only top-quality product, leaving less of it for the auction. These members felt that the direct sales should be discontinued. A second argument presented by these growers was that based on their previous experience, they would have to pay for losses of a program they did not want. They saw losses as a distinct potential in the long run because they felt that the dramatic increase in exports to the United States was due to the weakness of the Canadian dollar against the American dollar. One American dollar had been worth $1.17 Canadian in 1979–1980; $1.20 in 1981; $1.22 in 1982–1983; and $1.30 in 1984. They thought that sales to the United States would be reduced considerably if the Canadian dollar strengthened. This would lower the value of sales to the United States and would also cause a glut of product as producers exporting to the United States would try to sell their product in Ontario.

Larger buyers and sellers both talked about the need for the direct sales program. They said that they had to limit their business through the auction because the large volumes they needed to deal in altered prices significantly. Only by negotiating prices could they be kept in line with general market prices. Buyers pointed out the problem by talking about a large buyer from Buffalo, New York, who would come to the auction with a transport truck. Since he always left with a full truck, many buyers said that they did not bother trying to bid against him because prices got driven too high.

The customers of the direct sales program had never been specified by the board. Growers using the program liked the fact that it was selling product in the United States. They saw that market as having unlimited potential. Efforts by the trader to make sales in Canada had been limited by the manager of the OFGC. She felt that direct sales were hurting the auction. She had convinced the board that because the purpose of the direct sales program was to find new buyers, the direct sales program should only sell to new buyers. All existing buyers who wanted to set prices through nego-tiation were required to use the presale program.

A final issue was the construction of the new building. This idea had captured the interest of the members. Haefling had been instrumental in persuading the members of the "common sense" of having members invest in a building for the OFGC. At the November meeting much time was spent discussing what features should be incorporated in the new building. During the meeting, an outspoken member had asked: "And just who is going to pay for this monument to the board?" After the meeting, Stueben realized that the board had put little thought into either the marketing or financial implications of the new building.

As Stueben reflected on these issues, he wondered what he should do. Many members of the board and the OFGC were pushing for changes and all felt that they had valid solutions. Stueben felt that what was needed was a coherent set of changes that he could sell to the members as the appro-priate plan of action for the OFGC.

Attachment A

▄▄ THE ONTARIO FLORICULTURAL INDUSTRY

The floricultural industry was involved in the production, distribution, and retailing of flowers and plants. The three main types of businesses in this industry were growers, wholesalers, and retailers. Each type of business was linked with the others through sales transactions. The dollar value of product moving between the various businesses and final consumers is presented in Exhibit 8. Details on each of these businesses for the period 1979–1983 were as follows.

Growers

Ontario growers produced cut flowers, potted plants (foliage and flowering), and bedding plants. Overall production of cut flowers had declined by 1 percent per year over the past five years, while that of standard carnations and chrysanthemums—the major products—had declined by 7 percent per year as the Canadian market had turned to foreign suppliers. U.S. and Colombian producers had lower costs and were able to supply product for a much greater part of the year. Ontario's growers had held volume in other traditional cut flowers. Imports of high quality and new products from the Netherlands had also grown over time. Canadian growers started growing the new types of cut flowers about five years after the Dutch introduced them into the Canadian market.

Production of most potted flowering plants (chrysanthemums, poinsettias, lilies, hydrangeas, and azaleas) had increased by 10 percent per year over the last five years. Production of tropical or foliage plants had stabilized, while production of hanging baskets had peaked in 1981 and was still declining. The different product situations seemed to be related to markets served with the product. Potted flowering products had been moving into the United States, while the others had been sold only in Ontario. Production of bedding plants had increased at 7 percent per year over the last five years.

Most growers specialized in producing a limited range of one type of product. They felt that this let them develop the specialized knowledge

212

EXHIBIT 8   Value of transactions with the Ontario Floricultural Industry (millions of dollars) for 1983.

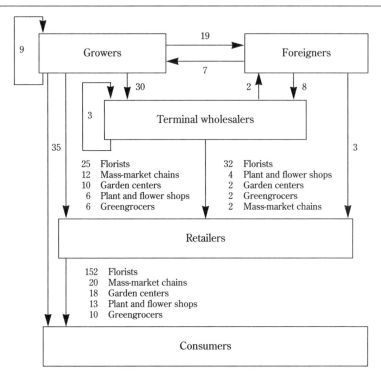

Source: An independent consultant to the floricultural industry.

needed to grow each product, although a grower may still experience grow-ing difficulties. It also helped spread some of the price and market risks associated with specialization. Growers usually grew the same products and thus gained security in knowing the difficulties involved. This also helped spread some of the price and market risks associated with specialization. Growers usually grew the same products for a long time because of the spe-cialized production knowledge they developed, the long production cycle for some products, and the security of knowing the product would sell.

Nearly all the commercial production in Ontario was produced in green-houses under controlled conditions. The publicly reported value of commer-cial sales in 1983 from Ontario's 3.6 million square meters of greenhouse grow-ers in Essex County near the west end of Lake Erie was 3,600 square meters, much larger than Ontario's industry average of 1,330 square meters. The area around the west end of Lake Ontario was the other major area of production. The 491 growers in this area had an average operation of 2,121 square meters.

Ontario greenhouses were largely family operations: 42 percent were sole proprietorships and 37 percent were family corporations. They used relatively small amounts of land. Thirty-eight percent of total greenhouse area was on farms with less than nine acres, and 76 percent was on farms with less than 69 acres. The greenhouse enterprise was the primary or secondary activity on these farms. Most greenhouse owners were happy with this size of business and did not plan to expand. They felt that expanding their businesses beyond what they could handle as a family created both labor and quality problems in production. Thus increased size did not mean lower unit costs.

Growers had several alternative ways of selling their products: (1) to independent wholesalers, (2) to growers who wholesaled their own product along with that of other growers (such growers, known as grower-wholesalers, are discussed in the next section), (3) to retailers, (4) to the public, and (5) to foreign customers. Sales could be made at the grower's or buyer's place of business or at one of two special market places, the auction of the Ontario Flower Growers' Cooperative or at the Food Terminal, a wholesale market on the outskirts of Toronto where farmers sold their produce, mostly fruits and vegetables, to retailers.

A single grower rarely sold in only one way. He preferred to sell several ways so that he could capture the advantages of selling to each. Selling to wholesalers provided some assurance of the amount and price of the product sold. Many wholesalers competed in southern Ontario, so the prices they paid were competitive. No grower relied on a single wholesaler, however, because the wholesalers' competitive situation had caused some to fail to meet their purchasing commitments to the grower or even go bankrupt. Most wholesalers were located close to growers and picked up product at the grower's greenhouse.

Selling through an auction provided growers with a ready market for any type, quality, or quantity of product. The auction required little time because it was held for a few hours several times a week. The grower got a feel for market prices and quality because all sales transactions were public knowledge. But prices at an auction could fluctuate considerably from one auction to the next, depending on what growers offered and what buyers wanted.

Selling directly to retailers involved a lot of time and expense as the grower searched out buyers interested in what he had to sell. The grower felt more secure with this method of marketing because he was seeking his own buyers for his product. Although prices were higher than selling to wholesalers, the gains were largely offset by high marketing costs, especially for the small grower.

Finally, selling directly to the public from the grower's greenhouse provided the highest profit margins and allowed the grower to stay at his site of production. Many growers liked marketing this way, but location near customers and some merchandising ability were important requirements.

The inability of many growers to meet these requirements had restricted the growth of direct sales to 4 percent per year.

The most important characteristic determining how growers sold was the size of their business. Large growers tended to market their own products. Negotiated sales could be a time-consuming way to sell, but the grower had to invest time and effort only when he wanted to sell. Moreover, his large production quantities made it important that he find a customer for his production. Large growers had enough financial resources that they often extended credit to buyers.

Most small growers relied on wholesalers and the auctions to help them market their products. They also sold product directly from their greenhouse. Most did so because they would rather spend their time dealing with production than marketing, and they did not have the earnings to hire someone to market their product. Their limited financial resources also meant that they liked to sell their products for cash. Finally, they wanted to be able to sell the small volumes of all qualities of product they produced.

Wholesalers

Wholesalers played an important role in linking supplies of floricultural products with retail demand. Several types of wholesalers carried out these activities. *Grower-wholesalers* grew and bought product from other growers. They tended to be large growers who wanted to assure a market for their own product. While their marketing costs were similar to the wholesalers' 20 to 25 percent markup, they were more profitable because, by growing their own product, they had assured supplies. This also made their growing activities more profitable as they were able to sell a greater proportion of their product at good prices. They sometimes used other growers' product to complement their own product line and to fill in when their own production was not enough to meet their customer needs. *Terminal market wholesalers* specialized in collecting and distributing product from various growers to various retailers. Of the two types, the former was more profitable because the growers earned the margins from growing and there was always some product available.

Most wholesalers were always searching all sources for top-quality supplies. They would bring it in from foreign sources if necessary, although this meant that the product was more expensive than local supply when it was available. They both relied on the OFGC auction by buying at it and competed with it by selling to retail customers who might buy at the auction. Most grower-wholesalers both bought and sold, so the reasons explaining how they acted in both activities must be considered. When they bought product from growers, they were able to line up deliveries of the desired quality of product in advance. They were also able to negotiate lower prices with growers because of their commitment to take the product. Wholesalers might meet part of their product needs by buying on spot markets. These markets were the Food Terminal, where they could negotiate on quality and price, and OFGC's auction, where they could bid on available product. Sometimes they got very good quality for their money at the auction; at other times good quality was scarce and available only at extremely high prices.

The main customers of wholesalers were retail florists. To satisfy florists' needs, wholesalers had to provide stable supplies of top-quality products at stable prices. By selling to florists, wholesalers got regular customers who paid premium places. Serving florists was expensive, though, because they bought little each time and had to be dealt with individually in their place of business. Wholesalers also sold to mass-market chains. These chains wanted good-quality product but in large volume for holiday or seasonal selling. Chains also expected to pay lower prices because of the volume they bought. Wholesalers sold to garden centers and other wholesalers as well. Here the conditions of sale were much more variable. One thing that stood out in all these transactions was that grower-wholesalers liked to sell good-quality product as their own and move their poor-quality products into markets where their product image would not be hurt.

A few of the largest wholesalers had been very active exporters of floricultural products in recent years. Virtually all exports went to the United States and were mostly potted plants. Ontario exports of these products had risen from $5 million in 1980 to $19 million in 1983—an increase of 57 percent per year. Reasons given for this dramatic growth were: (1) the high quality of Canadian product, (2) the low price of Canadian product, due in part to more advanced production technology and in part due to the declining value of the Canadian dollar, and (3) the availability of Ontario product during peak consumer buying periods in the United States.

The overall growth rate of 7 percent per year in dollar sales was expected to continue. Growers wholesaling product were expected to continue to do so as long as they felt that they could not find ready wholesale markets large enough to handle their large volumes without market prices declining.

Retailers

The retailing of floricultural products had changed considerably in recent years with changes in consumer tastes as well as changes in the retailing industry. The consumer market for floricultural products had been segmented by the retailers so that each segment was served by a particular type of retailer. The segmentation of retailing floricultural products had two implications for those providing retailers with products. First, each retailer attempted to buy products in the way most compatible with its retailing approach. Second, the fortunes of those serving each type of retailer would change as the size of the market segment served by that retailing approach changed. Details for each of the retailers follow.

Florists

Sales of retail florists in Ontario could be broken up into sales of cut flower arrangements (45 percent of sales), flowering potted plants (17 percent), loose cut flowers (14 percent), and foliage plants (13 percent). Nonfloricultural products accounted for the remaining 11 percent of sales. This breakdown of sales seemed likely to continue.

The successful florist had traditionally provided customers with high-quality products and many services. His customers were willing to pay high prices to get what they wanted. To keep them satisfied, the florist was also willing to pay a premium for quality and availability. The variability in sales over the year complicated his buying. High sales levels in May (Mother's Day) and December (Christmas) meant that his needs were not in concert with the production pattern of Ontario producers. Nor did the florist spend much time buying flowers and plants; his interest was in taking and filling customer orders.

Florists bought product from several different sources. Most florists bought cut flowers from three or four wholesalers whose trucks would come by the florist's shop. Traditional florists like to buy from wholesalers because they would deliver product to the florist's store, usually had a full line of products, guaranteed their products, sold for stable though high prices, and gave credit. A few florists bought cut flowers directly from foreign sources to get top-quality product unobtainable from Ontario growers. This activity was facilitated by some wholesalers who, acting as agents for foreign suppliers, charged florists a 10 percent commission on the cost of purchasing and shipping the product to Canada's major airport at Toronto. Even when cut flowers were available locally, foreign products were sometimes cheaper and of better quality. Florists bought most of their potted plants from local grower-wholesalers.

Some florists had shifted from the traditional to a cash-and-carry orientation. The buying behavior of these florists is described in the next section. In recent years dollar sales increases of florists had been only 4 percent per year.

Plant and Flower Shops

These shops grew out of the consumer interest in foliage plants in the mid 1970s. Plant and flower shops tried to sell high volumes by providing the customer with a large product range, including cut flowers, foliage plants, and bedding plants—all at low prices. They kept down their costs by offering few services and selling primarily on a cash basis. They also devoted a lot of effort to buying floricultural products because the cost of product accounted for a large part of their revenue. They tried to buy only products that would sell quickly and wanted to pay as little as possible for them. They had started buying better quality products as their customers were becoming more sophisticated and starting to look for quality.

Shops bought from several different types of sellers. Many bought at the OFGC's auction because it brought together many different varieties and qualities of product. Shop owners could compare the available product and get a good feeling for what their competitors were paying. They felt that products tended to be cheap at the auction but that they had to be fairly knowledgeable about the products to buy well. Complaints they had about the auction included the requirement that purchases be paid for in cash, the variable quality of product in sales lots, and the limited availability of quality product. Some also bought at the Food Terminal. There they had to negotiate their own deals. This allowed them to pick the quality and quantity they wanted, but they did not know what others were paying. Other problems with the Terminal were that floricultural products were sold for only part of the year, and that buyers had to work quickly to get the quality, quantity, and variety of products they wanted before they were sold. These shops were using wholesalers increasingly for unusual and high-quality items. Plant and flower shops appeared to be fully able to maintain their past growth rate of 10 percent per year.

Garden Centers

Garden centers or nurseries were located in suburban areas. Some innovative ones had extended their original activities beyond bedding plants, shrubs, and trees into potted plants, cut flowers, plant accessories, and craft items. Their approach to business made them appear to be the suburban equivalent to plant and flower shops. These centers, as a result, approached buying the same way as plant and flower shops. They were different in several respects, however. They sometimes had greenhouses on the premises, which let them buy larger quantities of potted plants than a plant shop could. They were also larger and could afford to carry buyers on staff. The overall result was that they preferred contractual arrangements with growers because they could negotiate lower prices due to the volume they bought, and they were able to buy product when they wanted it. They sometimes used the auction as a source for part of their needs. These centers promised continuing growth as suburban areas in southern Ontario continued to expand. In the past, they had grown at 8 percent per year.

Mass-Market Chains

Chain stores reportedly bought $9.8 million of floricultural products in 1982. Different types of chains marketed these products in different ways. Food chains marketed them as impulse items. A moderately priced potted plant fitted easily into the grocery budget as a single additional item which could be taken home with the groceries. Stores induced customers to buy these products by offering good-quality plants at low prices during the periods of the year when the public bought most flowers and plants. Other types of retail chains sold bedding plants in the spring as part of their outdoor department's product line and other plants (usually foliage plants) as special promotions.

Chains had been very successful in buying what they wanted because sellers sought them out. The large volume they bought was attractive to sellers, although sellers had to meet rigid product standards while receiving low unit prices. Chains sometimes required sellers to put their products in special packaging so that the product could withstand the extra handling that chains performed as shipments were delivered to their central warehouses and distributed from there to each store.

Chain stores sales had grown at 10 percent per year over the last few years, but they looked like they had the potential for greatly expanded sales if they could do two things. First, they had to improve product maintenance once it was placed in the store. Second, they had to develop customers' buying habits so that customers would purchase flowers and plants regularly.

Greengrocers

Greengrocers are small grocery stores with product lines similar to those of convenience stores. Most are owned and operated by ethnic families. They are found in the high-density urban areas of Toronto, whereas food chains are mostly in the suburbs. They also considered plants and flowers an impulse purchase. They often displayed these products on the sidewalk in front of the store. They offered both flowers and plants of low to average quality at lot prices.

Most greengrocers were only occasional purchasers and were not well informed about prices or qualities. When buying, they tried to buy product that looked like that of their competitors and was cheap enough that it could be competitively priced yet still provide a reasonable profit. Many bought at the OFGC's auction, where they could see what other greengrocers were paying and could buy the amounts and qualities they thought their customers wanted. Many also bought at the Food Terminal several kilometers south of the OFGC. They liked the convenience of buying flowers and plants at the same time that they bought produce. The dollar volume of greengrocer sales had grown at 12 percent per year, but it appeared that this rate would slow down, as many greengrocers had found increasing competition was driving down the profits on floricultural products.